Women in Family Business Leadership Roles

Daughters on the Stage

Mary Barrett

University of Wollongong, Australia

and

Ken Moores

Bond University, Australia

Edward Elgar

Cheltenham, UK • Northampton, MA, USA

Published by
Edward Elgar Publishing Limited
The Lypiatts
15 Lansdown Road
Cheltenham
Glos GL50 2JA
UK

Edward Elgar Publishing, Inc.
William Pratt House
9 Dewey Court
Northampton
Massachusetts 01060
USA

A catalogue record for this book
is available from the British Library

Library of Congress Control Number: 2009928609

ISBN 978 1 84844 215 3

Printed and bound by MPG Books Group, UK

Contents

Foreword

A snappy, incisive and thoroughly researched book, *Women in Family Business Leadership Roles* is a useful academic tool for those keen to understand how and why women operate in family businesses, a domain so often unwisely and mistakenly assumed to be run by men, with their wives labouring over the bookwork after finishing the dishes and their children's homework. *Women in Family Business Leadership Roles* successfully explodes that myth.

Professors Barrett and Moores are leading researchers into the machinations of the family firm. They combine the latest academic research with 13 case studies and explore various theoretical approaches to understanding the role of women in a family business, a domain where they have been quietly achieving for some time. They carefully examine an international sample of case studies and the characteristics of leadership and how they apply to women. The experience of innovation and the challenge of incorporating radical innovation as a means for preparing for the future are discussed, with deference to the expressed desire for the family firm to continue to exude the family feel with all its special advantages.

Barrett and Moores detail the factors which have led some to success, and pick over and examine the pitfalls. Social theories are compared and contrasted to help explain the differences between men and women, as well as how they behave generally and within the context of small, medium and large family firms.

Inevitably the book also explores female archetypes and the importance of popular perceptions of successful women—both for the women entrepreneurs themselves and for others. This text will be extremely useful in helping women—and their families—understand the dynamics of their family business.

Business is a life spent in detail, often described as the 'weeds'. It has to be, of course. Financial survival is a very detail-dependent business, and wrong assumptions, sloppy processes and unnecessary risk taking can all irrevocably damage a family business, especially one with limited financial reserves. Business people inevitably spend most of their time caught up in the detail; they often describe this as working *for* the business instead of the business working for them.

Women in Family Business Leadership Roles is an opportunity for women to step outside the all-consuming detail, look for the patterns of success and failure and understand when this is the result of gender or of other factors. It is a diagnostic, an explanation and a confirmation. I know all that will be welcomed by those in small business who often live and work in isolation from others in similar situations.

The case studies and examples of entrepreneurship and commercial successes are accompanied by a detailed look at how being female has made this different, if indeed it has. The book explores the lack of research on women in business and management and argues that the invisibility of women in business partly resides in the focus of business and communities on the 'heroic' approach. Previous analyses of women's experiences as entrepreneurs had been inadequate, further discouraging more investment in women.

The book presents a dazzling display of research exploring whether, and to what extent, women and their businesses differ from men and men-owned businesses; allegations about difference in management styles and risk adversity are also featured. While it does not deny the importance of having more women representatives in business, it certainly questions the impact of gender on their success. It points to a number of barriers, such as family background and family responsibilities, as well as those accursed assumptions about how women should behave and what makes them so special.

The subject areas are broad, but the figures, while more modest, build a convincing case for female entrepreneurship. The book starts from the premise that the successful entrepreneur must combine risk-taking with innovation and prudent management, and explores how women contribute to this within the confines of often small family businesses. It relies on the experiences and stories of women in family businesses, what sort of innovators they are and how women understand and use the continuity of 'sameness' so often associated with the successful family business.

But the book is much more than a theoretical trawl through the research gaps. It looks at the characteristics of leadership and how they apply to women, the experience of innovation as a means for preparing for the future and how the family business can be a way of incorporating radical innovation.

It is an expansive and detailed insight into what lies behind the successful businessperson. Men can learn as much from this book as women—almost.

Pru Goward
Leader, politician and passionate advocate for women in the mainstream

Contributors

Professor Mary Barrett (BA [Hons German] BA [Hons French] PhD MBA MAHRI MAIM) is Professor of Management at the University of Wollongong, where she is a member of the People and Organisations Research Centre. She is also a Research Fellow of Bond University's Australian Centre for Family Business. Professor Barrett began her academic career in languages and literature, and later worked in university administration, government and human resource management. Professor Barrett researches and publishes in the fields of family business, women in management (including women entrepreneurs), workplace communication and learning, leadership and management theory. She has published several books including, with Professor Ken Moores, *Learning Family Business: Paradoxes and Pathways* (Ashgate, 2002), and with Elizabeth Baker and Lesley Roberts, *Working Communication* (John Wiley, 2002). With co-editor Marilyn Davidson she published *Gender and Communication at Work* (Ashgate, 2006). Professor Barrett is a regular speaker at business and other conferences on gender, communication and family business issues. She and Professor Ken Moores are planning further research into family business, focusing on transgenerational learning.

Professor Ken Moores AM (BBus BEcon MSocSc PhD FCPA FCA FAICD) is Foundation Director of and Professor at Bond University's Australian Centre for Family Business—a centre he established in 1994. Dr Moores pioneered research and recognition of family business in Australia and has published internationally in accounting, finance, education and family business management. He co-authored, with Professor Mary Barrett, *Learning Family Business: Paradoxes and Pathways* (Ashgate, 2002), and continues to publish and present internationally in the family business field. In 2008 he was appointed to the Family Business Review Advisory Board and made a Fellow of the International Family Enterprise Research Academy (IFERA). Professor Moores also serves the family business community as a company director, a speaker at family business conferences, a consultant to family businesses and professional advisory firms, a judge of the annual Family Business Awards, and a member of the board of directors of Family Business Australia (FBA) Ltd. Professor Moores served as Vice-Chancellor and President of Bond University from 1997–2003, and prior to that as Dean of Business and Foundation Professor of Accounting. In 2005 he was made a Member in the Order of Australia for his service to academia and the accounting profession.

Pru Goward (MLA [NSW] BA [Hons Econ]) is the current State Liberal Member for Goulburn in the New South Wales Parliament in Australia and Shadow Minister for Women, Climate Change and the Environment. Ms Goward served as Executive Director of the Office of the Status of Women in the Department of the Prime Minister and Cabinet under Prime Minister John Howard from 1997, and from 2001 until 2007 as the federal Sex Discrimination Commissioner. In 2004 she was also appointed Commissioner Responsible for Age Discrimination. She was awarded a Centenary Medal in 2001 for services to journalism and women's rights and an Honorary Doctorate in Business Studies from Charles Sturt University. Ms Goward is the author of *A Business of Your Own: How Women Succeed in Business* (Allen & Unwin, 2001) and co-author (with David Barnett) of *John Howard: a Biography* (Viking, 1997).

Acknowledgements

We are grateful to many people who gave generously in helping us undertake the research that has produced this book. In particular, we would like to acknowledge BDO Kendalls, who sponsored the project and gave financial support for our research. Our interviewees also contributed generously by giving us their time and access to their firms. Our families, as always, gave us encouragement, practical help and the space to endure the tougher moments of authorship.

Mary Barrett and Ken Moores

1. Women, Leadership and Family Business

Family firms have long been important cogs in the engine room of private enterprise economies. Their stability and continuity, coupled with their innovation and rapid decision making, have provided reassurance for those seeking sustained growth and development of regional and national economies. Two features of family firms, which have recently received increased attention, can help us understand their economic contribution. First, researchers, advisers and policy makers have sought to understand entrepreneurship as practised by families in business. Second, they have tried to come to grips with the leadership roles women play in these firms. This book presents the results of research directed primarily at the second area, but it also offers some insight into the first. How do the experiences of women family business leaders help us better understand leadership and entrepreneurship generally? How do they contribute to knowledge of how family businesses function?

RESEARCH GAPS

A great deal is still not fully appreciated about leadership and entrepreneurship, especially how they play out in a family business context. This section surveys some of the gaps in our knowledge, and discusses how knowing more about women's experience might help fill them.

Leadership in a Family Business Context

Our earlier book, *Learning Family Business: Paradoxes and Pathways* (Moores and Barrett, 2002) discusses how successful CEOs in family firms went on a learning journey to leadership, in which they progressed through four stages:

L1 learning business
L2 learning our business
L3 learning to lead our business
L4 learning to let go our business.

Each learning phase was associated with a difficult paradox, which could only be managed—not made to disappear. We comment further later about what those paradoxes were and what management lessons they entailed. The important issue here is that the CEOs in that study were mostly male. Since then, women have been increasingly likely to be considered potential successors to the leadership of family firms. The *2007 American Family Business Survey*[1] points out, for example, that US family-owned businesses are growing both in terms of revenues and jobs, and they expect to continue doing so. Women often lead that growth, and have assumed leadership positions in family businesses at much higher rates than women in primarily non-family firms. According to the 30 April 2007 issue of *Fortune* magazine, women lead only 2.5 per cent of the Fortune 1000 firms, which are primarily non-family run.

Nelson and Levesque (2007) tested the conceptual ground that high-growth, high-potential firms might be better for women in governance, based on the evidence of recent success of women in start-up companies, the labour market strengths of the 1990s, and women's recent increasing levels of higher education in business. However, they found few significant differences in women's representation in governance between Fortune 500 firms and high-growth, high-potential firms. In contrast, the *2007 American Family Business Survey* shows an almost fivefold increase in the number of women leaders in family business since 1997, and almost one-third of family firms indicate they may have a female successor (Mass Mutual Financial Group, 2007). Dugan et al. (2008, p. 1) go further, asserting that 'while family businesses are still primarily a male domain, more women are running family businesses than ever before, and more aspire to leadership'. Evans (2005) notes, via the *Coutts 2005 Family Business Survey*,[2] which compares family and non-family businesses in England and Ireland on a range of factors, that 12.0 per cent of family businesses have women in chief executive officer or managing director roles, compared to only 3.0 per cent of non-family businesses. Twenty-one per cent of family businesses, compared to 17.0 per cent of non-family businesses, have female non-executive directors. Evans quotes Nicholson and Bjornberg from the London Business School, who argue that:

> Family businesses are creating diversity and a broader set of leadership skills by including women leaders in the top management teams. The fact that family businesses do this to a greater extent than non-family firms could be because they have access to talented women through different networks and are not pressurised by public shareholders to be conventional in terms of board selection. It may also be a sign that the traditionally 'invisible' influence of women in family firms has always been there but is now beginning to take a modern shape: as officially recognised positions of leadership (Evans, 2005, p. 11).

Findings such as these prompt further questions, such as whether women in family businesses follow a leadership journey different from men, and what any differences might mean. Until recently, it was more than likely women family business CEOs would have taken over the business by default, following some catastrophe such as the death of a partner or family business member, rather than consciously or unconsciously directing themselves towards leadership, as their male counterparts usually did. Therefore, we thought there would probably be both similarities and differences in women's experiences of attaining family business leadership compared to men's.

Approaches to Studying Women in Family Business

Researchers and business people alike have considered gender—and gender differences—in different ways. One approach, social feminism, is the framework for many previous studies, including Barrett (1995, 1998), Carter and Williams (2003), Fischer et al. (1993) and Johnson and McMahon (2005). Social feminism is closely linked to social learning, of which one theory, communities of practice, is an important explanatory framework in the present research. Broadly speaking, social feminism holds that, partly because of different learning experiences, women and men have different experiential backgrounds, and therefore different ways of thinking. In addition, and important for the question of whether women's and men's experiences in learning leadership differ, social feminism holds that in learning, management, leadership and so on, 'women follow different processes, but neither the male nor the female mode of knowing is regarded as innately superior' (Fischer et al., 1993).

An alternative approach, liberal feminism, underpins much other gender-focused research in business, especially into women executives or women seeking such positions in the family firm (for example, Cole, 1997; Dumas, 1989, 1990, 1992; Hollander and Bukowitz, 1990; Iannarelli, 1993; Lyman, 1988; Salganicoff, 1990; Sexton and Bowman-Upton, 1990). These studies often reveal instances of open (or more subtle) discrimination, which create barriers to women's advancement, and suggest how such barriers might be overcome to make better use of women's potential in the firm. The type of problem they discern, for example, how family firms maintain a 'glass ceiling', and the solutions they suggest, such as training women to develop personalities and attitudes more aligned with success, reveal their primary aim as helping women achieve equality with men. Their underlying liberal feminist assumption is that gender difference is associated with inequality, rather than the idea that women and men are 'equal but different'. Women will 'rise' to equal standing with men once obstacles holding them back are removed (Greer and Greene, 2003; Hurley, 1999).

Dumas adopts a broadly social feminist approach in her various studies of women in family firms (see Dumas, 1989, 1990, 1992). In examining daughters' pathways to leadership in family firms, she tries to understand what helps make leadership possible for women, rather than merely what prevents them assuming leadership roles. In several of her studies, but especially her research on women working with their fathers as managers in family firms, she uses a method similar to ours, examining women's behaviours and experiences and trying to generate theories 'from the ground up' about what they mean. Her research aim is also similar: to categorise the experiences of women in family firms. The categories she develops strongly emphasise psychological development and emotional factors: the 'invisible successor', 'Daddy's little girl', the 'silent voice' and 'caretaker of the king's gold', among others. Her findings about women's experiences also have a strong psychological emphasis. A summary of Dumas' results appears in Table 1.1.

Table 1.1 Daughters' Problems as Managers in Family Firms

Category	Description
Untapped resources	Daughters' strong skills and abilities represent a richness of resources which remains under-utilised.
Role conflict and ambiguity	Fathers frequently fail to recognise and utilise their daughters' skills and acknowledge their aspirations; they think their daughters' entry into the firm is probably temporary. Daughters need to contend with carryover conflict and ambiguity in their business roles in the firm and as daughters, leading to their being torn between their roles as daughters and their business roles.
Family/managerial conflict	Daughters' shifting identities and roles in the family firm threaten the identities and roles of other family or non-family members. For example, mothers (whether working in the firm or not) are threatened by the new closeness between fathers and daughters.
Interdependence	Some daughters eventually make a successful transition from being their father's (and their mother's) child working in the family business, to being an independent adult successfully integrated into the family business. This is typically linked to the father's need to give up some responsibility, often because of health problems.

Source: Adapted from Dumas (1990).

In a study which also has a strong psychological focus, Hollander and Bukowitz (1990) consider how women think about their identity when they occupy different positions in a family business. The authors start with the observation that women typically have difficulty reconciling professional success with 'feminine' success. In their minds, acting professionally is equated with being considered cold-hearted and calculating. In a family business, this dilemma means women turn their energies away from professional activity toward the 'family' or 'private' side of family business. Deciding to deal with difference by choosing a narrower sphere of activity entails a peculiar psychological advantage for women in family business, where both private family life and the professional side of the family business are seen as important: any kind of success, personal or professional, is equally valued. It is also harder for women to fail in family business: if there is a failure on the business side, it can be counterbalanced by success on the family side. Cole (1997, p. 357) points out that 'there is a belief that women in the family business continue to struggle with the traditional limitations imposed on them by others'. However, she also states that women themselves are at least partly responsible for their subordinate position: they develop devices to see other women as equally 'invisible', and are not always willing to proceed in their careers when they have the opportunity.

These studies all grapple with what gender difference and gender equality mean. As Curimbaba (2002) points out, aspects of many previous studies suggest gender difference is positive: for example, when women show more loyalty and concern than men do for the business or its founder, and more sensitivity and capacity for peacekeeping. However, difficulties arise when women's differences mean something needs to be accepted in the firm, for example, the difference of women needing more flexible schedules, differences in values placed on private and professional activities, differences in attitudes to career advancement. These difficulties attest to the longstanding prominence of the view that 'leadership is male', and that gender difference requires accommodation, rather than celebration.

Evidence of male advantage over women is common in entrepreneurship studies. Verheul et al. (2005) observe that at the macro level, female and male entrepreneurs differ in the type of entrepreneurial activity they engage in, and the ways they manage this activity. They found that women select different activities from men, choosing those that both genders see as less entrepreneurial. Women also view themselves as less entrepreneurial than men. However, these findings, while raising concerns about women's disadvantage, should also prompt critical questions. For example, what opportunities have women had to develop entrepreneurial skills and recognise and exploit business opportunities? How likely are they to know an entrepreneur or to have any other type of mentor? What opportunities do they have for learning that might help them overcome the fear of business failure that can inhibit entrepreneurial activity? The next chapter considers some international evidence about these and other questions, and the implications of a family business perspective on how they might be answered.

Our project considers these questions, rather than merely the simple and outdated issues of 'men versus women'. As Ahl (2004) shows, academic researchers are reluctant to reject a basic assumption that men and women entrepreneurs are essentially different, despite consistent research findings to the contrary. Ahl (2004, p. 184) points out that many researchers use three strategies to shore up this assumption against the evidence: stressing small differences between men and women while ignoring similarities and large overlaps; proclaiming women entrepreneurs to be exceptional women when finding that men and women entrepreneurs are more similar than different; and constructing 'the good mother', an alternative, 'feminine' entrepreneurship model. The present project is sceptical that inherent differences in men's and women's approach to leadership and entrepreneurship exist. We nevertheless want to pay special attention to women's experiences of leadership and entrepreneurship in the context of family business, to seek a more complete and therefore better understanding of all three phenomena.

Understanding female vantage points may also suggest how family businesses might make better use of the totality of resources at their disposal to build 'familiness' and sustain competitive advantage. 'Familiness', or the various forms of family-based relatedness, is increasingly recognised by researchers such as Habbershon and Williams (1999) and Miller and Le Breton-Miller (2005) as a source of competitive advantage available to family firms. We discuss 'familiness' in more detail later in this chapter.

Women as Leaders and Entrepreneurs

Other reasons for the relative absence of female vantage points in studies of entrepreneurship and leadership include how researchers have tackled these concepts in the past. Typically, trying to discover and illustrate 'a women's viewpoint' on entrepreneurship, leadership, management and so on has meant taking male approaches as the norm (Billing and Alvesson, 1994; Brown, 1979; Bruni et al., 2004; Collinson, 2003; Collinson and Hearn, 1996; Sinclair, 2004, 2007). Consequently, few female perspectives exist because they are seen in terms of differences from this assumed male norm, rather than investigated in their own right. Viewing the contexts in which women's entrepreneurship takes place—of which family business is one—has been limited in similar ways.

Definitions of entrepreneurship, which tend to determine how we think about and study it (Gartner, 1990), have also tended to screen out female vantage points. Bull and Willard (1993) argue that we still lack a unifying economic theory of entrepreneurship capable of providing a generally acceptable definition of entrepreneurial activity. What we do know about it, according to Ogbor (2000), is derived from the theories of 'creative destruction' which originated with the nineteenth century economic theorist

Schumpeter, the theories of enterprise creation by Collins and Moore (1964) and Knight's (1964 [1921]) theory of risk. In all these authors' works, the distinctive feature of entrepreneurial activity is the entrepreneur's capacity for opportunity recognition and innovation. However, this was seen primarily as a quality of the person, rather than as a set of practices. As a further consequence, entrepreneurship is seen as an activity primarily undertaken by men. Fulop and Linstead (1999) point out that archetypal models of entrepreneurship are based on success stories about men, especially those with a 'command and control' management style. Consequently, 'heroic', male-oriented models of entrepreneurship have dominated both academic debate, as well as the 'advice' literature on entrepreneurship. We discuss below an approach to entrepreneurship that cuts through these difficulties, and allows the phenomenon of corporate entrepreneurship to be considered part of entrepreneurship in general.

Similar problems have occurred with theories of leadership. The dominance of the 'great person' view of leadership, typically a 'great man' view, continues in much academic theorising, as well as in the general 'advice' literature (Fletcher, 2004). The 'great man' view persists despite the efforts of prominent feminist theorists such as Gilligan (1982), Kanter (1977) and Rosener (1990) to elucidate so-called 'female' models of leadership and explain why they are more appropriate for organisations in the twenty-first century. Through the 'great man' understandings of leadership, training for leadership roles has meant that women need to adapt their styles of leadership to male norms (Barrett and Davidson, 2006).

The View from Other Disciplines

The gender-related problems and limitations we observe with studies of entrepreneurship and leadership echo what has happened in other academic disciplines. As Curthoys and Docker (2006) point out about history, until very recently, this discipline was 'profoundly gendered'. Early studies seeking to rectify this situation focused on how women were oppressed or excluded from various fields of human activity. However, such studies often relied on a male-defined conceptual framework for various human activities. Consequently, these studies made women appear as victims—or at best, passive recipients of events, simply reacting to male pressures. However, historians, especially female historians, eventually became interested in the ways women had actively created and changed their environments. By the mid 1970s a considerable body of historical work had accumulated which focused on women's ideas and actions, not just how these things were constrained.

History now has a strong practical and theoretical focus on women. However, in academic studies of entrepreneurship, business and management, relatively little work has so far appeared specifically on women. Why the delay? Reed (1996) surmises that reflective studies on the social construction of gender issues in business and economics simply started late compared with other academic disciplines. When studies of women's entrepreneurship eventually came along, they tended to make points similar to early studies in feminist history, arguing that a lack of attention to women entrepreneurs was a result of men's traditional dominance of the academic community, and that attitudes and studies that focused on the 'heroic' approach to entrepreneurship had rendered women invisible. At best, analyses of women's experiences as entrepreneurs was inadequate, biased or distorted (Ferber and Nelson, 1993).

Previous Remedies

Even when it was agreed there was a problem, entrepreneurship researchers and textbook authors were not necessarily unanimous about how to fix it. The remedy in textbooks, as Baker et al. (1997) point out, was usually to try to take a gender-neutral approach to studying entrepreneurship. In practical terms, this was rather simplistic: authors presented an equal proportion of case material on women in business as on men. This paints over the issue by assuming that the drivers of entrepreneurship for men and women are always (or even typically) similar, that their representation in industry is comparable, that the problems they face are essentially identical and so on.

Research suggests none of this is true. For example, beginning in the 1980s, researchers investigated whether and to what extent women and their businesses differ from men and men-owned businesses (Belcourt, 1987, 1990; Birley, 1989), whether and how women's management styles differ from those of men (Chaganti, 1986; Dobbins and Platz, 1986; Folker and Sorenson, 2000), whether women business owners are more risk-averse than men (Carland and Carland, 1991; Carter, 1989; Fagenson, 1993; Fischer 1992), whether women are less interested than men in growing their business quickly (Cromie, 1987a, 1987b; Hisrich, 1986) and to what extent women are more interested than men in fitting their businesses into their existing lifestyle (Hisrich and Brush, 1983). Despite efforts to represent entrepreneurial women as 'just as entrepreneurial as men', over time, the entrepreneurship and business leadership literature has tended to move back to relying on men for case examples.

Moore and Buttner (1997) took a different approach by looking at women entrepreneurs in the context of legislative attempts in the 1970s and 1980s to promote equal opportunity for women. They found that entrepreneurship represents many women's attempts to escape the corporate glass ceiling—that unseen yet powerful barrier which persists in preventing talented, ambitious and hard-working women from reaching the top of the corporate ladder. By creating their own ventures, women could circumvent the whole issue and *start* at the top. Moore and Buttner's approach, taken up by many other researchers, represents genuine progress in the attempt to understand women's entrepreneurship on its own terms. However, it typically focuses on women who left uncongenial corporate environments, and does not address the experience of women who start businesses for other reasons.

CURRENT RESEARCH DRIVERS

The Global Public Policy Push

Moore and Buttner (1997) point to another reason that research into women's entrepreneurship gained momentum in the 1980s: public policy and general public interest began to be influenced by the claim that female entrepreneurship was an important economic and social phenomenon in many countries both domestically and internationally. This interest has continued, with the US Census Bureau now gathering more detailed data about women-led firms, which enabled organisations such as the US National Women's Business Council to report recently that:

> Women-led firms—businesses that are run on a daily basis by a woman or women who own a plurality, but less than a majority, of a business—number just over 1 million, and add 2.5 million jobs and $300 billion in revenues to the 6.5 million majority women-owned firms already counted by the Census Bureau. In total, then—adding in majority women-owned firms—there are 7.5 million women-owned or women-led (WOWL) businesses in the United States (as of 2002), employing 9.6 million workers and generating $1.2 trillion in revenues (US National Women's Business Council, 2007, p. 3).

OECD attention has also focused on women and their firms. As the growing frequency of international symposia organised by academic and public policy bodies during the 1990s and early twenty-first century shows, strenuous efforts are underway to discover how more women business owners might be persuaded to grow their firms. As Thompson and McHugh (1990) point out, female entrepreneurship is linked to globalisation through the 'excellence' movement, and this accompanied notions of female (read 'better') approaches to leadership and human resource management. The founder and managing director of the Grameen Bank, Muhammad Yunus, won a Nobel Prize in 2006 for making microcredit available to poor people, especially women, in Bangladesh. This third-world example endorses the notion that women make good—perhaps even superior—entrepreneurs.

The Regional Public Policy Push

Brush et al. (2006) indicate that research and public policy attention to the phenomenon of women's entrepreneurship continues to increase, with researchers trying to understand how women entrepreneurs' needs and interests may (not must!) differ from those of their male counterparts. They are simultaneously widening the traditional arenas of inquiry into women-owned enterprises to include regional and ethnic concerns. For example, Prowess, the UK-based organisation which promotes women's enterprise support, recently celebrated its fifth anniversary with an event in the British Houses of Parliament, releasing a new analysis: State of Women's Enterprise in the UK (Harding, 2007). The report shows the rate at which women enter self-employment is rising at a faster pace than for men. Nevertheless, women are still less likely than men to start their own businesses. The report also found some significant regional differences, which point to the need for localised support for firm creation. Finally, it argues that much remains unknown about entrepreneurship rates and challenges in the BAME (black, Asian and minority ethnic) communities. In the light of these findings, public policy action needs to shift from the earliest stages of entrepreneurial activity, to:

> ...look at the ways in which women can be taken along the "enterprise journey" from this early stage through to high growth where appropriate, systems and structures that combine both the supply-side interventions with demand-side support and mentoring help to address process issues that underpin women's enterprise in the UK (Harding, 2007, p. 3).

But Where is the 'Theory Push'?

As many critical management theorists point out (for example, Bruni et al., 2004; Collinson and Hearn, 1996; Sinclair, 2004, 2007;), we ought to be cautious about treating claims about the inherently special nature of female entrepreneurship, and its sudden rise in Western countries, as objective facts. Curran and Blackburn (2001) suggest that it is also too easy to get caught up in 'phenomenon-driven' research, where topics such as personal factors, resources, financing, strategies and performance are brought to the agenda by policy makers seeking a particular result, instead of being driven by results from earlier theory building.

In the rush to promote women's entrepreneurship, and discover how to remove or counter liberal feminism-based barriers (personal factors, resources, strategies and so on), we still have not yet taken time to discover more about what women's experience of entrepreneurship actually is. Just as early feminist studies in history focused mainly on women's oppression, studies of women leaders, managers and entrepreneurs were often too narrowly confined to issues such as the difficulties of balancing work and family. The number of studies which do this for men is very small. Studying women in business to find out how they balance work and family reinforces the idea that women's natural place is in the family, and that their involvement in leadership and management, new venture creation, corporate entrepreneurship and so on are secondary concerns. This is another implied model of entrepreneurship and leadership as inherently male. Women entrepreneurs become interesting mainly to the extent that they contrast with what is seen as normal for women.

The 'entrepreneurship and leadership are male' approach also does nothing to discourage the frequent stereotyping of women entrepreneurs, such as the 'iron lady'—the woman who is tougher and more determined than any male boss. This stereotype suggests to potential women entrepreneurs that they will need to 'beat the boys at their own game' if they are to enjoy business success. Relevant to the realm of family business, Bruni et al. (2004) point to the limitations arising from over-attention to the myth of the woman who marries the boss and becomes the heiress. This seductive individual is prejudged to be self-interested and threatening to the business' long-term future, and likely to milk the business instead of building its assets.

Another myth is pertinent to family business: that of the woman whose husband dies suddenly, leaving her alone either to sell the family business or discover a latent entrepreneurial talent and take the business to even greater heights. It is possible to find many examples of both these archetypes of women family business owners. Such stories may be inspirational to women thinking about starting their own firms (Olsson, 2006); however, neither view presents a full picture of women's leadership and entrepreneurial contributions to family business.

Incorporating Women's Experience into Entrepreneurship

This book deals with the concept of entrepreneurship in the light of these myths and research limitations, but works from a broad view of the concept. Brush (2006), de Bruin et al. (2007) and Hurley (1999) point out that if we accept that gendered aspects to entrepreneurship exist (say because of society's norms being focused on women's family roles), we may also miss aspects of women's entrepreneurship that are positive, create value and can teach us more about entrepreneurship generally. We probably also miss 'the more silent feminine personal end' of new-venture entrepreneurship (Bird and Brush, 2002, p. 57), and delete in advance any consideration of how women might act as corporate entrepreneurs—that is, how they act entrepreneurially within existing firms.

Regardless, definitions of entrepreneurial activities as they relate to both new and existing corporations are strikingly inconsistent (Chrisman and Sharma, 1999). Broad views of entrepreneurship are more sensible, and should include corporate entrepreneurship, if we are to examine as-yet-unspecified issues around women's experience of both concepts. Along with Chrisman and Sharma (1999), who in turn follow Collins and Moore (1970), we define independent entrepreneurship as 'the process whereby an individual or group of individuals, acting independently of any association with an existing organization, create a new organization'. In contrast, corporate entrepreneurship is 'the process whereby an individual or a group of individuals, in association with an existing organization, create a new organization or instigate renewal of innovation with that organization' (Chrisman and Sharma, 1999, p. 18).

Our view of these concepts (and others which emerge in the study) will incorporate the experiences of women themselves. The women we spoke with in the course of our research experienced leadership and entrepreneurship in ways broadly similar to how they were traditionally discussed concerning men. For example, they saw leadership as involving strategic thinking, providing direction to staff and serving as a role model to them, having courage, integrity and so on. For women—no less than for men— entrepreneurship involved engaging in various processes of innovation, creating new ventures (or substantially developing existing ones), taking calculated risks and so on. These are classic concerns of entrepreneurship, but we found some new and interesting ways they manifest in women's experience. Our specific interest is to observe how women act as leaders and entrepreneurs in the real-life, messy and highly specific context of a family business—and to do this both with and without reference to how men in the family business have performed these roles.

GETTING TO THE ESSENCE OF FAMILY BUSINESS

Just as with leadership and entrepreneurship, the literature contains no single definition of a family business. Table 1.2, below, which summarises more than 40 years of theoretical viewpoints, indicates the breadth of views on the issue.

Our research does not require a universal definition of family business (notwithstanding its impossibility), because of the range of countries from which we drew our data (Chapter 3 elaborates on aspects of our sample). Nevertheless, it is useful to define common foundational characteristics of family firms. One is the notion that family firms—in contrast with non-family firms—consist of three overlapping subsystems: family, business and ownership (Gersick et al., 1997; Hoy and Vesper, 1994).

But how different are family firms from non-family firms regarding other dimensions? Chrisman, Chua and Sharma (2003) probed this question by reviewing various dimensions of family business including (but not limited to) the basis of firm ownership, management, structures and strategies, performance, ethics and succession planning. However, the magnitude of the differences between family and non-family businesses on these dimensions is subject to the 'family business' definition adopted and, as Table 1.2 shows, so far, no final definition has been agreed.

Table 1.2 Selected Family Business Definitions from the Literature

Reference	Family Business Definition
Chrisman et al. (2005, p. 557)	Family involvement is only a necessary condition; family involvement must be directed toward behaviors that produce a certain distinctiveness before the business can be considered a family firm
Chrisman et al. (1999, p. 25)	Governed and/or managed with the intention to shape and pursue the vision of the business held by a dominant coalition controlled by members of the same family or a small number of families in a manner that is potentially sustainable across generations of the family or families
Sharma et al. (1997, p. 2)	Governed and/or managed on a sustainable, potentially cross-generational, basis to shape and perhaps pursue the formal or implicit vision of the business held by members of the same family or a small number of families
Westhead and Cowling (1997, 1998)	[Members of the firm] have undergone an inter-generational transition, and speak of themselves as a family firm. More than 50 per cent shareholding owned by family, 50 per cent of the daily management team are family members
Litz (1995)	Ownership and management are concentrated in a family unit [in which] individuals within the firm seek to perpetuate or increase the degree of family involvement
Smyrnios and Romano (1994, p. 5)	a) More than 50 per cent of the ownership is held by a single family; b) more than 50 per cent of the ownership is held by more than one family; c) a single family group is effectively controlling the business; and d) a significant proportion of the senior management is drawn from the same family
Carsrud (1994, p. 40)	A firm's ownership and policy making are dominated by members of an 'emotional kinship group' whether members of that group recognize the fact or not
Daily and Dollinger (1992, p. 126; 1993, p. 83)	Two or more individuals with the same last name are listed as officers in the business and/or the top/key managers are related to the owner working in the business

continued overleaf...

Table 1.2 continued...

Reference	Family Business Definition
Stoy Hayward (1992, p. 3)	The family body has a considerable impact on the ongoing and future operations of the business. A business can also be considered to be a family business where any one of the three following criteria are true: a) more than 50 per cent of the voting shares are owned by a single family; b) a single family group is effectively controlling the firm; and c) a significant proportion of the firm's senior management is drawn from the same family
Donckels and Fröhlich (1991, p. 149)	Family members in one family own 60 per cent or more of the equity in the business
Handler (1989, p. 262)	Major operating decisions and plans for leadership succession are influenced by family members serving in management or on the board... indicates that current family involvement in the business, even though these family members may not necessarily be in line for succession, would qualify the organization as a family business
Lansberg et al. (1988, p. 2)	Members of a family have legal control over ownership
Ward (1987, p. 252)	The business will be passed on for the family's next generation to manage and control
Dyer (1986, p. xiv)	Decisions regarding the firm's ownership or management are influenced by relationship to a family (or families)
Rosenblatt et al. (1985, pp. 4–5)	Majority ownership or control lies within a single family and in which two or more family members are, or at some time were, directly involved in the business
Davis (1983, p. 47)	A family business results from the interaction between two sets of organization, family and business, which establishes the basic character of the family business and defines its uniqueness
Barry (1975, p. 42)	Practice is controlled by the members of a single family

women's (as well as men's) skills is likely to increase the competitive advantage of businesses generally, including family businesses, but also that each gender should build on the specific resources available.

Rugman and Verbeke (2002) summarise four characteristics of resource-based views of the firm:

1. The firm's ultimate objective is to achieve sustained, above-normal returns, as compared to rivals.
2. A set of resources, not equally available to all firms, and their combination into competences and capabilities, are preconditions for sustained superior returns.
3. Competences and capabilities lead to sustained superior returns, to the extent that they are firm-specific (that is, imperfectly mobile), valuable to customers, non-substitutable and difficult to imitate.
4. From a dynamic perspective, innovations, especially in terms of new resource combinations, can substantially contribute to sustainable superior returns.

While this resource-based framework gives the essence approach a theoretical foundation, the essence approach is considered difficult to use in a practical sense, especially because 'family-based relatedness' is a difficult resource to measure. This is why most prior research has favoured a 'components of involvement' approach.

Despite such difficulties, this book relies on the essence approach to family business. This is because it has recently yielded important insights about how the 'familiness' of family business—contrary to previous assumptions that 'familiness' is a source of sluggishness and inflexibility—can actually lead to competitive advantage for family firms. We acknowledge that 'familiness' has yet to be definitely articulated for the purposes of theory-building. Accordingly, we employ the term to communicate those valuable, rare, inimitable and non-substitutable features of a family business' resource base, especially those associated with its learning and entrepreneurial orientations.

Table 1.3 Characteristics of Family Businesses

Quality	Meaning
Continuity	Stability and focus
Community	Clannish behaviour
Connections	Dependence on powerful partners
Command	Independence from shareholders which allows quick and unorthodox action

Source: Adapted from Miller and Le Breton-Miller (2005).

As Habbershon and Williams (1999) show, 'familiness', when linked with 'entrepreneurial orientation' and 'learning orientation', forms an important part of the resources available to the firm. Miller and Le Breton-Miller (2005) made a similar finding. From a qualitative, inductively focused analysis of 46 successful and 24 unsuccessful family businesses, they found four qualities to be characteristic of all: 'continuity', 'community', 'connections' and 'command'.

Table 1.3 summarises what each entails in terms of meaning and practice.

To take the first 'C' as an example, 'continuity', the desire for the long-term continuity of the business manifests itself in family business members' statements such as, 'We intend to keep the business in top shape for later generations of the family' or 'We manage the company for the long run'. More important, it is substantiated by practices such as unusually generous investments in the future of the business, and in capabilities central to its mission, as well as in the long apprenticeships and tenures given to managers—first, to instil values and craft, and then to implement these over an extended period (Miller and Le Breton-Miller, 2005, p. 518). The 'four Cs' have both positive and negative aspects: Miller and Le Breton-Miller found that successful family businesses made much more use of the positive aspects of each C, and unsuccessful firms leaned towards each C's downside. This growing interest in the 'familiness' of family business as a source of competitive advantage suggests a further reason for revisiting women's contribution to family firms. That is, rather than only trying to develop solutions to problems of women's psychological domination or potential, or actual problems of discrimination, the four Cs approach suggests we should consider how women leaders and entrepreneurs may also contribute to their family firms' potential strategic competitive advantage.

New Firms May Aspire to Continuity

A further point warrants consideration in relation to the four Cs. Its importance lies in its implications for the range of firms which is appropriate to study. While we may think of family firms as long-lived, a desire for continuity is not limited to firms in a second or later generation. As Litz (1995) and Sharma (2004) assert, even new ventures can be defined as family businesses if they are founded with the intention to continue them as family firms. The intention of continuity may not be particularly well formulated when the business is founded. Sometimes it is only when the second generation expresses an interest in being part of the business in the future that the continuity of the firm as a family firm is noticed. Taking an 'essence' view of family business means we can include women leading first-generation family firms (and not merely those leading second-generation or later firms) in our investigation of how women in family business function as leaders and entrepreneurs.

Some Early Findings on Familiness

Good theoretical grounds exist for taking an essence view of family business when looking at women in the context of family firms. There are also solid empirical reasons for being concerned with 'familiness' in our discussion of leadership and entrepreneurship in family firms. As noted earlier, it makes sense to include the expansion and renewal of existing firms in our definition of entrepreneurship, partly because increasing attention is being paid to the competitive advantages arising from the 'familiness' of family businesses, many of which are sustained over long periods (Habbershon and Pistrui, 2002; Habbershon and Williams, 1999; Habbershon et al., 2003). Empirical work also justifies the view that family firms serve as training grounds for the next generation of entrepreneurs. Carr and Sequeira (2007), for example, in their survey-based study of 308 business people in a southwest US city, found that prior family business exposure directly and indirectly increased respondents' entrepreneurial intent. This occurred even when family business exposure was defined broadly to include having had a parent who had ever owned a business or having ever worked in a family member's business.

Kellermanns and Eddleston (2006) also took a 'family' perspective on corporate entrepreneurship, examining the degree to which corporate entrepreneurship in family firms was influenced by family members' willingness to change, the current level of generational involvement and family members' perceived technological opportunities. They also considered strategic planning as a moderator of these factors, and found that strategic planning led to higher levels of corporate entrepreneurship in organisations where only one family generation is present. However, contrary to their predictions, they found that strategic planning had little effect on the corporate entrepreneurship of multi-generation family firms, and that multi-generation family firms that undertook relatively little strategic planning actually appeared to have the highest level of corporate entrepreneurship.

The reasons for this unexpected finding are unclear. Kellermann and Eddleston speculate that the lower level of strategic planning in multi-generation family firms may result from the greater political activity needed to accommodate the diverse interests and ambitions of people in such firms, or that the greater level of professionalism and formalisation typically associated with multi-generation firms may simply make strategic planning less important. Regardless, their finding is important to the task undertaken in this book because it suggests that, contrary to popular opinion, first-generation family firms do not necessarily become less entrepreneurial over time, nor are multi-generation firms always the least entrepreneurial. As Litz and Kleysen (2001) suggest, entrepreneurship can be found in both first-generation and later-generation family firms, while other family firms may lack entrepreneurial spirit across many generations. This in turn suggests that knowing more about the operation of family factors, including family members' specific roles, will help in understanding how family firms engage in corporate entrepreneurship and realise its benefits.

Other family aspects to have attracted empirical investigation include whether the firm is a) founder-centred, b) a sibling/cousin consortium or c) an open family firm (Salvato, 2004). In a founder-centred firm the founder still plays a centrally powerful role. In a sibling/cousin consortium firm the second, third or later generation holds majority ownership and plays a central managerial role; this leads to intense interplay between siblings and cousins. In contrast, open family firms are established companies where no single family or group of related families possesses a majority ownership. Top management do not usually perceive them as family firms, although some family influence may be present, so decisions are influenced more by business imperatives and less by family influence (Salvato, 2004, p. 69).

In seeking correlates of entrepreneurship (that is, firm action relating to product market and technological innovation, risk taking and proactiveness), Salvato (2004) considers four variable sets: individual CEO characteristics, family firm issues, ownership structures and organisational characteristics. He claims that elements of all four variable sets are important for fostering entrepreneurship in family firms, but that how each could function as an entrepreneurship lever varies with the type of family firm. In founder-based family firms, attention should be focused on the founder's previous experiences and on their family, and allowing second-generation family members to take an active role in entrepreneurial processes. Founder-based family firms should also develop an active board of external directors, involving investment companies in ownership, and especially, fostering employees' contribution through value-based compensation. The entrepreneurial potential of sibling/cousin consortiums can be enhanced by broadening successors' leadership experiences in unrelated activities. However, successors' previous experiences in the same industry may actually have a negative influence on entrepreneurship. The level of entrepreneurship in open family firms could be enhanced by ensuring a relatively large number of managers (to let several promising innovative ideas emerge), increased venture capital participation and discouragement of ownership by inactive managers (Salvato, 2004, p. 75). Thus this study also underlines the importance of managing aspects of founder and later generation involvement to maintain the family-controlled firm's entrepreneurial spirit.

Zahra (2005) makes a finding broadly similar to the studies by Carr and Sequeira (2007), Kellermann and Eddleston (2006) and Salvato (2004), discussed above. Zahra's study uses agency theory to highlight key correlates of risk taking among 209 US family firms involved in manufacturing. The results show that family ownership and involvement promote entrepreneurship, whereas the long tenure of CEO founders has the opposite effect. This result suggests managers need to capitalise on the skills and talents of their family members in promoting entrepreneurship and selective venturing into new market arenas.

These studies did not specifically address gender issues in family firms, although Salvato (2004, p. 75) claims that his findings for founder-based family firms hold for both male and female founders. Nevertheless, all three studies indicate the importance of understanding how women—as well as men—learn the skills of leadership and entrepreneurship in family-controlled businesses. This will provide a more nuanced understanding of the issues that confront women entrepreneurs generally, including their capacity to start new ventures and to maintain and develop existing ones.

GUIDING PRINCIPLES OF OUR STUDY

We have already argued that more remains to be discovered about women entrepreneurs. We have also pointed out the value in using an essence approach to defining family firms. These two ideas are closely linked to the principles that guided us in carrying out our study. They include focusing on issues arising from the intersection of 'family' with 'business', including larger as well as smaller family firms in the study; sticking with a 'doing', rather than a 'being' approach to entrepreneurship; and staying close to our data sources, in terms of the ideas people in family business espouse and the practices they actually carry out.

Linking Family and Business

One way to avoid predetermined views of 'male' and 'female' approaches to family business management and leadership is to move directly to issues arising from the intersection of 'family' and 'business'—two topics which, as is often observed, need not necessarily come together. The wish to understand the effects of this incidental (rather than necessary) link has spurred much family business research and drawn attention to many peculiarities of family businesses, such as their strategic focus on stewardship for later generations (for example, Anderson and Reeb, 2003; Corbetta and Salvato, 2004; Davis et al., 1997; Salvato, 2002). A focus on stewardship appears in some of the largest family firms. Marilyn Carlson Nelson, now in her sixties, recently succeeded her father as CEO of the giant travel firm Carlson, which has approximately $US7 billion in annual revenue. Its brands include Radisson Hotels and Resorts and T.G.I. Friday restaurants. The firm is one hundred per cent family owned. Carlson Nelson is dedicated to fulfilling her father's wish to keep the firm family owned until at least the fifth generation:

> I have to be steward of the Carlson companies to continue to earn the support of the rest of the family and our employees who are the key stakeholders. Because I am

not the founder, I must work with the family group to ensure [that] they receive economic and psychological value from the company that is equal of better than what they will get from other investments (cited in Halamandaris and Halamandaris, 2004, p. 93).

Family firms' conservative approach to risk also receives much attention in the academic literature (for example, Bartholomeusz and Tanewski, 2006; Chandler, 1990; Gedajlovic et al., 2004; James, 1999; Meyer and Zucker, 1989; Schulze et al., 2002; Zahra, 2005). Linked to this, family firms' closely held ownership structures have provoked research into a variety of agency issues (for example, Blanco-Mazagatos et al., 2007; Carney, 2005; Daily and Dollinger, 1992; Denis et al., 1997; Fama, 1980; Fama and Jensen, 1983; Geeraerts, 1984; Jensen and Meckling, 1976; Randøy and Goel, 2003).

Our own previous work considers the implications of the special way people working in family businesses typically view their firms, describing them as 'just like any other business, except...' The 'except' is invariably followed by an unusual feature of the family business environment which arises from the intersection of 'business' and 'family'. Looking at how women deal with the vagaries and paradoxes of 'familiness' when it is joined to 'business' moves the discussion closer to a variety of classic and fruitful preoccupations of family business research.

Including Large and Small Firms

Including both large and small family firms in the study is another way we avoided some typical problems seen in the existing literature on women entrepreneurs. Previous research on women business owners mostly focuses on women's presence in small and medium enterprises, rather than large businesses. Studies of female business ownership (for example, APEC 1998 ; Brush et al., 2006) in both developed and developing countries found that women typically operate businesses only in sectors with lower barriers to entry and with the help of skills learned through gender socialisation. The risk is that future research may focus solely on what women are assumed to 'lack' in small firms: status, networks, credibility and capital. The very term 'lacking' reveals an implicit norm based on 'large' male-owned firms, which are assumed to be 'rich' in these things, and therefore other resources of women's firms risk being overlooked.

To look at the issue another way, taken together, family businesses' contribution to the international economy is large (Astrachan and Shanker, 1996; Jaffe and Lane, 2004; Morck and Yeung, 2003). In the Australian context, and even using a narrow definition of family business, the *Business Longitudinal Survey, Australia, 1994–95 to 1997–98* (BLS) shows that at least half of all businesses are family businesses (ABS, 2000). Australian family firms are also estimated to have a combined wealth of $A3.6 trillion, and employ 50 per cent of the private sector workforce (Smyrnios and

Walker, 2003). They constitute approximately 67 per cent of the small and medium enterprise (SME) sector in the Australian economy (Kotey, 2005). Moreover, not all family firms are small: over half of Australia's top 500 private companies, including names such as Boyd, de Bortoli, Kidman, Linfox, Myer and Packer are family owned (Matterson, 2002). Many large— if not the very largest—family firms in Australia and elsewhere have women who are CEOs or run major business units within them. Accordingly, our study includes the experience of women in established family firms of well over 100 employees, as well as the experience of women in family-based small or medium-sized enterprises.

In Entrepreneurship, It's What You Do, Not What You Are

Following the advice of Gartner (1988, 1990) to avoid stereotypes in the study of entrepreneurship, this book closely examines what women in family business do, rather than simply what they are. Our three analytical frameworks, which Chapter 3 discusses in detail, are helpful in this respect because they focus on problems and activities. For example, our 'four phases of learning family business' framework (Moores and Barrett, 2002) focuses on how family business leaders experience and learn to cope with a series of dilemmas and paradoxes in managing family firms. It makes no *a priori* claims about whether women and men are the same or different in how they do this. Our task here is to consider how women in family business encounter and deal with these phases, and how they do this in ways similar as well as different from men.

Sticking Closely to the Data

Last, but most important, we are guided by the experiences and stories of women in family businesses. They are better placed to let us know, for example, about their experience of innovation—whether this takes the form of groundbreaking and heroic change, or more subtle ways of preparing their businesses for the future. They are better qualified to let us know how maintaining the status quo—and the continuity or quality of sameness associated with the 'familiness' of family business—is increasingly being recognised as a source of competitive advantage (Anderson and Reeb, 2003; Miller and Le Breton-Miller, 2005), and how this can be a way of incorporating radical innovation into a family business culture.

This chapter considered some of the research gaps, problems and general principles that guide and inspire this book. The next chapter explores data about the situation of women entrepreneurs worldwide, and argues that understanding how women learn the skills of leadership and entrepreneurship in the family business setting can illuminate issues that confront women entrepreneurs generally.

NOTES

[1] *American Family Business Survey* (2007): www.ffi.org/images/misc/FFI_familybusiness.pdf
[2] *Coutts 2005 Family Business Survey*: www.coutts.com/files/family_business_survey.pdf

2. A Global Perspective

With the growing attention to women's entrepreneurship which Chapter 1 discusses, there is increasing interest in the profile of women entrepreneurs in the international context, and in how women everywhere may be encouraged to start new businesses. This interest focuses especially on how women can be encouraged to start opportunity-based (rather than necessity-based) firms—that is, how they can choose to be an entrepreneur as one of several desirable career options, rather than take that path through lack of other opportunities. Here we add insights from the empirical research findings which Chapter 1 discusses, about the value of a family business background for creating capacity and interest in entrepreneurship. This chapter sets out some recent findings about characteristics of women's entrepreneurial activity worldwide and discusses them in the light of the potential of family businesses as training grounds for entrepreneurship.

THE GLOBAL ENTREPRENEURSHIP MONITOR (GEM)

The data for this chapter is drawn from the Global Entrepreneurship Monitor (GEM), a not-for-profit academic research consortium that aims to 'make high quality international research data on entrepreneurial activity readily available to as wide an audience as possible' (GEM, 2008). Specifically, it aims to 'measure differences in the level of entrepreneurial activity between countries, uncover factors determining national levels of entrepreneurial activity and identify policies that may enhance national levels of entrepreneurial activity' (Allen et al., 2008, p. 8). The GEM is the largest single study of entrepreneurial activity in the world. Following its inception in 1997, it has reported annually since 1999. The 1999 report covered 10 countries, its most recent report for 2007 covers 42 countries, and 48 were expected to participate in 2008.

To date, four special reports, based on data from the 2004, 2005, 2006 and 2007 GEM surveys, have been devoted to analysing women's entrepreneurship on a worldwide basis. Specifically, each aimed to: a) measure the level of women's entrepreneurial activity across countries, b) understand why women become involved in entrepreneurial activity, and c) suggest policies to increase women's involvement in entrepreneurship (Minniti et al., 2005, p. 11).

The next sections examine the value of bringing a family business perspective to GEM findings about five topics relating to male and female entrepreneurs:

1. participation in early-stage entrepreneurial activity
2. necessity and opportunity-based entrepreneurship
3. the influence of work status on entrepreneurship
4. the influence of education on entrepreneurship
5. factors influencing perceptions of the entrepreneurial environment, including knowing someone who has recently started a business, perceiving opportunities in the near future, believing you have the skills and knowledge to start a firm and fear of failure.

Participation in Early-Stage Entrepreneurial Activity

Table 2.1 summarises data from the GEM reports of 2004–2007 inclusive on the prevalence of men's and women's early-stage entrepreneurship in low, medium and high-income countries. The GEM defines early-stage entrepreneurship as ownership of a business aged 42 months or less. For 2006, data for low and middle income countries was not reported separately. The 2007 report distinguishes between low and middle-income countries in Europe/Asia and Latin America/Caribbean. Allen et al. (2008) draw attention to the regional and cultural differences between these two parts of the world which have a major impact on early-stage entrepreneurship with respect to gender.

For all country income groups, in no year did the level of women's entrepreneurial activity surpass that of men. Moreover, in most years, men in high-income countries were almost twice as likely to be early-stage entrepreneurs as women. For example, in high-income countries in 2007, 8.2 per cent of men were early-stage entrepreneurs, compared to 4.3 per cent of women. The gap is still wider in low-income countries.

Concerning the results for 2004, Minniti et al. (2005) comment that a stable ratio of female-to-male entrepreneurship across countries suggests that:

> ...entrepreneurial attitudes are influenced by some universal factors and that, when making decisions with respect to starting a new business, women and men are influenced by many of the same variables. However, the fact that male entrepreneurship rates are systematically and significantly higher than female entrepreneurship rates also indicates that these factors do not influence both genders necessarily in the same way or with the same intensity (Minniti et al., 2005, p. 17).

This observation points to one of the objectives of this book: the value of understanding women's experience of entrepreneurship, especially in the family business context, separately from that of men.

Table 2.1 Early-Stage Entrepreneurial Activity by Gender and Country Cluster

Year			Country Income Level	
		Low	Middle	High
2004	Women	12.5	3.9	6.4
	Men	18.2	6.3	9.0
2005	Women	–	6.6	4.7
	Men	–	9.2	8.8
		Low/Middle		High
2006	Women	10.7		4.0
	Men	14.6		7.6
		Europe/Asia	Latin America/ Caribbean	
2007	Women	7.6	14.4	4.3
	Men	11.7	19.6	8.2

Note: All figures are percentages of the population aged 18–64. Each country's representation in the sample is weighted according to population size.

Source: Adapted from Allen et al. (2007), Allen et al. (2008), Minniti et al. (2005) and Minniti et al. (2006).

Necessity and Opportunity-Based Entrepreneurship

Table 2.2 summarises international differences according to country income groupings for the two primary reasons respondents to the GEM surveys gave for their involvement in entrepreneurial activities—opportunity and necessity. Opportunity entrepreneurship estimates the number of people who started their own business as one of several desirable career options; that is, starting a business reflected their desire to take advantage of a business opportunity. Necessity-based entrepreneurship estimates the number of people who started their own business because other employment options were absent or unsatisfactory.

The figures in Table 2.2 represent the combined percentages of three groups of people aged 18–64 in the population of each country: nascent entrepreneurs, early-stage entrepreneurs and established business owners. Nascent entrepreneurs are actively involved in setting up a business that they will own or co-own, which has not paid salaries, wages or any other payments to the owners for more than three months. Early-stage entrepreneurs are owner-managers of a new business that has paid salaries, wages or any other payments to the owners for between three and 42 months. Established business owners run a business that has paid salaries, wages or any other payments to the owners for more than 42 months.

Table 2.2 Opportunity and Necessity-Based Entrepreneurship by Gender and Country Cluster

			Country Income Level		
Year			Low	Middle	High
2005	Women	Necessity	–	2.55	0.54
		Opportunity	–	4.63	3.09
	Men	Necessity	–	2.94	1.02
		Opportunity	–	6.36	5.77
			Low/Middle		High
2006	Women	Necessity	3.99		0.59
		Opportunity	7.17		3.40
	Men	Necessity	4.20		1.06
		Opportunity	10.53		6.84
			Europe/ Asia	Latin America/ Caribbean	
2007	Women	Necessity	2.22	5.33	0.83
		Opportunity	4.35	7.15	3.56
	Men	Necessity	4.50	0.51	1.18
		Opportunity	7.35	12.38	6.85

Note: All figures are percentages of the population aged 18–64. Each country's representation in the table is weighted according to population size.

Source: Adapted from Allen et al. (2007), Allen et al. (2008) and Minniti et al. (2006).

Table 2.2 shows that, like most men, most women start a new business in order to pursue an opportunity. Nevertheless, across all country clusters during 2005–2007, necessity entrepreneurship was much more widespread among women than men. For example, in high-income countries in 2007, 6.85 per cent of men were opportunity-based entrepreneurs, compared to only 1.18 per cent who pursued necessity-based entrepreneurship. For women in the same group, the percentages were 3.56 and 0.83 respectively. The disparity was especially marked in low-income countries in 2006 and low/middle income countries in Latin America and the Caribbean in 2007.

These findings have important implications when we consider family firms' 'training ground' role. As the empirical studies discussed in the previous chapter show, exposure to a family business increases entrepreneurial intentions and behaviour, whether these are oriented towards maintaining and developing an existing family business which will pass to future generations, or starting a new firm. Accordingly, family firms are likely to provide skills in opportunity recognition and development, directing potential entrepreneurs towards opportunity, rather than necessity-based entrepreneurship.

Entrepreneurship and Work Status

Table 2.3 shows the extent to which being involved in early-stage entrepreneurial activity is associated with women entrepreneurs' work status; that is, whether they are working, not working, have retired or are students. Early-stage entrepreneurs are defined in the same way as above.

Table 2.3 shows that from 2005–2007, the likelihood of women being involved in entrepreneurial activity was three to four times higher for those who also were employed in a waged job (whether full or part-time), compared to those who were not working or who were retired or were students. For example, in high-income countries in 2007, 6.0 per cent of women who were working were early-stage entrepreneurs, compared to 1.5 per cent who were not working and 0.8 per cent who were students. As the authors of the GEM reports on women's entrepreneurship consistently comment, working may give people access to resources, social capital and ideas which help them to establish an entrepreneurial venture.

During 2005–2007, the employment patterns of women involved in entrepreneurial activity were broadly similar between country income clusters, except that the rates of non-working women, students and retired women participating in entrepreneurship were significantly higher in middle-income countries (2005) or low/middle-income countries (2006 and 2007). The reports' authors say this is because the lack of safety nets and social welfare for unemployed women in middle or low/middle income countries forces them to start necessity-based businesses. The phenomenon is even more evident for women entrepreneurs in the Latin American and Caribbean low/middle-income group, whose data are displayed separately for 2007. This group of countries shows a much larger percentage of women starting companies, regardless of employment status. This probably reflects the higher rate of necessity-based entrepreneurship among women in this region. Broadly similar relationships between work status and participation in early-stage entrepreneurial activity are observed for men as for women.

Table 2.3 Female Early-Stage Entrepreneurial Activity by Work Status and Country Cluster

Year		Country Income Level		
		Low	Middle	High
2005	Working	–	12.3	5.8
	Not working	–	3.9	2.4
	Retired/students	–	3.8	1.0
		Low/Middle		High
2006	Working	12.3		5.7
	Not working	3.9		1.2
	Retired/students	3.8		0.7
		Europe/ Asia	Latin America/ Caribbean	
2007	Working	1.4	2.2	6.0
	Not working	3.4	9.4	1.5
	Retired/students	1.1	6.3	0.8

Note: Figures represent percentages of female early-stage entrepreneurs aged 18–64. Each country's representation is weighted according to their population size.

Source: Adapted from Allen et al. (2007), Allen et al. (2008) and Minniti et al. (2006).

The findings highlighted in Table 2.3 also point to the value of learning in family firms. As evident in the research cited in the previous chapter, family firms are well-documented as being sources of financial resources, social capital and ideas for their members. They may also employ family members who are as yet uncertain what career they will choose, or who need temporary employment for other reasons. Even when they are not formally employed in the family firm, family members often spend considerable time in it, and this often promotes business ownership in the longer term. Thus, family businesses often blur the usual distinctions in work status, while simultaneously building family members' entrepreneurial skills.

Entrepreneurship and Education

Table 2.4 presents data on women entrepreneurs' educational level by country income group for the years 2005–2007.

Table 2.4 Female Early-Stage Entrepreneurship by Education and Country Cluster

		Country Income Level		
Year		Low	Middle	High
2005	Some secondary	–	45.0	27.8
	Secondary	–	20.0	19.6
	Post secondary	–	17.0	17.7
	University graduate	–	15.9	32.9
			Low/Middle	
2006	Some secondary		36.5	25.2
	Secondary		26.4	24.8
	Post secondary		25.4	14.9
	University graduate		11.8	35.0
		Europe/ Asia	Latin America/ Caribbean	
2007	Some secondary	39.2	34.1	21.6
	Secondary	24.6	32.1	28.4
	Post secondary	16.8	23.4	21.6
	University graduate	19.4	10.4	28.4

Note: Figures represent percentages of female early-stage entrepreneurs in the population aged 18–64. Early-stage entrepreneurship is as defined earlier. Each country's representation is weighted according to population size.

Source: Adapted from Allen et al. (2007), Allen et al. (2008) and Minniti et al. (2006).

Educational level typically influences the type and level of people's opportunities for employment, and so can indirectly affect women's entrepreneurial behaviour. However, beyond this, the direct influence of education on women's entrepreneurial activity is complex and varies between countries. Table 2.4 shows that, on average, and in all three years 2005–07, women early-stage entrepreneurs in high-income countries were better educated than those in low or middle-income countries. For 2005 and 2006 in high-income countries, more than half of women entrepreneurs had completed their secondary education, and more than one-quarter had graduated from university. In low or middle-income countries in 2006, the percentage of women early-stage entrepreneurs with less than a completed secondary education was considerably higher than in high-income countries. In 2007 the percentage of early-stage entrepreneurs with less than a completed secondary education in the low/middle-income Latin American and Caribbean group was 34.1 per cent, and 39.2 per cent for the low or middle-income European and Asian group.

Even though confirmed data are not available, the educational profile of women leaders of family business firms is unlikely to differ substantially from that of the general population of women entrepreneurs. However, a consensus is emerging in the family business literature on succession, which argues that family businesses typically try to ensure their successors are highly qualified, both formal education and relevant experience in the family firm and elsewhere. Understanding the dynamics of women's formal and informal learning outside and inside the family firm should contribute to our understanding of how women assume leadership positions in family firms.

Perceptions about the Entrepreneurial Environment

The GEM reports examine entrepreneurs' personal perceptions and knowledge as well as their demographic circumstances. While these perceptions may be subjective—even biased—they are important for the present study because Minniti and Nardone (2007) found that they correlate significantly with an entrepreneurial 'mindset'. Accordingly, the GEM surveys asked respondents a) whether they personally knew entrepreneurs who had started a business in the last two years, b) how they perceived the business environment in terms of the opportunities it offered them, c) to what extent they believed they had the requisite knowledge for business start-up and d) whether fear of failure would prevent them from starting a business.

Knowing Someone Who Had Started a Business in the Previous Two Years

Table 2.5 compares female and male entrepreneurs and non-entrepreneurs in terms of whether they personally knew an entrepreneur who had started a business in the previous two years.

In family businesses, knowing an entrepreneur on a personal basis often occurs simply because of the environment one is born into. While the original entrepreneur may be a member of an earlier generation, the next generation of potential leaders is typically strongly aware of the founder's values, strategies, business philosophies and so on. This book probes how these values, strategies and business philosophies work themselves out for women who aspire to be leaders of family firms. The mini-cases of Kobkarn

Wattanavrangkul and Letizia Tufari which follow illustrate how family
businesses can help women acquire business acumen by having an
entrepreneur in the family. For Kobkarn, the entrepreneur was her father;
Letizia was inspired by her mother's example.

*Table 2.5 Knowing Someone Who Had Started a Business in the Previous
Two Years*

Year		Country Income Level		
		Low	Middle	High
2005	Female NE	–	31.8	30.5
	Male NE	–	40.9	38.4
	Female ESE	–	60.6	57.5
	Male ESE	–	67.4	68.3
		Low/Middle		
2006	Female NE	35.2		26.6
	Male NE	41.7		35.4
	Female ESE	61.3		55.5
	Male ESE	65.4		62.5
		Europe/ Asia	Latin America/ Caribbean	
2007	Female NE	36.5	34.1	27.9
	Male NE	43.6	46.8	36.5
	Female ESE	54.2	56.9	56.6
	Male ESE	76.8	68.2	60.4

Note: ESE = early-stage entrepreneur. NE (non-early-stage entrepreneurs) includes people who
have never established a business and owners of businesses that have paid salaries, wages or
other payments for more than 42 months. Figures represent percentages of female and male non-
entrepreneurs and entrepreneurs aged 18–64. Each country's representation is weighted
according to their population.

Source: Adapted from Allen et al. (2007), Allen et al. (2008) and Minniti et al. (2006).

Table 1.2 continued...

Reference	Family Business Definition
Channon (1971, p. 161)	A firm [is] held to be a family firm if: a) a family member is a chief executive officer; b) there have been at least two generations of family control; and c) a minimum of 5 per cent of the voting stock is still held by the family or trust interests associated with it
Church (1969, p. 211)	The whole capital is privately held, practically all the important and administrative posts are filled by members of a single family
Donnelley (1964, p. 94)	A company is a family firm when it is closely identified with at least two generations of a family and when this link has had a mutual influence on company policy and on the interests and objectives of the family

Source: Irava (n.d.) unpublished PhD thesis (in progress).

Litz's (1995) definitional construction cuts through this complexity. He suggests that family business can be defined using two complementary approaches: a structure-based approach and an intention-based approach. The structure-based approach defines the family firm by considering the various elements of how it is owned and managed; while the intention-based approach is based on the values and preferences of the family firm's members towards family-based relatedness. This 'structure versus intention' distinction lies behind the 'component involvement' and 'essence' approaches to defining family business. The 'essence approach' (Chrisman et al., 2005) states that family components—typically, ownership, governance, management and transgenerational succession—are insufficient on their own to define a firm as a family business. These components must be directed towards behaviours that produce a certain distinctiveness if a firm is to qualify as a family business. The distinctiveness asserted in the essence approach can be ascribed to the family presence and the existence of 'familiness' resources (Habbershon, 2006; Habbershon and Williams, 1999; Habbershon et al., 2003) within the family business.

'Familiness', Women and the Resource-Based View of the Firm (RBV)

According to resource-based views of the firm, the firm's or individual's unique bundle of resources contributes to competitive advantage (Alvarez and Busenitz, 2001; Barney, 1991). The essence approach implies that 'familiness' is part of the nature, characteristics and potential of a family firm's unique resource base. An RBV approach is also compatible with our perspective on gender matters. It suggests that finding the best use of

Mini-Case—Entrepreneurial Exposure

Kobkarn Wattanavrangkul is Vice-President of Toshiba Thailand Co. Ltd. Kobkarn was born into Thailand's royal family, but was raised through the ranks of the family company, Toshiba Thailand, on her father's 'no privilege' code. This close acquaintance with an established entrepreneur gave her both a solid work ethic and exposure to the firm and its networks, which in turn developed her insight into the business. Several promotions later, she gained her current post of Vice-President. Her business acumen became clear during the 1997 crash. Rather than succumbing to the crisis, Toshiba Thailand actually launched a range of acclaimed information technology products under Kobkarn's leadership. This helped the company develop further. It emerged from the crisis in good standing and has gained further strength since then.

Source: Adapted from *Leading Women Entrepreneurs of the World* (2004).

Mini-Case—When the Next Course is a New Career

Letizia Tufari, co-founder with her mother of Venturi's Table, a corporate cookery events business, appeared to have a dream career in front of her. She had completed her business degree at Warwick University, had a high-flying job at Pfizer and was on track to become sales director of a major blue-chip firm. But something was missing. As she put it, 'I really enjoyed working at Pfizer, but I just started realising that I didn't want my boss' job, and I didn't want my boss's boss's job. One day I just thought, *Shoot! Where am I going with this?*'

She considered taking time out, and studying for an MBA, then decided she wanted to try running a small business. Her mother, Anna Venturi, had already run a successful cookery school and catering company called Italian Secrets for ten years, and Letizia thought she might 'gatecrash' that business. Her mother was hesitant at first, warning her daughter against leaving the job security and good salary at Pfizer. But when Letizia made it clear she was definitely leaving her job, her mother snapped her up and they started Venturi's Table together. Almost three years on, mother and daughter enjoy repeat business from firms such as Google and Microsoft, and are projecting just under £1 million turnover next year.

Source: Adapted from Dewing (2008).

Perceiving Market Opportunities

People's perceptions that unexploited market opportunities exist often spur their entrepreneurial activity. Nevertheless, people vary markedly in the extent to which they are alert to such opportunities. Table 2.6 presents data for 2005–2007 on the extent to which early-stage entrepreneurs and people not engaged in entrepreneurial activity perceive current market opportunities.

Table 2.6 indicates that from 2005–2007, early-stage entrepreneurs had much more confidence than non-entrepreneurs that good market opportunities would be available to them soon. For example, in high-income countries in 2007, 64.6 per cent of male entrepreneurs and 56.7 per cent of female entrepreneurs reported this confidence, compared to 35.4 per cent of male non-entrepreneurs and 33.5 per cent of female non-entrepreneurs. However, for the most part, male early-stage entrepreneurs expressed more confidence about this than female early-stage entrepreneurs. Male non-entrepreneurs were also more confident about this issue than female non-entrepreneurs within the same country income cluster.

Table 2.6 Perception of Good Market Opportunities in the Next Six Months

| Year | | Country Income Level | | |
		Low	Middle	High
2005	Female NE	–	29.7	31.8
	Male NE	–	33.4	38.4
	Female ESE	–	62.6	55.6
	Male ESE	–	60.1	63.3
		Low/Middle		
2006	Female NE	34.0		32.2
	Male NE	38.1		38.6
	Female ESE	62.8		57.6
	Male ESE	68.0		59.0
		Europe/ Asia	Latin America/ Caribbean	
2007	Female NE	30.9	29.1	33.5
	Male NE	33.7	44.1	35.4
	Female ESE	50.3	67.1	59.7
	Male ESE	57.4	70.9	64.6

Note: ESE and NE are as defined for Table 2.5, above. Figures represent percentages of men and women aged 18–64. Each country's representation is weighted according to population size.

Source: Adapted from Allen et al. (2007), Allen et al. (2008) and Minniti et al. (2006).

The GEM presents opportunity perception simply as a broad measure of entrepreneurial confidence, but many scholars discuss it in a more fine-grained fashion. Hills (1995), for example, differentiates between various stages of dealing with an opportunity. Recognising an entrepreneurial opportunity was probably preceded by various search strategies and prompted by various cognitive cues. Recognising an opportunity precedes evaluating it, a process that differs according to whether the opportunity is being evaluated 'in general', or as one to which the entrepreneur or a private equity financier themselves might devote funds. At the process level, innovation is closely related to opportunity. As with the literature on opportunity, the literature on innovation is broad, discussing types of innovation (for example, Kanter, 1989), the adoption of innovation (for example, Collins et al., 1988), managing innovation (for example, Christensen, 1997) and the scope of innovation (for example, Cooper, 1999) and so on.

Researchers have not often studied family businesses to discover what they reveal about opportunity or innovation. However, Craig et al. (2006), in a ten-year longitudinal study of family firms' strategy, systems and environment for innovation, shows that family firms place considerable importance on innovation practices and strategy. This is at odds with the perception that family firms' typical concern to include family goals in their performance measures means they are less concerned with promoting innovation. Dibrell and Craig (2006) studied a specific area of innovation strategy: the incorporation of the natural environment into firms' strategic processes. They show that family firms are better than non-family firms at facilitating environmentally friendly firm policies that are associated with improved firm innovation and greater financial performance. Other studies (for example, Craig and Lindsay, 2002) found that emotional attachments to family assets may interfere with the innovation process. All this suggests that understanding how female (as well as male) entrepreneurs in family businesses deal with opportunity and innovation can illuminate the entrepreneurial process as a whole.

Mini-Case—Growing the Opportunities for Growth in a Family Business

Mallika Srinivasan is General Manager of Tractors and Farm Equipment Company (TAFE), a $US750 million tractor firm incorporated in 1969 at Chennai in India. Mallika Srinivasan entered the family business in 1986 at the age of 27. She credits the expert guidance of her father and the support of her team as major factors in her capacity to transform TAFE into a high technology-oriented company.

Today, the company occupies a niche as the leading tractor manufacturer in India, but it has also expanded into engineering plastics, panel instruments, automotive batteries, gears, hydraulic pumps and farm implements. The company has a long alliance with Massey Ferguson (now a part of Agco, USA), and plans to export fully constructed tractors to Agco. Mallika Srinivasan's commitment to research and development, her capacity to recognise and exploit opportunities and develop strategic alliances for the family firm, including during times of economic downturn, has contributed to the firm's growth from a company with a turnover of Rs 850 million when she joined it to a current turnover of Rs 12,000 million.

Source: Adapted from *Indian Heroes*, n.d.

Table 2.7 Has the Required Knowledge and Skills to Start a Business

		Country Income Level		
Year		Low	Middle	High
2005	Female NE	–	36.0	35.6
	Male NE	–	46.3	49.5
	Female ESE	–	81.8	84.2
	Male ESE	–	85.4	89.8
		Low/Middle		
2006	Female NE	40.7		32.9
	Male NE	49.6		46.3
	Female ESE	83.4		86.5
	Male ESE	86.5		92.4
		Europe/ Asia	Latin America/ Caribbean	
2007	Female NE	30.2	54.8	36.2
	Male NE	41.0	68.8	49.5
	Female ESE	76.5	86.4	85.5
	Male ESE	83.5	92.1	88.7

Note: ESE and NE are as defined for Table 2.5, above. Figures represent percentages of men and women aged 18–64. Each country's representation is weighted according to population size.

Source: Adapted from Allen et al. (2007), Allen et al. (2008) and Minniti et al. (2006).

Having the knowledge and skills to start a business

Entrepreneurship scholars (for example, Carland and Carland, 1992; Chen et al., 1998; Delmar and Davidsson, 2000) repeatedly found that entrepreneurs and non-entrepreneurs differ on attributes such as self-confidence, and that people's beliefs in their capability to perform tasks influence how entrepreneurial intentions and actual behaviours develop—including starting a business. In addition, being confident in one's skills to start a business increases entrepreneurial alertness and leads to the creation of more new firms. However, these effects may be asymmetric across genders (Verheul et al., 2005).

Table 2.7 presents data on the extent to which early-stage and non-entrepreneurs perceive they have the required skills to start a business, and indicates that both male and female early-stage entrepreneurs have consistently greater confidence that they possess the necessary skills and abilities to start a business than people who have not previously started a firm. However, and echoing earlier results, men typically perceive that they have greater knowledge and skills than women, whether or not they are engaged in entrepreneurial activity. For example, in high-income countries in 2007, 88.7 per cent of male and 85.5 per cent of female early-stage entrepreneurs said they had the knowledge and skills to start a business, compared to 49.5 per cent of male and 36.2 per cent of female non-entrepreneurs. Thus, the findings of Table 2.7 are consistent with Tables 2.5 and 2.6: people already engaged in entrepreneurial activity probably have an advantage over those who are not. As noted in the previous chapter, exposure to a family business can be a good way of acquiring these valuable skills and abilities.

Mini-Case—Recycling Her Work Experience

Cheung Yan, co-founder with her younger brother of Nine Dragons, a paper recycling company, is cited as the richest woman in China. She worked in the paper recycling industry in the People's Republic of China before moving to Hong Kong in 1985 to start her own paper recycling firm. She had just $US4,000 when she began the company, but the firm now exports to the US, the Middle East and several Asian countries.

Ms Cheung had low start-up capital, but she held a substantial intangible asset: her extensive industry experience meant she had already thought deeply about how to get mainland Chinese manufacturing companies to accept recycled paper in place of straw, which at the time dominated paper as a raw material in box container production. At that time, paper recovered in China had a high moisture content, which made it unviable for reuse in paper-based manufactured goods.

> Ms Cheung's challenges in growing her firm included overcoming such technical problems and, just as importantly, marrying Chinese and Western management approaches. She had dealt with precisely these issues in her previous job.
>
> *Source*: Adapted from *CNN Talk Asia* (2007).

Fear of Failure

To start a business, people must be reasonably free of concerns that it might fail. The three previous items: knowing an entrepreneur, perceiving market opportunities and having the skills to start a business, should all help to alleviate fear of failure. However, the GEM surveys also ask respondents directly about how much they fear failure. Table 2.8 presents GEM data for 2005–2007 on the extent to which fear of failure would prevent business start-up.

Table 2.8 suggests that fear of failure correlates highly with entrepreneurial activity, although country context may mitigate this. From 2005–2007, male and female early-stage entrepreneurs consistently feared failure less than non-entrepreneurs. For example, in high-income countries in 2007, only 27.1 per cent of male early-stage entrepreneurs and 26.1 per cent of female early-stage entrepreneurs said that fear of failure would prevent them from starting a business, compared to 38.2 per cent of male non-entrepreneurs and 43.4 per cent of female non-entrepreneurs. Noticeably, more than one-third of women who engaged in no business activity expressed fear of failure. However, while these patterns are qualitatively similar by gender, a higher percentage of females than males would let fear of failure prevent them from starting a business. In 2005 and 2006, fear of failure was significantly higher for women than men in low or middle-income countries. In 2007, fear of failure was significantly higher for women than men in both low/middle-income country groups, particularly among European and Asian low/middle-income countries, where women entrepreneurs (42.6 per cent) expressed fear of failure at almost double the rate for women early-stage entrepreneurs in Latin America and Caribbean low/middle-income countries (22.5 per cent). However, in European and Asian low/middle-income countries, women entrepreneurs expressed fear of failure at the same rate as women in high-income countries not engaged in entrepreneurial activity.

The authors of the GEM reports on women's entrepreneurship for 2005, 2006 and 2007 speculate that women's fear of failure might be higher because they are more likely to perceive no other job alternatives. The results for necessity and opportunity-based entrepreneurship in Table 2.2 reflect a similar finding. Female and male entrepreneurs who live in high-income countries and are motivated by opportunity expressed the least fear of failure, possibly because these groups have other work alternatives and live in countries with higher per capita incomes. Thus, country context may have a powerful influence on entrepreneurial motivation.

Table 2.8 Fear of Failure Would Prevent from Starting a Business

	Country Income Level		
Year	Low	Middle	High
2005	–	29.7	31.8
	–	33.4	38.4
	–	62.6	55.6
	–	60.1	63.3
		Low/Middle	
2006		40.2	44.0
		33.0	39.1
		33.6	21.3
		24.3	25.8
	Europe/ Asia	Latin America/ Caribbean	
2007	40.2	36.0	43.4
	33.7	28.6	38.2
	42.6	22.5	26.1
	23.9	17.1	27.1

Note: Figures represent percentages of men and women aged 18–64. Each country's representation is weighted according to population size.

Source: Adapted from Allen et al. (2007), Allen et al. (2008) and Minniti et al. (2006).

In combination with the three previous GEM findings about perceptions of the entrepreneurial environment (knowing an entrepreneur, perceiving market opportunities and having the skills to start a business), having a family business background seems likely to promote chances of entrepreneurial activity and success. Knowing an entrepreneur, perceiving market opportunities and having business start-up skills all tend to reduce the likelihood that a new venture would fail. Since having a family business background heightens the likelihood of all three of these positive factors, it is also likely that having a family firm background would tend to reduce fear of business failure, especially fear that would prevent a potential entrepreneur from starting a business in the first place.

Mini-Case—Putting Opportunity in the Bag

In August 2007, 35-year-old Amanda Briskin sold her leather goods and accessory company Mimco for approximately $AU45 million. She started Mimco in 1996 with the equivalent of $US5,000 and a design for two handbags. Briskin broke many rules building her business. Many Generation Ys spend approximately 10 years in a profession before branching out on their own. In contrast, Briskin spent just two years in a marketing and operations role in an information technology company before she left at the age of 24 and used her savings to start Mimco, inspired by her childhood name Mim. Briskin came from an entrepreneurial, determined family. Both sets of grandparents were Holocaust survivors, with one pair running a property development business and the other a manufacturing business. Briskin's family business background instilled confidence in her as a business owner and encouraged her to seek and develop a perceived entrepreneurial opportunity.

Source: Adapted from Gome (2007).

CONCLUSIONS

The findings from the GEM reports demonstrate many similarities and overlaps between male and female entrepreneurs. Tables 2.1–2.4 confirm that men and women act entrepreneurially for basically similar reasons, but contextual factors within and across countries affect the profile of women's and men's entrepreneurship. These contextual effects become evident when we compare necessity and opportunity-based entrepreneurship between women and men, the rate of entrepreneurship between working and non-working women and women entrepreneurs' level of education in different countries. Tables 2.5–2.8 suggest that, with few exceptions, people already engaged in entrepreneurial activity have various advantages with respect to current and future entrepreneurial activity, compared to non-entrepreneurs. They are typically more likely to know an entrepreneur, perceive good market opportunities being available soon, believe they have the skills to start a business and fear failure less than non-entrepreneurs.

This empirical evidence strengthens the point that Chapter 1 makes, supporting Ahl (2004): that we should reject *a priori* assumptions that men and women entrepreneurs are essentially different. While Tables 2.1–2.8 show that male entrepreneurs may enjoy certain advantages or exercise certain entrepreneurial propensities to a greater extent than women entrepreneurs, these differences might be related to aspects of the economic environment or other contextual factors, not to fundamental differences between men and women. This is further confirmed by the observation that female and male entrepreneurs across countries have more in common with each other than either group does with members of the non-entrepreneur population.

These findings about women's—and indeed men's—perceptions of and confidence in themselves as actual or potential entrepreneurs reinforce the studies which Chapter 1 cites about the effects of a family business background on entrepreneurial motivations and behaviours. These studies suggest if we understand what being exposed to a family business means, we should gain new and special ways of understanding the learning journey to entrepreneurship. These lessons may include how entrepreneurs—women as well as men—manage the fear associated with starting a new business or taking over an existing one, how they learn to recognise and exploit market opportunities, and how they gain skills and knowledge for the varied tasks of firm leadership and entrepreneurship.

The next chapter explains the analytical frameworks which helped us explore and understand the nature of the entrepreneurship journeys of family business women in a variety of countries.

3. Frameworks and Method

This book explores leadership and entrepreneurship in the light of women leaders' experiences as leaders and entrepreneurs in family firms. While seeking understanding of women leaders' experiences, we also aim to extend understanding of leadership and entrepreneurship generally, and how these skills are learned. This chapter explains how we undertook the study and the three main analytical frameworks we used.

BUILDING THEORY

Whetten (1989) argues that the essential ingredients of a value-added contribution to theory are explicit treatments of Who? What? Where? When? Why? and How? The greatest of these, he claims, is Why? Other researchers have started to explore 'why' and 'how' businesswomen's experience is the way it is. Even with the limitations discussed earlier, this literature is useful as a starting point. Women entrepreneurs in family business are, after all, a subset of women entrepreneurs in general. In light of recent claims that women are now more routinely considered as potential leaders and successors in family businesses (for example, Allen and Langowitz, 2003; Dumas, 1998; Sharma, 2004), and considering the new interest in 'familiness' of family businesses as a potential contributor to strategic competitive advantage, it is time to revisit women's contribution to family business, especially in leadership or entrepreneurial roles. How do women contribute to the 'familiness' of family firms, and consequently, improve firm performance?

The Value of a Case Study Approach

Varying views exist about how best to set about answering questions about family businesswomen's roles and experiences, their contribution to familiness as a resource and so on. Sharma (2004) points to the need for theoretically oriented large-sample studies to understand the role of women in family firms. While such large studies will no doubt be undertaken in due course, it is also valuable to continue with smaller studies of women's experiences—and to use a case study approach for this. As Eisenhardt (1989) points out, the case study is a research strategy that focuses on understanding the dynamics present within single settings, and is particularly well suited to researchers examining new topic areas. The case study is especially appropriate as a research tool for examining family business, a relatively new topic area, and women's leadership and entrepreneurship in family business, a still newer one.

Along with many other case study theorists, Eisenhardt (1989) argues that case studies are useful, inductive strategies for building theories that are novel and testable. The present research is more interested in developing an in-depth understanding of the nature of women's experiences of family business leadership and how they see their contributions, than trying to develop laws about this for later testing. Numagami (1998) argues that, in management studies, it makes little sense even to search for invariant laws—management issues always incorporate such a variety of contextual factors that achieving universal wisdom or certainty is impossible. Nevertheless, a deeper understanding of family business women's experiences of leadership and entrepreneurship should also help us determine what approaches are likely to make these roles more possible for women, as well as how women's leadership and entrepreneurship contribute to the health of family business.

Case studies are useful in other ways too. Siggelkow (2007, p. 21) argues that at least three important reasons to do case study research exist: motivation, inspiration and illustration. Case studies of women in family business may motivate new research questions; for example, if women's experiences and approaches in family business roles show consistent contrasts with men's experiences, this would motivate more nuanced studies of how and why they differ, implications of the differences for firm performance and so on. Case studies on women in family business may demonstrate why understanding women's roles as family business leaders and entrepreneurs is important, so that family business owners can make productive use of the full human resource base available to the firm, perhaps to achieve some form of competitive advantage. A further inspirational reason for studying women in family businesses is that cases grounded in real-life examples are likely to be appealing to researchers and family business members alike. Knowing the detail of women's experiences and how they succeeded may inspire others to follow them.

According to Siggelkow (2007), case studies let us get close to constructs and illustrate possible causal relationships more directly. This illustrative function of case study work is especially applicable to our topic. Researchers such as Dumas (1998) argue that women who are psychologically dominated by their fathers are less likely to succeed to leadership roles in the family firm. Her view is borne out by findings such as those from Allen and Langowitz (2003) and the Center for Women's Business Research (2006): female-owned family firms in the US are more likely than male-owned family firms to choose a successor, and that women leading firms are much more likely to include a woman as a possible successor. While the statistics produced by these and other studies are telling, they are even more convincing if we see them played out in an empirical setting. This book closely examines some examples of women in a family business who are—or were—very close to their fathers, perhaps even psychologically dominated by them. We investigate what factors in that situation can exclude women from a leadership role, and are likely to help women attain leadership, despite the difficulties.

OUR METHOD

This section overviews what we did and why—from the assembling of our case samples to how we conducted the interviews and analysed them.

Assembling the Sample: Focusing on the Topic of Interest

Consistent with an in-depth case approach as described by Eisenhardt (1989) and Silverman (1985) and Yin (1984), among others, we took a purposive approach to assembling our sample of cases. That is, rather than using the statistical sampling approach characteristic of large-scale survey-based research, we sought out cases we thought would be theoretically useful for our study.

To be theoretically useful, individuals and their roles in their firms needed to represent one of two possibilities: an 'illustrative' case, or a 'stretch' or 'limiting' case (Silverman, 1985). An example of an illustrative case is a family business woman who already occupied a role that strongly suggests leadership or entrepreneurial activity in family firm, such as a founder, a CEO or some other designated senior role. However, 'stretch' or 'limiting' cases are equally important, because they allow us to examine leadership or entrepreneurship where we might not expect to find them, or where they appeared in unusual guises. Examples of 'stretch' or extreme types in our sample are women who led their own firm, but had deliberately avoided seeking to head the original family firm. Other 'stretch' cases, were women who saw themselves—and who others saw—as exercising leadership in a family business without being either a founder or CEO. We wanted to see to what extent these women also demonstrated leadership—even entrepreneurial leadership—perhaps in a less acknowledged and formal way, and whether their experiences were similar or different from those who held more recognised leadership roles.

Assembling the Sample: Ensuring Diversity

While choosing cases that clearly illustrate leadership and entrepreneurship or provide opportunities for testing their theoretical boundaries was important, so was the inclusion of a more general diversity of cases. This section outlines some of the ways we ensured diversity in our sample.

Diverse Roles and Aspirations

The women in our study occupied a range of family business roles. They also varied in terms of whether they hoped to make a career in the family firm. Some came from family business backgrounds and had reached—or hoped to reach—a position of leadership in the firm that they had known as children or in which had already spent much of their working lives. Others with similar family business backgrounds had started their own new ventures. Like those who had stayed with the family business, these women hoped the firms they had started would continue into later generations. Recalling the 'essence' perspective on family business, this means these new firms can be considered as family businesses. Other cases in our sample presented different roles and aspirations, for example, women who had never expected to be a leader in their firms, but who had taken over a family business following a male relative's death.

The two founders who were CEOs but no longer hold this role are Brenda and Deborah (see the top-left quadrant of Table 3.2, below). They were both succeeded by a family member, who, in Brenda's case, was a son, and in Deborah's case, a daughter, Robyn. We first consider her story as part of Deborah's, but also discuss her later as a CEO in her own right. She appears in the right-hand lower quadrant as a non-founder CEO. The founders who were currently CEOs (see the top-right quadrant of Table 3.2) include both women who grew up with a family business background and women who did not.

Diverse National Backgrounds

We gathered participants at family business and other conferences, through formal and informal business networks. The sample includes women from such diverse backgrounds as Canada (this participant had dual citizenship in Egypt), the United States, Saudi Arabia, Lebanon, Hong Kong and Australia. The diversity of our participants' national backgrounds also allowed us to look closely at how aspects of country context affect women's entrepreneurialism.

Diverse Firm Products and Services

The firms in our sample handled a wide variety of different industry products and services, from traditionally 'male-image' firms such as machinery manufacture, plastic moulding manufacturing, supermarkets and car sales, to industries less obviously male dominated. One firm, a home-help agency, relied on a traditionally female skill set. This aspect of the sample, while not a major focus of our study, is interesting, because some previous literature (for example, De Tienne and Chandler, 2007) examines whether the 'male-dominated' or 'female-dominated' image of the industry in which a firm is located affects men's and women's propensities to create new ventures, their level of innovation behaviour and their management style. As noted earlier, Verheul et al. (2005) found differences in these areas along gender lines.

Table 3.1 lists the participants along with their firm's industry sector.

Table 3.1 Industries Represented by Participants' Family Firms

Name	Industry Sector
Brenda	Motor vehicle retailing
Cass	Wholesale/retail (fruit and vegetables)
Deborah/Robyn	Personal services (home care)
Ellen	Clothing manufacturing
Felicity	Personal services (funeral directing)
Gloria	Machinery manufacturing
Hannah	Food retailing (supermarkets)
Ingrid	Machinery manufacturing/real estate
Jane	Publishing
Miriam	Business services (marketing consulting)
Nancy	Business services (management consulting)
Sue	Roof manufacturing

Note: Names of the interviewees are disguised.

Diversity of Firm Size and Generation of Management

The previous chapter details how we had included women who run large firms as well as the small and medium-sized firms more commonly associated with women entrepreneurs. Table 3.3 shows the size of firms in our sample by number of employees and the current generation of firm management.

Diversity of Role in the Firm

Given the current attention to women entrepreneurs and the traditional focus on succession as the dominant problem in family business studies, we included both women founders and women from existing family businesses who reached the CEO position. Within these two categories, we included cases where generational succession was not yet an issue, as well as instances of where it had already taken place. The latter included both mother–son succession and mother–daughter succession.

A snapshot of our sample, categorised by founder/non-founder, and CEO/non-CEO status of the participants, appears in Table 3.2.

Table 3.2 Participants by Founder/Non-Founder and Ceo/Non-Ceo Status

	Non-CEOs	CEOs
Founders	Brenda, Deborah	Jane, Ellen, Miriam, Nancy, Hannah
Non-founders	Felicity, Sue, Gloria, Cass	Robyn, Ingrid

Table 3.3 Participants by Size of Their Family Firm and Firm's Generation of Management

	Fewer than 20 Employees	21–100 Employees	More than 100 Employees
Owner is from first generation of management	Ellen, Miriam, Nancy, Hannah		Deborah/Robyn Cass
Owner is from second generation of management		Gloria, Jane	Brenda, Ingrid
Owner is from third generation of management		Felicity	Sue

'Stretch' Cases

The 'stretch' cases—interviewees who had neither started a family business nor moved into formal leadership roles—appear in the lower-left quadrant of Table 3.2. These cases were in some ways the most interesting of all for what they showed about attaining leadership—or not attaining it. Most of these women had a family business background. They included one interviewee, Gloria, who, according to many people close to her, was clearly a leader. She had played an entrepreneurial role in the family business she had grown up in, expanding its revenue, introducing new products and developing effective marketing strategies. Despite this, she had never held the CEO position in the family business and finally left it to start her own firm. Felicity, in the same quadrant, is quite a different 'stretch' case. Despite her prominence as a speaker on women's leadership and the importance her job title suggests, Felicity said she was overlooked for a leadership role in her family firm. Consequently, she lowered her career aspirations in the family firm. Yet another interviewee in this quadrant, Cass, claimed never to have sought leadership in her family firm and would not allow us to describe her as a leader. Yet she had taken the major role in devising strategy for the family firm, pulling off a major turnaround in its fortunes after a financial crisis had brought it almost to bankruptcy.

Interview Methods

One or both researchers visited each participant at their business premises or their home, or arranged to meet her in some other private area, such as a meeting room at a conference venue. In each case we explained that we were interested in the experiences of women as they learned their roles within a family business. We asked each interviewee simply to tell us her story, how she had got to where she was. In that way we avoided 'priming' the participant—another important principle of case research. We let interviewees know we had previously studied how men learned to lead family firms, and wanted to include women's experiences to ensure our model was complete.

In accordance with the case study method, which requires researchers to seek to enter into and empathise with the viewpoint of the person whose story they elicit, our approach was to try to understand how each participant saw her own story and her place in the family business, and to try to understand the participant's view of how and why she had or had not reached a position of leadership in the business.

Analysing the Data

Case study proponents (for example, Silverman, 1985) recommend that investigations be done in a systematic, close-up and meticulous way. Accordingly, we used NVivo, a computer program for qualitative research, to code the case histories and other data in detail, according to the issues that participants raised in their stories, their family situation, data about their firms and so on. Later, we examined these issues from the viewpoint of wider themes that recur in the family business literature and other research areas, especially social approaches to learning. The Appendix gives more detail about how we did the analysis.

Valuing the Variety of Participants' Experiences

From the outset, our analysis revealed more difference and complexity in family business women's experience than much of the previous literature suggests. For example, we found considerable variety in what family members had done to influence whether or not a participant achieved a senior role. Some family members helped; others hindered. We also found that some standard ideas took on new facets in the family business context. An example was the value attached to mentoring—long a staple of the corporate literature on how women can advance their standing as leaders and managers. Participants varied in their views about whether mentors were more valuable inside than outside the family firm, whether family members made good mentors and so on. We also found a variety of opinion about the value of the learning done in traditional 'female' support roles in the family business.

Interviewees did not always share an understanding of certain terms, nor did they necessarily understand them in the same way as the academic literature defines them. This was not necessarily a problem; it might be useful for illuminating of the phenomenon under study. For example, the interviewees' varying understandings and experience of specific concepts, such as 'visibility', 'innovation' (and even 'leadership') led us to examine and re-examine these terms to understand how they defined contrasting approaches to attaining leadership in the family firm. These varying understandings, together with other evidence from the interviewees' firms, contributed to a picture of how a particular participant had gained a central role in her original family firm or another one, such as the one she started.

Most of our participants attempted to construct a 'stage' or firm context that suited their approach to leadership. This in turn prompted us to use the metaphor of the theatre to understand and describe our participants' experiences. Like a stage in a theatre, the leadership stage might be large or small, allowing more or fewer people to share it. This also influenced how the 'lead roles' were played. The spotlight might already shine on a participant at centre stage, or she may have needed to seek it out. The leadership stage, or context, also influenced whether and how the leader could manage the spotlight—the heightened visibility in the family firm which almost invariably came with the role.

The 'essence' approach to defining family business we chose seemed well suited to our analytical approach. Rather than sifting through the fine detail of firm's ownership and control structures to make arbitrary decisions about when participants had attained firm leadership, we could move directly to how participants themselves saw and understood issues of management, leadership, entrepreneurship and so on in their firms, and how changes in their situations affected how they evaluated their achievements and aspirations.

FRAMEWORKS USED

When considering the themes which emerged from our case histories, three main analytical frameworks helped us understand what was going on: our four learning phases of family business (Moores and Barrett, 2002), Wenger's (1999, 2000) concept of a community of practice and Curimbaba's (2002) typology of heiresses' roles in family businesses. The first two frameworks emphasise the social aspects of learning in organisational settings. Curimbaba's framework helped us to classify the changes many participants pointed to in their relationships with their family firms over time.

The next section reviews the learning phases of family business. These phases are our starting point for discussing similarities and differences between this sample of women leaders and our earlier findings, which we derived primarily from a sample of men. Following this, we discuss how family businesses in general function like communities of practice, and the implications of this for nurturing a learning orientation in family firms. Finally, we consider Curimbaba's findings about the roles of 'heiresses'— second or later-generation women in family firms—and how they influence the likelihood that women will act as leaders and entrepreneurs in family firms.

The Phases of Learning Family Business

In our earlier study, we found successful family firm CEOs encountered a series of unique paradoxes (Moores and Barrett, 2002). They needed to manage the paradoxes because they could not be made to disappear. Exploring, understanding and trying to manage these paradoxes characterised a learning journey in which they progressively learned business (L1), learned our business (L2), learned to lead our business (L3) and learned to let go our business (L4).

Learning Business (L1)

The first stage, learning business, involves leaving the family firm to learn functional business techniques, and more importantly, the personal disciplines needed for business. The priority of this stage is thus business and personal proficiency. This learning is better done outside the family firm. We call the paradox associated with this phase the 'inside–outside' paradox, because CEOs agreed that, while the eventual heir needs to have worked elsewhere to be proven worthy of a place in the firm's senior management, the heir's departure is also a threat to the survival of the firm as a family firm. The person who leaves the family business setting to learn about how to run a business may never come home. Nevertheless, 'going outside' is so important to a future family business leader's learning that, despite the risk to family firm continuity, the pathway through the 'inside–outside' paradox is to go outside anyway.

Learning our Business (L2)

The second phase, learning our business (L2), encompasses learning the special qualities of a family business, especially those of the family business which the heir would eventually lead. This phase involves a second paradox: 'continuing differently'. Its priority is to perpetuate values; that is, to maintain a sense of continuity that allows owners and customers alike to see the business as 'the same' family business—even while it evolves to deal with a changing world. The pathway through the paradox is for family firm leaders to keep the basic philosophies of the business intact, rather than the detail. They need to learn the family firm's special qualities and values as well as the financial value the marketplace attaches to these qualities.

Learning to Lead Our Business (L3)

Learning to lead our business is the third phase. The aspiring family firm leader needs to acquire a 'helicopter view' of the firm and its life-cycle stage, in order to develop plans for its future. Again, this phase creates a paradox. We call it the 'informal formality' paradox, because family firm leaders need to professionalise the firm as it grows, which often means formalising many aspects of its operations. Simultaneously, they need to maintain the firm's qualities of 'familiness' which are part of its competitive strength. The priority becomes achieving the perspicacity needed to maintain these delicate balances. We found there are no simple pathways through the 'learning to lead' paradox; leaders needed to work out their own approach.

Learning to Let Go Our Business (L4)

The final (L4) phase we call 'leading in order to let go the family firm'. When planning succession in the family firm, leaders need to anticipate the firm's needs when they will be no longer there, manage their own and family members' varied ambitions regarding the firm's future, and plan a productive non-leadership role for themselves. While these are difficult tasks, there are pathways through them. Leaders need to develop a timeline for their retirement, and create systems to develop the leaders who will come after them. Finally, they need to stick to the plan.

Table 3.4 summarises the four phases. We could say that all firm leaders encounter these phases. Business leaders in general need to learn personal and functional skills and to appreciate the special qualities of the firms they run. They need to know how to run their firms along more professional lines as they develop. Eventually, all will need to know when and how to leave their firms. However, in family firms, the paradox of each of the four learning phases arises from the collision of two fundamentally different social entities: family and firm. Dealing simultaneously with the contrasting qualities and demands of these two social entities creates the special learning tasks for family firm leaders.

Table 3.4 The Four Phases of Learning Family Business

Learning	Priority	Paradox	Pathway
Business	Proficiency	Inside–outside	Go outside
Our business	Perpetuating values	Continuing differently	Keep philosophies, not details Learn the market value of family business values
To lead our business	Perspicacity	Informal formality	No simple pathways
To let go our business	Prescience	Leading by leaving	Develop timeline for retirement Create management development systems Stick to the plan

Source: Adapted from Moores and Barrett (2002).

LEARNING: A SOCIAL PERSPECTIVE

Our second social view of learning is derived from the concept of a community of practice, as developed by Lave and Wenger (1991), Wenger (1999, 2000) and Wenger and Snyder (2000). Other theorists have developed the concept further for particular contexts. For example, Brown and Duguid (2000) consider the importance of organisational learning and tacit knowledge in the development of technological innovation. Wenger (1999, 2000) points out that the way most of us know even objective realities (such as that the Earth is round and orbits the Sun) is not because we have carried out formal experiments, but because we belong to various communities of practice. These communities, taken together, comprise 'a complex social, cultural and historical system, which has accumulated learning over time' (Wenger, 2000, p. 226). Learning in communities of practice mostly happens informally, by more experienced members of the community handing on their knowledge to less experienced members.

The Family Business as a Community of Practice

Family businesses resemble communities of practice in many ways. Wenger and Snyder (2000) describe communities of practice as groups of people informally bound together by shared expertise and passion for a joint enterprise. Family businesses are also based on informal, non-business links, such as blood ties and ties of affection, and a variety of self-organising principles which overlay and often dominate those dictated by business (Moores and Mula, 2000).

The history of communities of practice further reveals their links with family business. According to Wenger and Snyder (2000, p. 140), communities of practice had their origins in the corporations of metalworkers, potters, masons and other craftsmen of classical Greece, and later, the guilds of the medieval period. They exercised a social purpose, bringing members together for celebrations, and a business function, training apprentices and spreading innovations. Family businesses are even older organisational forms, and many family enterprises are among the most enduring of today's successful firms. Like the guilds and other 'apprenticing' organisations (which were often located within family structures), family businesses function both as businesses and as entities quite unrelated to business. They train their members and facilitate innovation and entrepreneurship both inside and outside their own boundaries, and bring people together for activities which occur in families with no specific goals or shared interests in a business. Craig et al. (2006) and Dibrell and Craig (2006) discuss similar innovation activities within family businesses.

Successful family businesses most resemble communities of practice in the passionate, informal, free-flowing quality of their approach to solving problems. From our earlier research into what members of family businesses say about the nature of family firms, we were continually struck by the frequency with which family business members told us that family firms are 'just like any other business except...' The 'except' was invariably followed by a characteristic that sets the 'family' nature of the enterprise firmly apart from its non-business counterpart. As we showed briefly just now and in our earlier book, this 'except' lies at the heart of the intractable paradoxes of family business leadership. However, the same paradoxes point to how members of family firms typically work informally to make decisions, come up with ideas, implement them in creative ways and so on.

Learning in Communities of Practice: a Matter of Belonging

Wenger (2000) points to three dimensions of a community of practice which need to be established and sustained in a healthy way if the community itself is to endure: belongingness, boundaries and identity. Belongingness comprises three special modes: engagement, imagination and alignment, to use Wenger's terms, which are vital to sustaining learning in communities of practice. The same applies in the family business setting. We discuss the three belongingness modes first because of their importance to family business learning, and then turn to boundaries and identity.

Engagement

Engagement simply refers to people doing things together to identify gaps in their knowledge and work together to address them (Wenger, 2000, p. 231). Our earlier book contains many family business leaders' recollections of spending time in the family firm, especially early in their lives. Watching and taking part in providing the family firm's service or product was a prelude to understanding how the firm could build on its early successes. Here we ask whether women have the same possibility of simply 'doing things' in the family firm as a way of learning it. Are other experiences just as important?

Imagination

Imagination is necessary at several levels, from the individual to the entire community of practice. It entails 'constructing an image of ourselves, of our communities, and of the world, in order to orient ourselves, to reflect on our situation, and to explore possibilities' (Wenger, 2000, pp. 227–8). Our previous book (Moores and Barrett, 2002) argues that in family business, this capacity to reflect and develop a helicopter view of the firm is gradually developed over all four learning stages, from the earliest 'going outside' phase to 'learning to leave' the firm in retirement. Our interest is how women in family firms imagine or develop a vision for the firm. How do they continue its entrepreneurial orientation and renew this vision over time? How do women imagine themselves in leadership roles, and how do others imagine such roles for them, if they do so at all?

Alignment

Communities of practice demand alignment, or 'making sure that… local activities are sufficiently aligned with other processes so that they can be effective beyond the community of practice members' own engagement' (Wenger, 2000, p. 228). In a family business, the firm's values, from simple hard work, to providing superior customer service, to making sure the business serves the long-term interests of the family—are linked to its alignment dimension, and these values help integrate the often diverse perspectives of its members. This prompts the question of whether and how women leaders in family firms manage to continue a set of values for the firm which accord with those of the founder or, alternatively, how they come up with a new set of values with which others in the firm can align themselves.

Designing Healthy Communities of Practice: Issues for Family Firms

Wenger (2000) argues that those trying to build a healthy learning community need to ensure that three general dimensions of the community—its level of learning energy (enterprise), its level of trust (mutuality) and its degree of self-awareness (repertoire)—are nourished by its three 'belongingness' modes: engagement, imagination and alignment. Similar observations are made in the family business literature about how family businesses need to be managed. The next section uses a series of tables to show how the learning energy (enterprise), trust (mutuality) and self-awareness (repertoire) dimensions relate to the belongingness modes of engagement, imagination and alignment in communities of practice in general and family businesses in particular.

Belongingness and Learning Energy

Table 3.5, below, summarises Wenger's arguments about the impact of belongingness modes (column 1) on the learning energy of communities of practice in general (column 2), and then compares them with frequent observations about how family businesses learn (column 3).

Belongingness and Trust

Wenger (1999, 2000) stresses the value of trust (mutuality) as a basis for learning, yet too much trust can give rise to problems in any learning community, including the family firm. Table 3.6 shows the impact of Wenger's three belongingness modes (column 1) on the trust dimension of communities of practice (column 2) and on trust issues in family firms (column 3).

Belongingness and Self-Awareness

Those interested in creating healthy learning communities should take into account members' self-awareness or 'repertoire'; that is, how members consciously or unconsciously held ideas about themselves influence their practices. Table 3.7 summarises how the 'belongingness' factors can influence self-awareness in learning communities in general, and in family firms in particular.

Given the growing interest in familiness as a source of family firm advantage, we were particularly alert to whether one or more of the belongingness factors (engagement, imagination or alignment) lay at the heart of interviewees' experience of being part of their family firms, whether one or more belongingness factors influenced their approach to leadership and so on.

Table 3.5 Belongingness Dimensions and Learning Energy

Belongingness dimension	Learning Energy in Communities of Practice	Learning Energy in Family Firms
Engagement	What are the opportunities to negotiate a joint inquiry and important questions? Do members identify gaps in their knowledge and work together to address them?	By preferring to employ family members, rather than recruiting widely, family firms were traditionally seen as limiting their knowledge base. Thus, knowledge gaps could be larger and the capacity for members to investigate them together could be limited. Remedies lie in including incorporating expertise from outside the family.
Imagination	What visions of the potential of the community are guiding the thought leaders, inspiring participation and defining a learning agenda? What picture of the world serves as a context for such visions?	What potential does the family firm see for itself? For example, does being a family firm connote a small entity, or is there an intention also to grow the business side of the family firm? How do growth intentions link to the values of the firm established early in the family firm's history? How will these values be sustained at later stages of the firm's development?
Alignment	Have members articulated a shared purpose? How widely do they subscribe to it? How accountable do they feel to it? How distributed is leadership?	Do members of the family firm share a view about the appropriate relationship between family and business, and how the two will be managed? Do members all get the chance to help determine what this view is?

Table 3.6 Belongingness Dimensions and Trust

Belongingness Dimension	Trust in Communities of Practice	Trust in Family Firms
Engagement	What events and interactions weave the community together and develop trust? Can members raise troubling issues during discussion?	Family firms were observed as having fewer needs than other firms to develop trust, since many shared goals arise through family membership. Nevertheless, issues of trust—between founder and successor, or between siblings—often arise at succession.
Imagination	What do people know about each other and about the meanings that participation in the community takes in their life more broadly?	Founders of firms often do not know enough about what other members hope for from participating in the family firm. They also often fail to think about how they can contribute to the firm after they have stepped down from its leadership—advising but not interfering in the next generation's leadership.
Alignment	What definitions of roles, norms, codes of behaviour, shared principles and negotiated commitments and expectations hold the community together?	Divisions of labour, what name family members use for each other at work, 'rules' about whether 'talking about business' is off-limits over dinner and so on, are norms often consciously and strongly adhered to in family firms.

Table 3.7 Belongingness Dimensions and Self-Awareness

Belongingness Dimension	Self-Awareness in Communities of Practice	Self-Awareness in Family Firms
Engagement	To what extent have shared experience, language, artefacts, histories and methods accumulated over time, and with what potential for further interactions and new meanings?	Family firms typically embody shared experience and history; some make it part of their public face to the world. But difficulties can arise when shared experience and commitments—even to important values such as quality—become too entrenched and rigid, making them difficult to view objectively and reinterpret if necessary.
Imagination	Are there self-representations that would allow the community to see itself in new ways? Is there a language to talk about the community in a reflective mode?	Members of family firms need the ability to understand the firm's values, but also ways of talking about (and if necessary, reinterpreting) these values in ways that will be comprehensible to new members, especially the next generation, who will be charged with 'continuing the firm differently'.
Alignment	What traditions, methods, standards, routines and frameworks define the practice? Who upholds them? To what extent are they codified? How are they transmitted to new generations?	Can people inside and outside the family firm, both family members who might want to work in it one day, and those who simply deal with the firm as customers, creditors, suppliers and so on, understand and endorse its family traditions? This is often crucial when members of the younger generation need to tell their partners about the meanings and attractions the firm holds for them.

Two More Facets of Learning Communities: Boundaries and Identity

Wenger (1999, 2000) discusses two other aspects of a learning community: its boundaries and its identity. These also influence the community's health and viability. Because boundary and identity themes of various kinds also recurred in interviewees' discussions about their relationships with their family firms, we discuss these topics briefly here.

Boundaries

A learning community's boundaries are its points of articulation with the rest of the world. They arise from the discontinuities between those who were participating in the community and those who were not, as the learning required to cross them demonstrates. They serve to define the community, though they are typically fluid and unspoken (rather than rigidly defined)— much like the boundaries of organisational units sanctioned by management. The connections made in order to span boundaries may also be a source of new learning (Wenger, 1999, pp. 103–4). Boundaries are also important in family business, as evidenced by the amount of time and energy family members sometimes spend in deciding who is part of the family firm and who is not.

The chapters which follow consider how family firm boundaries helped or hindered interviewees' learning goals—how they were created and protected, and the balance they presented between rigidity and permeability. For example, were the firm's boundaries permeable enough to permit learning for its members and future leaders? Or did they turn members inward, cutting them off from learning opportunities outside and preventing fresh ideas from entering?

Identity

Identity refers to the way knowing is an act of belonging to a community (Wenger, 1999, 2000). What constitutes the 'right way' to do something may differ vastly from one learning community to another, without members necessarily being aware of it. Similarly, in family firms, knowledge gained in the broader business world often turns out to be worthless if it is not consistent with what family firm members value; that is, if it does not contribute to the family firm's existing sense of its identity. We sought how the women we interviewed tried to reinforce (or alternatively, change) the firm's identity, the ways family firm members felt they 'knew' things, and what problems they encountered when they tried to bring in new ways of knowing.

A Word of Caution

The preceding discussion drew attention to many conceptual and practical resemblances between communities of practice and family firms. However, not everything about how family firms function links them to communities of practice. Family firms are still firms, and as Wenger (2000) points out, corporations rarely—if ever—function as a single community of practice. Because of their size and the way management controls their functioning, corporations generally cannot be true communities of practice. Particularly in large firms, several different communities of practice may exist within specific functional areas. This is true for family firms too, and we made the point earlier that family firms are not always small. Therefore, we might expect to find more than one community of practice within family firms—just as we would in non-family corporations. Nevertheless, our observations suggest that the functioning of the inner management core of even a large family business shares many aspects of a community of practice. Communities of practice cannot be created in a vacuum, and in a family business, as our Chapter 1 definitions show, there is also no vacuum or clean slate. Rather, complex histories and family relationships overlay and reinforce business relationships, all driving a shared knowledge base.

We now consider our third analytical framework: Curimbaba's (2002) typology of heiresses' roles in family businesses.

FAMILY BUSINESS WOMEN'S ROLES

In her study of family businesses in Brazil, Curimbaba (2002) distinguished three typical roles for daughters ('heiresses') in family businesses: 'invisibles', 'professionals' and 'anchors'. She found that the woman's birth position in the family and the number of men in the same generation and in the extended family greatly influenced these roles.

Invisibles

The invisible family business woman is typically part of a large nuclear family containing many sons. The daughters are usually in the middle and have older brothers, so the daughters are not seen as necessary to include as successor managerial staff. They were not prepared for a professional career in the business and tend to care more about the job itself than the business, and this makes it difficult for them to identify with managers or entrepreneurs. For them, the company was a stock of previously accumulated wealth which they should not be kept from enjoying. Their invisibility gives them flexibility, which allows them the freedom to leave the family business and return as they wish. They can only move away from being invisible by filling roles in which women's 'feminine traits' are seen as adding value.

Anchors

Anchors are women from families with predominantly female offspring, with few men in any generation. With great visibility inside the family business, they became essential for its continuity, despite passing through phases that tend to reduce their significance. Nevertheless, they are never considered completely unnecessary. They readily adopt the company's spirit, but occasionally confuse their own objectives and the company's, although the company tends to be the primary object of their energies. They value the family business setting as one where being a successful executive does not require them to give up their concept of femininity.

Professionals

Professionals work in mature family companies with complex ownership structures, where a reasonable number of men, but not an overwhelming majority, also work. They typically join the family company as the result of an opportunity when they could make a particular contribution to it. Their participation is often initially a way to resolve some type of conflict in the family part of the system, but after that, no one intervenes to push their careers further. They are extreme adherents to 'professionalism', always trying to separate family from business, and strongly believe that merit is something universal, valid and clear in all contexts. This means they sometimes fall foul of political tactics used by others to advance, particularly men.

In contrast to many other studies, which provide snapshots of women's roles as they appear in a particular firm, Curimbaba is interested in how women in family firms often move between the various roles. This was one reason Curimbaba's findings resonated with our own exploration of how women learn and move into leadership roles. Curimbaba also identifies how some movements between roles are more explicit, which the family is more likely to recognise as entailing an aspiration towards leadership, such as the movement from being an invisible to a professional or an anchor. Other moves are subtle and occur more discreetly over time. Examples include an anchor who has lost importance and becomes an invisible, an anchor who has become more of a professional, or a professional who has become invisible, perhaps because she views her role in the family business as a market position.

A high-profile example of a woman who moved from an invisible to an anchor role is Katharine Graham, who, in the late 1960s, took over the CEO role of the *Washington Post* following her husband's death. Under her leadership, the newspaper, which had been losing both financially and in terms of its standing as a paper of repute, gained market share and an international reputation for courage when it covered the Watergate break-in that led to the impeachment of President Nixon. Many attributed the paper's strength to its new, female leader.

A New Role: Entrepreneur

Curimbaba (2002) limits her analysis in two ways. First, while she seeks to understand the extent to which women get to play key management roles in family firms, her focus is on describing and understanding the experiences of women who are daughters or granddaughters of the founder. She does not deal with women who aspire to or actually fill leadership roles—including that of CEO in the family firm. Second, and related to this, she deals exclusively with longstanding family businesses, because of her interest in how structural issues affect women's roles in the firm. Consequently, her implicit definition of a family business does not include a firm that a woman founds.

The importance of these aspects from our perspective is that Curimbaba's focus on structural factors indicates that a 'components of involvement' perspective on the family firm underpins her research. As we discussed earlier, this is a narrower perspective on family firms than our 'intention-based' or 'essence' view, which holds that new ventures may also be family firms, provided the founder intends the firm to continue into later generations. While the component perspective is necessary for Curimbaba in light of her interest in family structure, it means her descriptions of women's roles are silent about whether and how they may apply to family businesswomen who aspire to firm leadership or are already acknowledged as leaders, who perhaps even founded the firm. Our choice of an 'essence' or 'intention-based' definition of family business allows us a wider view of the dynamics of women-led family business than Curimbaba takes. However, it also means we need to look beyond Curimbaba's focus on birth order issues, such as the number of available men in the second or later generations of the family. The next five chapters examine interviewees' experiences as leaders and understand how they got there.

A SYNOPSIS OF THE PLOT

Examining interviewees' experiences as family firm leaders is a detailed exercise. Therefore, like a synopsis of a play for theatregoers, here is an overview of the story we will tell.

Four Ways to Become a Leader

Four typical ways of 'being on the family business stage' as a leader emerge from our analyses. We labelled them:

1. stumbling into the spotlight
2. building your own stage
3. directing the spotlight elsewhere
4. coping with shadows.

'Stumbling into the spotlight' concerns the experiences of women who unexpectedly find themselves leading the family business. In one case this was through the death of the male founder, in another because no one else would start the business for which our interviewee so urgently saw the need.

'Building your own stage' deals with women who have a family business background, but who are either excluded from succession to the leadership of the family firm or deliberately avoid that path, preferring to create their own firms, which they plan to continue as family businesses.

'Directing the spotlight elsewhere' groups together interviewees who led the family firm by not appearing to do so. Several took great pains to disguise their own contributions and make it seem that someone else was the main leader.

'Coping with shadows' characterises the leadership of family business women who spent a long time securing a senior role in the family business against longstanding opposition, or who must deal with a difficult legacy from an earlier leader.

The first three ways of being on stage characterise various kinds of successful leadership in the family business context. We deal with them in Chapters 4–6. The fourth approach, coping with shadows, may lead to success, although this remains uncertain. It is the subject of Chapter 7.

Leadership Sometimes Eludes Family Business Women

A fifth relationship within the family business stage also emerged. It reflects the experiences of women who recognised that, despite earlier hopes, they never really attained a leadership role. These women typically started out in ways similar to other interviewees, and sometimes even had the formal trappings of leadership. Chapter 8 Becoming invisible is about those women who once aspired to leadership in the family firm, but lost the battle or gave up the struggle.

The theatrical metaphor of being on stage and under a spotlight links these titles. These metaphors seemed apt because we were struck by how many participants—especially in the first three groups—found that leadership involved moving from relative obscurity in the family firm to a position of centrality and strong visibility. They were like actors moving quickly or more gradually from behind the scenes to a prominent position where their every move was watched. Several mentioned how they became aware of their increased influence on others in the firm, and even how their casual speech and actions were scrutinised for new meanings. Others, as we shall see, resisted being perceived as being at the centre of things, and deliberately directed attention towards other people while maintaining or even increasing their influence in the firm. Some still struggle to gain and maintain their place at the centre of the action. Still others, especially the participants in the final group, did not manage to secure themselves a place on the stage. While they said that they had regrets about this, they were also relieved not to have to deal with the glaring spotlight of leadership.

What does 'being on stage' feel like? How is the experience similar or different for the various women leading family firms? Are there similarities as well as differences between cases where the leadership learning process took a long time, for example, where the interviewee spent many years as an understudy to a predecessor, and one whose journey to the top job happened suddenly and drastically? What does leadership mean? Is it only a matter of gaining—and then learning to deal with—a fancy job title and the visibility that goes with it? Or is it influenced by the kinds of learning that precedes leadership? What is it like to be sidelined, to have had dreams and expectations of moving into a prominent role and to know now that it will probably never happen? Are there antecedents of failure as well as success that are discernible in the early experiences of those who do not make it to leadership? These questions and more arise in the next five chapters.

4. Stumbling into the Spotlight

This chapter considers two interviewees who found themselves thrust onto the leadership stage. Like actors without a script, they needed to improvise to meet the demands of their role. However, as we see when we compare their experiences using the family business learning phases, community of practice and women's roles frameworks, both found they knew more about the stagecraft of leadership than they had given themselves credit for.

BRENDA

Brenda succeeded to the leadership of the family motor dealership business when her husband died suddenly. She did not have a family business background. Before opening a motor dealership with her husband she worked in jobs requiring 'feminine' skills such as sewing, rather than jobs that would orient her to business:

> Brenda: I was once the sewing adviser for [a major Australian department store].

Brenda was acutely aware of her lack of functional business skills when she took over the business. She stressed during her interview that neither she nor her husband had ever expected her to run the business; they had both always seen her only as a 'support person'. For Brenda, the experience of attaining leadership was short, sharp and difficult. She felt she had stumbled inadvertently into a blinding spotlight where she did not know what she was supposed to do or say, and her mistakes would be obvious to all around her. Her 'audience' was hostile, especially at first. She experienced overt discrimination from men in business, and from their wives who regarded her as a threat:

> Brenda: I look at myself and the ostracising I had and you will never know how I was laughed at. Wherever I went it was, 'Why don't you go home and look after your kids? Do you really think you can run a motor dealership? Of course you can't.'

DEBORAH

Deborah was the founder of a home-care business that she started when she was a first-time mother. It now operates nationwide. The idea for the business came from the situation that without her family nearby to lend a hand, she struggled to keep up with her housework as well as look after a new baby. While Deborah was not thrust into the new venture spotlight as suddenly as Brenda, the idea on which she eventually based her business still arrived as a surprise:

> Deborah: I had a six-week-old baby, I wasn't about to start a business. It [the idea for the home-care service] just grabbed me and said, 'This is what has to be done, you have to do it'.

The name of the service—which suggests the kind of divine yet practical help in the house all new mothers need, also 'just occurred to her'—another vision from above.

While at the time of interviewing, Deborah was not systematic in researching her business idea, she had a strong sense of its importance: she saw it almost as a directive from heaven. Despite being convinced that a home-care service would be valuable to many people, Deborah did not initially see such a service as a business opportunity. In contrast to the standard notion of an entrepreneur spotting and immediately exploiting a potentially lucrative gap in the market, Deborah first tried every other way she could think of to get the service started:

> Deborah: I just thought this is what should be and I tried, I tried to talk everyone I knew into it. I said, 'It has to be... it has to be given life—this private agency behind help for young parents... I talked to [local council], but they just laughed.

Brenda's friends were scathing about the idea of her running a business; Deborah's friends had a similar lack of faith in her business idea:

> Deborah: All my friends said, 'But Deborah, who would use it?' I mean, they all had older children. They didn't have a six-week-old baby. I said, 'Look, I've got this fantastic idea. It would be a wonderful home helper agency.' And they said, 'Who'd use it? You know, we all have mothers and aunties...' But I didn't. What about all those people travelling around the world who are relocating? They don't have family support... [but they said], 'You're wasting your time. Do it as a hobby.'

Eventually, Deborah needed a push from her husband to realise that only she could start the business.

> Deborah: My husband actually was the instigator. He came round and said, 'I'm so sick of hearing about this [name of the business]—either do it yourself or shut up.'

Like Brenda, Deborah's previous experience of business was patchy at best, and unrelated to the kind of service she wanted to start. Her husband owned a business in which she helped out, but she saw it as his firm, separate from her own interests. Her father had also run a business, but this was not a positive learning experience for Deborah. She remembered how ill-suited her father was to business, and regarded his ad hoc management style as a lesson in how not to do things:

> Deborah: He had inherited this business along with his two brothers. Not one of the three of them was a manager. So they were thrown in. He was the eldest and assumed the running of the business, but hated it. He had never wanted to run the business and got out of it as soon as he could reasonably retire, having raised the kids.

Through watching her father and uncles, one of Deborah's strongest management philosophies was a commitment to planning. She knew the chaos that could occur if it was unclear whom the leadership spotlight should move to after the main actor left the stage. Deborah related how she took most of her major business decisions by trying to imagine how things would be in the firm at some future time. She said that she was still amazed that the firm had grown large enough to continue after her departure:

> Deborah: I am just very aware that we are just not here forever. I looked at my three daughters and thought, 'Well, they're happy enough. If something happens to me, they can always get in a manager'. But this business or whatever it is I'm building will be sold and they will split the proceeds from it. I never imagined it would go on beyond my lifetime.

While Deborah always acknowledged her mortality and the need to think ahead—this was the major characteristic of her leadership—it took a while for her to become fully aware that, with four children and a major firm, she needed to deal with succession issues in a planned way. Rather like her unsystematic approach to starting the business initially, Deborah's approach to succession did not include designating someone to take over the CEO role:

> Deborah: I thought that none of my children would be interested in the business. I have three daughters and a son. My son was certainly not and never will be interested in this type of business. He's very macho and he's a builder and he likes to knock around with the boys, you know, in the nicest way... I thought as an interim measure, the girls should know [about the business] because... I've always been very aware of my own mortality. When you are a mother you realise what will happen. If I get hit by a bus tomorrow, I've got four children, I've got a home. I've got to have some plan... where the children are going to go to school, what they are going to do with their lives. And I started to write things down, you know, this is what I would like to see my children do: to go to a private school, public school, whatever... You might not die until you're ninety-nine but you take the precaution of writing your will when you're thirty-five.

She eventually settled on her third daughter, Robyn (whom we meet again in Chapter 7), by a process of trial and error: she simply tried out each of her daughters in the firm and encouraged those whose performance did not align itself with the firm's values to leave. While Deborah may not have had a well-defined set of core competencies and skills which her eventual successor needed to attain, the succession process was based on the core philosophies of familiness she developed. This played out in Deborah's clash with her second daughter, who was keen to streamline the business operations, but clashed with Deborah over how they should manage staff:

> Deborah: My second daughter said, 'You are way out of date. Bring in some computerisation for the accounts.' So my second daughter came in. She and I are temperamentally different, and after two years she said, 'You know what I'd do? Sack the lot of the staff. You and I could run this show on our own'. And I said, 'Well, that's not really the way to run a business.' She said, 'Well, I can't stand it. You mollycoddle them, you look after them… I'd sack the lot.' So I thought, this is not going to work. So I said to her, 'You can't do that, you can't have that attitude in front of the staff.' So we agreed to disagree and she went off to do her thing…

Her third daughter, Robyn, also had a capacity for introducing new computer systems, and her goals in doing this were probably not very different from those of Deborah's other daughters. However, Robyn accepted her mother's approach to business, including her so-called 'mollycoddling' approach to the staff—which might be called familiness—to create employee loyalty. She was happy to continue her mother's personal approach to running the business, but just a little differently to allow the business to operate in a more professional way.

> Robyn: I've made lots of changes in the last twelve months, significant changes in operations. But that wasn't because I felt that Deborah was doing anything incorrectly or wrongly. But in the time I had I was able to observe and I was trying to think of how we could become more profitable… I have just seen a way of streamlining things, improving systems, upgrading technology, upgrading our staffing… and staff's ability to cope with certain situations. I've brought in additional staff training and really it's come down to a lack of time for the two of us to try and make these changes. But now I've got additional staff, put on an operations manager and a chief financial lass who have taken a lot of my other work which I was doing prior to Deborah's step-down as CEO. So I've got a bit more time.

Robyn used this additional time to work on the business' strategic direction:

> Robyn: I can see what the next twelve months is going to bring and I've had [a consulting firm] up to do a health check on the business for me to give me ideas of where we've got to fill up holes. We've got a business plan that's being developed with their help… We are here, and we want to get up here…

She also worked out how to expand the firm without stretching its resources too far, something her mother was nervous about:

> Deborah: I was very nervous about handing things on because I was taking on more and more and I thought, 'Well, I have to be aware of this...' I mean, I couldn't handle at that time any more than the five offices...

> Robyn: It wasn't a rapid expansion anyway, we did it very, very slowly, and we would do a little bit at a time...

> Deborah: But it was rapid for me before you came. In '85 I opened two franchises and had to train them, go round and visit them, bring them over for training here. I mean, it was enough for me to run the business in two offices here without having to focus on people in Perth, you know...

Chapter 7 contains more about Robyn's priorities, where we consider her approach to leading the firm that her mother started. Here, we compare Brenda's and Deborah's experiences as family firm leaders, starting with how they dealt with the phases of learning family business.

DISORDERED LEARNING

Both Brenda and Deborah found their leadership paths were highly condensed, and carried out in a sequence different from those we found typical for men in family businesses.

Learning Business (L1)

As Chapter 2 discusses, the first learning stage (L1) entails learning personal disciplines such as self-reliance and self-control, and how to be accountable to someone else for results. Brenda learned these personal discipline skills before she and her husband had even started the business, and well before she came to lead the firm on her own. However, acquiring them was not part of being groomed for a management career: Brenda and her husband had seen Brenda as the support person and him as the boss. Moreover, when Brenda eventually took over the firm, she was yet to learn several functional business skills, such as finance.

Deborah also had a somewhat improvised approach to moving into the spotlight of family business leadership. She also did not plan to be a businessperson; rather, she had a strong sense of a service that she and other new mothers needed, which no one else was willing to provide. Like Brenda, she had not 'learned business' (L1) before she started one. In contrast, the men we spoke to typically recalled that part of being groomed for business leadership meant they acquired business proficiencies during the first (L1) learning phase, through formal study, as an employee in someone else's business or both. This other firm was always an adequate distance from the family firm so as to permit the learner to make mistakes and learn from them somewhere other than the organisation they would eventually seek to lead.

Learning Our Business (L2)

Learning our business (L2) is usually also undertaken early, well before the learner has any formal leadership role in the family firm. Our first study (2002) suggests that future leaders learn the special qualities of the family firm (L2) both during their childhood and later on, typically after they return to the family firm. Many participants in that study talked about how, as children, they absorbed their parents' work ethic, their concern for quality, their willingness to innovate, take calculated risks and so on. Later, after spending some time outside the family firm, the potential leader began to learn and appreciate its culture in a more conscious, business-oriented way.

Brenda made another unconventional learning leap in the L2 phase by simultaneously developing a business and creating its distinctive culture. Brenda was surprised by what she achieved through quite simple measures, which she was aware might have sounded naïve to outsiders. Her preferred approach was simply to ask her staff for suggestions about how to solve problems. This contrasts with the conventional top-down approach to management typical in her industry at the time, where managers develop strategies and handed them down to staff. In addition, she simply adapted her skills as a housewife, since a housewife needed to be 'a bit of an economist' to balance the budget and keep the household afloat.

Deborah also used a staff-centred approach, creating a distinctive culture for her business (L2) based on caring for staff, even mollycoddling them. She did this as she went along, rather than by implementing ideas she had absorbed earlier, by the process of osmosis that resulted from long-term exposure to an earlier family business' practices. Thus, like Brenda, she had to learn—and even create—her family business' culture while simultaneously creating the firm.

Learning to Lead Our Business (L3)

Our previous study (Moores and Barrett, 2002) describes how the third learning stage (L3), learning to lead, requires developing a 'helicopter' view of the business to understand its stage of development, its place in its industry, the stage it has reached in its lifecycle and so on. In Brenda's case this meant producing a financial strategy that would secure profitability for her nascent firm as quickly as possible.

Brenda developed her financial strategy by managing resources as would a careful housewife used to living frugally: she asked herself and her staff what she needed to do to ensure that revenue exceeded expenditure. Without knowing it, Brenda was managing what she experienced as a lack of legitimacy for her nascent firm. Zimmerman and Zeitz (2002, p. 414) define firm legitimacy as a 'social judgment of acceptance, appropriateness, and desirability'. It is a vital resource for new ventures, as important as capital, technology, personnel, customer goodwill and networks. This is because it helps overcome the 'liability of newness' (Stinchcombe, 1965) which sinks so many not-yet-profitable ventures. Zimmerman and Zeitz point out that formal qualifications, accreditations, testimonials and so on are important in new firms that need to present themselves as legitimate players in the market. We saw earlier the lack of social acceptance Brenda encountered as a female businessperson. She also had no formal qualifications for firm leadership in the male-dominated auto industry. These issues meant Brenda was under more than the usual pressure to present her firm as a profitable—hence socially legitimate—player in the market. Despite her apparently naïve approach to finance and to firm leadership in general, Brenda managed to achieve profitability fairly soon, quicker than other, similar firms.

To a lesser extent, Deborah also had to deal with legitimacy issues: her friends found it difficult to take her business idea seriously. She too achieved firm legitimacy simply through growth, slowly realising she was running an entity large enough and strong enough to continue after her. This in turn belatedly forced her to take family succession planning seriously. Brenda and Deborah had successfully completed the first three learning stages, though in an unconventional order—at least compared with what is typical for men being groomed for family business leadership. Nevertheless, the unusual learning sequence meant they had some important gaps in their leadership learning and had to work hard to bridge them.

Letting Go the Family Business (L4)

At the time of interview, Brenda and Deborah were the only interviewees who had gone through the fourth (L4) learning stage: learning to let go the family business and deal with the transition to a successor. Our earlier research—and the sheer quantity of family business literature devoted to the topic—suggest this is the most difficult stage of all. To manage succession, leaders who have often grown up with the idea that they are the 'anointed one' must try to imagine themselves as willing outcasts from the firm at some future time, and work out a new relationship with the firm once the handover to a successor is complete.

In contrast to many founders who are unwilling to let go, both Brenda and Deborah managed the succession process firmly, if not easily. Brenda had a clear idea about who amongst her children would be better suited to running the firm, and stuck to this through the 'inevitable jealousies'. She was equally resolute about exercising her prerogative to make a transfer decision based on the market value of the firm. On the negative side, Brenda was also aware her son lacked the rapport with staff that she had so carefully developed. Anticipating that the business might not continue in his hands over the long term, and to manage his siblings' disappointment, Brenda insisted on selling the business to him at its full market value:

> Brenda: It's taken me twelve months to bed down the deal with [her son]... He was looking at trying to get a bargain, and I was looking at a commercial transaction... There has been a bit of to and fro, and anger, but it's a matter of learning to keep your cool with the family. With the other two there were certain jealousies and envies because [he's] got it now.

Deborah's experience shows that relinquishing the spotlight gracefully also requires skill and grace on the part of the successor, not just the incumbent leader.

Deborah had tried out each of her daughters as a possible successor, but had never created a precise timetable for the handover. Seventeen years passed from the time Robyn entered the firm and when she took over its leadership, and in that time, Robyn never once asked Deborah when she would step down. In a private discussion with us away from her mother, Robyn commented on how she managed to let the spotlight gradually shift to herself and away from Deborah. She did this in a natural way, rather than trying to force the process, despite the formidable waiting period:

> Robyn: Everyone says, 'Oh gosh, it took her long enough to hand over'... I've really been running the business for probably ten years. I mean, on the operations side of things, I knew what every office was doing and internally... she was overseeing everything and, you know, she was finding it very frustrating and I think that's one of the things in the end...
>
> Interviewer: Did you ever say to her, 'Why don't you move over now?'
>
> Robyn: No, never. No. I knew that eventually she would. I could tell that she was getting irritated. She was less tolerant of the staff. I knew she was considering it. It wasn't a complete shock to me at all.

At the time of interviews, Both Brenda and Deborah had fully retired from their leadership role in the firm, something many family business founders never achieve. However, Brenda was continuing her involvement in the business as a kind of ambassador for it. According to Sonnenfeld (1988), being an ambassador is a positive way a departing leader can manage the two important barriers to exit: the 'hero's stature', the unique position of power that top leaders hold and the hero's mission and 'heroic mission', the unique ability to run the business that the leader often feels they have. CEOs may be more or less troubled by the prospect of relinquishing their heroic stature and their heroic mission, and how they manage these feelings of loss determines their approach to retirement. The following four approaches to retirement, adapted from Sonnenfeld's typology, illustrate both dangerous and more benign possibilities.

> Monarchs are the most troubled by both barriers to exit from the business. They do not leave until forced, and this may happen only through death or a 'palace revolt'.

> Generals long for their lost heroic stature. They leave only when forced, but finally do so willingly. However, they plan to return.

> Ambassadors are the least troubled by either barrier to exit. They leave willingly and maintain contact with the business in an advisory capacity. Their exits are graceful.

> Governors are similarly untroubled by exit—at least on the surface. Their approach to leaving is to rule for a bounded period only, making a clean break when the moment for exit comes. They then genuinely carry out the clean exit strategy and maintain little contact with the business thereafter.

Source: Adapted from Sonnenfeld (1988).

In summary, monarchs and generals have least mastery over heroic stature and most frustration with the process of exit from family firms. Monarchs and generals are prevalent in family firms and have contributed to the wealth of research literature on succession difficulties. Ambassadors and governors, in contrast, manage their heroic stature much better, and are relatively untroubled by the impending loss of their heroic mission.

Brenda had become well known in social and charity circles in the capital city where the family firm was based, and she hoped to maintain the business' prominence by remaining associated with it. Nevertheless, she recognised her ongoing role probably added to her son's difficulties because she, rather than he, remained the public face of the business.

BUILDING A COMMUNITY IN WHICH TO LEARN

Chapter 3 outlines some common features of family businesses and communities of practice, and how the belongingness dimensions of a community of practice help it sustain itself by increasing its learning energy, trust and self-awareness. This makes it even more remarkable that neither Brenda nor Deborah did much learning in a pre-existing learning community. Brenda did not experience the firm she and her husband started as a learning community—she was simply a support person for it.

Community of practice theorists (for example, Wenger, 1999, pp. 103–6) show how members of one learning community can pass on skills to another when the two communities' boundaries are permeable enough. This kind of useful boundary-crossing was never possible for Brenda, whose female friends and the business community in general were sceptical—even hostile—to her as a businessperson. Deborah also encountered scepticism, if not hostility; other people had trouble understanding her business idea. Building a community from scratch while learning its operations is always difficult. Brenda said that she 'never felt she could say to the bastards that she was on top of this', and Deborah was still surprised her business ever grew large enough to outlast her tenure in it.

After being plunged into the leadership spotlight, for a long time, Brenda and Deborah lacked a sense of their 'learning trajectory'; that is, a clear view of how they had gradually developed their businesses, their leadership skills, management philosophies and so on (Wenger, 2000, p. 241). For both, but especially Deborah, the interview in this project was one of the first times they had attempted to clarify to themselves just how they had created their identity as business leaders. Perhaps this lack of a sense of a learning trajectory was the result of their turbulent experience of the learning stages, which did not occur in the conventional order or at a steady pace.

Belongingness through Engagement and Imagination

Both Brenda and Deborah created a learning community primarily through creating belongingness. However, they used different modes of belongingness: Brenda favoured engagement; Deborah relied on imagination.

Brenda: Engagement

In Wenger's terms, Brenda relied heavily on engagement to build a learning community in her family business. Her approach to problem-solving was to do things with her staff, and encourage them to share responsibility when dealing with tough times. Also, the way that staff, rather than Brenda, could decide who was worthy of being in the community (they even carried out necessary sackings) is typical of the 'boundedness' of engagement—how engagement defines actions as competent in the community (Wenger, 1999, p. 175). However, Brenda's talent for engagement also made her concerned for the son who succeeded her as CEO. She doubted he shared her capacity to solve problems by working them out jointly with his staff. Instead, he tended to be isolated from them, relying on his own knowledge—contrary to the type of learning approach that works in a true community of practice:

> Brenda: He then [after taking over the firm] had to feel the brunt of his staff, getting the best out of his people, doing deals, keeping within budgets, buying cars, etc... And the point was, he found he couldn't do it all by himself. He knew a lot— or thought he did. What he really had to learn was how to produce the results by getting people to work as a team. It only took one person not to follow up and the deal was lost. He had to learn not to blame that person, but to blame himself for not making sure they knew what they had to do...

Deborah: Imagination

Deborah lacked the support of her friends when she talked about her business idea—they simply could not understand why Deborah thought it was so urgent to set up a home-care agency. In addition, the communities of practice where Deborah might have learned leadership and management skills—the businesses run by family members—were negative examples. Nevertheless, her friends' scepticism only reinforced her commitment to her business idea. Her uncles' poor performance as managers prompted her to think about a deliberately contrasting set of norms, roles, expectations and so on, based on planning and conscious efforts to build familiness.

All this points directly to Deborah's preferred belongingness strategy in her community of practice: imagination. Deborah's original vision defined the idea for her firm, her learning agenda and her management philosophy. In the end, it even provided a tacit job specification for Robyn, her successor.

Evolving Roles: From Invisible to Anchor to Entrepreneur

Brenda and Deborah both ran first-generation ventures, family businesses 'by intent'; thus neither is an 'heiress', the term Curimbaba (2002) uses to describe women who manage family firms started by a member of an earlier generation. All Curimbaba's roles, whether invisible, anchor or professional, are ways of describing female managers—not leaders—of family firms. Nevertheless, many aspects of Curimbaba's invisible and anchor roles fit Brenda's and Deborah's experiences. They also fulfil a role that Curimbaba's typology did not anticipate: that of entrepreneur, a person who creates new organisations or renews existing ones.

At first, Brenda filled what both she and her husband saw as a somewhat low-status role in her husband's firm; she was 'just a support person'. She took over the family business in a thoroughly unexpected way, because she needed to support her family after her husband's death. Her education and career had given her 'feminine' skills that most people—and Brenda—regarded as unrelated to motor vehicle retailing. She, like others, attributed her leadership difficulties to being female and, to a lesser extent, her lack of an appropriate background and formal education for business management and entrepreneurship. In this she resembles Curimbaba's invisible female manager.

However, even as a support person, she did not regard the firm as a source of privileges, or believe she was free to come and go from it as she wished. Her husband's death quickly changed her to an anchor: someone indispensable in the firm and from there she rapidly revealed a budding entrepreneurial identity. Even before taking over running the firm, she showed a propensity for calculated risk taking and a conviction that risks are worthwhile. Brenda, rather than her husband, negotiated the bank loan they needed to start their business, after she put together the collateral to show the bank, making it appear bigger than it really was. The decision to start the firm was more hers than his:

> Brenda: He [her husband] was certainly nervous about it—more than I was, probably. He always said to me that he didn't want us to bite off more than we could chew, but I could tell even then that it was now or never. If we hadn't taken the plunge then, maybe we never would have. And then we'd have always wondered whether we'd lost the opportunity to go it on our own.

Deborah also started her own firm, but at first she was more spontaneous about it than entrepreneurial, in the sense of consciously seeking out and developing an opportunity. Even the way she formulated her business idea was spontaneous—as a 'call from heaven'. While intensely focused on the details of running the business and developing it in accordance with her vision since then, at another level, she was reluctant to acknowledge its growth. She shied away from referring to her firm as an 'empire', which may be a way of coping with being 'condemned to success' and tied to the business, both common problems for anchors. Also typical of anchors is Deborah's feeling that she had no need to find any other major career focus than the business.

Neither Brenda nor Deborah ever expected to take a key role in a family firm; in that sense both were originally invisibles. Later, as anchors, they moved in the direction of leadership, and since then have acted out their personal identities as entrepreneurs. The process was never easy. Both were thrust into—and then learned to manage—the *visibility* that comes from being centre stage in their firms and even beyond, and they learned how to relinquish the firm in favour of the next generation.

CONCLUSIONS

Brenda and Deborah moved into the leadership spotlight in different ways. Brenda made the move suddenly and through a personal catastrophe; Deborah did it less suddenly, but still in an improvised way. Neither was a 'method' actor who could consciously draw on past business experience and thoroughly rehearse her role. As founders, neither had the opportunity to model her leadership on someone in a business she already knew, much less try it out in a separate firm (for instance, a subsidiary of the family firm), which could serve as a training ground. They had to make up the moves as they went along, drawing on unrelated experience. Neither had a close relationship with a mentor, whether inside or outside the business. Consequently, we can say that both Brenda and Deborah were 'thrust into the leadership spotlight'. Nevertheless, both learned to control the spotlight and eventually to move it onto someone else—their chosen successor. Chapter 9 distils how their experiences and learning, along with those of other participants, helped to generate more general propositions.

The next group of interviewees, in contrast to Brenda and Deborah, all actively drew on their experience of growing up with a business background. However, they were discouraged from entering the business world, especially the 'original' family business. Our next chapter is about women who 'build their own stage'.

5. Building Their Own Stage

The four interviewees in this chapter—Jane, Nancy, Miriam and Ellen—are all entrepreneurs: they have created new organisations. Thus, they directly link our study with today's increasing academic and public policy attention to women entrepreneurs. Miriam and Nancy came from a family business background, although neither had ever taken a senior role in the family business. Jane's father was an independent professional; Ellen's father had extensive corporate experience. This chapter's first interviewee, Jane, founded a business in close collaboration with an experienced mentor. The others, despite the extensive business experience in their family backgrounds, all mentioned obstacles that even now would rule out succession to a leadership role in a pre-existing business, including the 'original' family business in the case of Miriam and Nancy. Nancy never even wanted to enter the family firm. Nevertheless, all four said that they hoped the firms they started would continue as family businesses. This makes them family business owners 'by intent'. Like many family business owners, they indicated that they would be happy if their children carried on the business they started—provided the children demonstrated the skills and desire to do this.

What is it like to start a firm 'against the odds', separately from an existing firm in the family background? All four interviewees in this section constructed their own stage; that is, started their own business apart from and in some ways in opposition to, their previous experience of business. We start with Jane, who did the building work with the help of a close business mentor.

JANE

Jane's journey towards starting her own corporate publishing business was long and circuitous. Superficially, she seemed an unlikely candidate for a career in business. She had no family business background, although her father and other members of his generation were independent professionals: doctors, lawyers, architects. Neither her birth position in the family nor her choice of university course initially hinted at a future business career.

Jane: I have three older brothers, none of whom are professionals or in business. I'm the youngest of four and the only daughter. And the most educated in terms of formal education... I have a Masters degree in Russian politics...

She had always felt strong pressure from her parents, particularly her father, an oral surgeon, to achieve highly, even more so than her brothers:

Jane: My father was particularly determined that just because I was a girl meant nothing; that I had to achieve just as much as anybody else did, in fact probably more... I remember being 14 and crying to my mother saying, you know, I've got to really do well because, you know, Dad really expects me to. And it was good that he expected me to, because that challenged me very well. But yeah, it was always a pressure... Then it became more of a pressure later on because my brothers who worked in business didn't do well, and I was the one who did really well... There was no expectation... it wasn't even discussed that I'd get married and have kids and not have a career.

Jane's initial career activities and choices pointed in no particular direction for long, though she pursued them with great intensity while they lasted. She was not particularly reflective about the goals she chose—she saw having a goal and going all out for it as an end in itself. She chose to study Russian politics because 'politics had always been her passion', and because she was told that a degree in politics was a good way to get into the diplomatic corps. However, having reached this goal, her rapid change of direction was typical:

Jane: I applied in my last year of my Masters degree for the diplomatic corps and got accepted. And the day after I got accepted I said, 'I'm not going to do this.' He [the representative of the diplomatic corps] said, 'What do you mean you're not going to do it?' And I said, 'They don't promote on merit, they promote on how long you've been there... That's not me. I don't want to go into somewhere where I'm not going to be recognised for my merit.' He said, 'What are you gonna do?' and I said, 'I have absolutely no idea because since the age of twelve this is what I wanted to do'... I took a lot of time walking up and down a beach crying, because I had no idea what I was going to do.

Her next career moves seemed just as haphazard. Her thesis supervisor employed her as a research assistant to work on a book about the history of one of the political parties in New Zealand. This led to her interviewing current and former political figures all around New Zealand. This in turn led to her being invited to organise the junior members of the political party which had commissioned the original book. Jane accepted this task mainly because she had nothing else to do.

Jane: So I did that for two and a half years... So at twenty-two, I was sitting on National Council receiving papers on... I guess on... how to structure the Young Nationals and what they should be doing. I didn't have a job description, they just gave me an office and said, 'Well, work out what you need to do, go and do it and tell us what you're doing'.

Jane became frustrated when it was clear the Young Nationals were never going to be taken seriously as a policy-making body. She was employed again as a research assistant for a book on the history of Australian entrepreneurship, and took over writing it when the original author became too busy to do it. Then she was invited to stand for political office in New Zealand. But in her own view she was, at 25, 'single, and too young and too naughty' to contemplate a job in politics. So again she found herself unsure what to do next.

It becomes clear only later how all these apparently unconnected jobs contributed to the personal, product and industry skills needed to develop a business in publishing. On the personal side, Jane learned the self-discipline to complete major tasks. She also gained the confidence to believe she would be judged on her abilities. She had no difficulty approaching senior, busy people and getting them to help her. Even more important, she learned not to become caught up in the detail of any project or transaction, but to keep moving towards the next one.

> Jane: As soon as I've got the contract, I pick it up and move on. You know, because... in the business, I'm the person who negotiates the major contracts and does the deals.

Because she was used to processing large amounts of information and reducing it to a concise and palatable form, she also knew how to pick other people with this skill:

> Jane: In terms of ending up in publishing, I mean, I know how to write. I know how to research. I know how to take a huge pile of information and condense it. So, in terms of this particular business, contracting writers and that sort of stuff, it's very valid. I can make a very good assessment about how long I think someone should take, about what they should be doing, about what should be coming out the other end.

Even so, when Jane was first asked to write more corporate histories, she was only vaguely aware that this represented a business opportunity. She resembles Deborah in this respect: her eventual business partner, Simon [name disguised], had to point out to her that she could make a business out of people's requests that she write their firms' corporate histories.

> Jane: I guess over a period of about a year and a half I could potentially have picked up maybe a dozen books to write. And I thought, well, I could do that. And that'd be classed as a cool job. You know, spend my life writing interesting books about interesting people... and then I met Simon and I interviewed him. He'd just sold [a large and well-known Australian travel business] and at the end of the interview he said, 'Well, what are you going to do next?' and I said, 'Oh, I don't

know, but a number of people have asked me to write their books for them and I really don't want to do that. I thought I might organise to get them done'. And he said, 'Well, you'll have to get yourself a business plan and come back and have a chat with me.' Because I didn't have a business plan... I said, 'Well, I've got all these people that are interested and I reckon that I could get this amount of money for it', and he said, 'Oh, okay, well let's see if we can start a business and make some money out of it'. And that's literally how it happened. And I think I still have that first shocking business plan in my desk.

The meeting between Jane and her mentor was as serendipitous as her previous projects. Simon was 60 years old and had just sold a successful firm, but he did not want to be left with nothing to do. The new business was a result of combining 'his money and her idea'. Jane, despite her varied, intense and highly focused learning experiences, initially had even less knowledge of business practice than many of the other participants in our study. She had no idea at all about business, let alone a publishing business.

An important role of Jane's new business partner and mentor was to put her in touch with people who would help her develop her skills in publishing.

Jane: He said, 'Well, you're gonna have to learn, and you're gonna have to learn fast.' So he sent me off to a printer and he sent me off somewhere else and two days later I came back and I could put together a budget... so I've had the best MBA. I think that's the easiest way to describe it.

Simon introduced Jane to prominent publishers as well as representatives of other industries, so this spread the mentoring function widely. Simon also insisted on basic corporate disciplines from the outset:

Jane: In terms of corporate disciplines we had quarterly board meetings. We still do, did from the day we started... And interestingly, also... whilst we were still a private company, we got our annual figures audited. So we always presented our board with audited figures. Audited reports.

However, before this, Simon brought together Jane's energy and self-discipline, her knowledge of writing and her capacity to get people to do what she wanted, and added his knowledge of how to set up and run a business. All Jane knew at this stage, rather like Robyn in Chapter 7, was that she was a good leader, that she was articulate, that she could sell a concept. She had become aware of her leadership skills because of her experience with getting a difficult group of people to work together:

Jane: I'd led groups of people when I was doing stuff in politics. I had a group of Young Nationals that I had to try and get together who hated each other, who didn't like talking to each other. Then I led at school. I mean, I guess I took control of things and always have done. So I don't know whether that's necessarily a good leader, but I take control of things. And I sort things out.

Having started a business from scratch, Jane had to decide what values would underpin its operations.

Jane: We have a company motto which is 'Do as you say'. Pretty corny, but one of the key values of this business is that we will do what we say we're gonna do. From returning phone calls to delivering something… When we say we're gonna do it, I mean, just right down to very basic levels through to very big levels. If we say we're gonna deliver something by a certain date, it's delivered by a certain date.

While she said this value came from Simon, she always felt it to be of the utmost importance. She also valued fairness and recognised the links between fairness and trust:

Jane: We have a principle that you sign the contract and you put it in the drawer. Because if you ever have to refer to it you've got a problem.

Jane also needed to learn how to take a strategic view of the business, preparing for and introducing change. In short, she needed to learn to work on the business, rather than only in it. Looking back, Jane realised that she gradually acquired strategic leadership skills under Simon's tutelage. He always reminded her that 'you don't make real money by doing all the work yourself. You have to employ people, and deal with the pain of that'. Jane now tells other women business owners this, echoing Simon's words. However, she did not always have this degree of confidence. She recalled her first experience of employing someone, a receptionist:

Jane: I stayed awake for days worried about how I was gonna make sure that this person got paid. Not that we didn't have the money, but it really worried me, you know, now I was responsible for somebody in a job. Me I could handle, but now I had another person. I had to really make sure that you know, there was business coming in the door, so I felt extraordinarily responsible.

Thanks to her mentor, Jane's confidence in her ability to solve problems in the business and ensure its long-term future grew:

Jane: Now I don't worry about employing people or not employing people. I just think it's business. It's a numbers game now… I've sat next to a highly successful businessman for 15 years and I've learned every day.

Jane said that she felt that she was still in the process of developing a long-term strategic direction for the business. It was too small for her to relinquish all operational involvement in it, so she did not work solely on the business, rather than in it. Nevertheless, she was getting used to confronting change:

Jane: I guess what's happened for us in the last 18 months to two years is that I've worked more on it [the business], and had to move us into other areas because our

Even her friends told her, 'Go and get some nice little job somewhere'. She knew what the business needed: debt reduction and growth, but had little idea of how to achieve it:

> Brenda: I had debts to pay and wages to meet; the overheads were high. I had the opportunity of encouraging them [the staff] to get a bigger bottom line and discussing: 'How can we do it? Where can we cut corners?' But I had no specific idea of what they [the staff] should do.

Brenda's solution was to build on her female skills as a housewife where, as she said, 'You become a bit of an economist'. She asked the staff what should be done to reduce costs and improve profitability, and what sort of rewards they would want for achieving it. Her major strategy for ensuring the firm survived was to build equity in the business faster than other dealerships were doing:

> Brenda: I was paying the debts back quicker than I had to. And I was taking the profits and putting them into debt reduction and growth. I thought to myself, well, this is great, because that property has got to grow into something that's worthwhile. If I wanted to grow, I had a better chance of getting another loan. So it worked. It worked with finance companies who then wanted to know me. For five years there, it was touch and go, but they could see that I was too proud, far too proud to let anybody believe I was going to fizzle out.

However, it was a long time before Brenda felt she had the full confidence of others in her firm. Another problem was to gain the trust of the network organisation of which her firm was a part. Referring to them, Brenda commented that there was never a time when she could say, 'I don't need to worry about these bastards anymore. I'm on top of this'.

Because of her sudden entry into the top role, Brenda did not have the opportunity to absorb and appreciate the firm's culture gradually before taking over its leadership. She created that culture as she went along. The way Brenda developed her firm's culture and its strategic direction was simple, but far from obvious in the motor retailing industry during the 1970s. She asked her staff for help:

> Brenda: And I used my staff. They found the solutions and then they owned the idea of the solutions.

The solutions Brenda's staff came up with included deciding themselves when a member of their team should be sacked, and actually carrying out the sacking themselves.

mainstream areas were okay, but they weren't growing. So Simon and I spent quite a bit of time thinking, what else can we do, where else can we go. We've changed. We still do mainstream parts of what we've always done, but we're doing a whole bunch of different things that we wouldn't have even thought of two years ago, and that's largely because I've decided that that's what we needed to do—or we needed to do it from a business point of view. But where we went and how we did those things, that's where I've put a lot of my energies.

Jane's mentor Simon taught her to recognise when it was time to change the business' direction and not be frightened by this. Flexibility became a quality of the business as well as its leader. As Jane stated, echoing Simon's mantra when they started the business:

Jane: We weren't a publishing company, we were a business. We happen to publish books, but basically, we're a business.

Finding new directions for the business became one of her primary sources of enjoyment in it:

Jane: I get my jollies out of developing new concepts. I got bored with doing corporate history, so I've developed new concepts as I needed them for the business. Now I can do that with my hand tied behind my back. So, my challenges are: I want to create different things that haven't been created before and get them out to the market in a way that hasn't been done before.

Several things converged to require Jane to change her style of involvement in the business. Changes in the publishing market pointed to the need to be flexible about the business' products. Her mentor's health was deteriorating and he would soon need to scale back his involvement in the business.[1] At a personal level, Jane wanted more time with her son. All this meant that Jane had to act as a mentor for others in the business. In talking about this, she spoke about what she was doing by herself, instead of speaking of herself and Simon as 'we', as she had earlier in the interview. After much effort, she found a person whom she was starting to train as an operations and project manager. She hoped that later, he would also undertake more entrepreneurial functions in the business:

Jane: I'm really the one in the business that does that [now] and the only way he [the new project manager] is gonna learn is to do it with me. From the time that I have the first initial meeting with people or even when I'm brainstorming concept development—because normally I would sit and do it on my own—now every time I'm doing something like that, I drag him in and say, 'Come on Andy [name disguised], I need to talk to you about this'. Because he also needs to get an understanding of the assumptions I'm making, because I haven't got this written down anywhere, there's no sort of process…

Jane agreed that there were no manuals to help her new operations manager develop the conceptual skills needed to develop her business. This meant Jane had to articulate many things she had probably forgotten she had ever learned. She was creating a 'learning trajectory' for her operations manager:

> Jane: There's a whole range of assumptions that I just naturally think about, and so with him there, I have to articulate those. He's saying, 'Well, why did you do it that way?' So that's the way that's going to happen. And he'll do things differently from me and that's okay, but he needs to understand that we've done that before and it didn't work, and he might say, 'Well, maybe we'll do it this way'.

At the time of interview, it was still too early for Jane to predict what form the business would take in the long term, or whether she would hand it on to her young son, though this was an attractive option. Jane's business was thus a family business by intent. However, for now, she was pleased to make her son aware of the benefits of being in business for yourself, especially independence. As she explained to him:

> Jane: 'Because I work for myself I can leave whenever I want to, and I can pick you up from school and I can do all sorts of things that I couldn't do if I worked for somebody.' So, he understands the hard work and also I guess the flexibility of being your own boss.

She also helped him understand the basics of business:

> Jane: When I say, 'I think I got a really good contract in today', he says, 'Well, how much is it?' and I go 'That', and he says, 'That's a lot of money'. And I go, 'Yeah, but we don't get to keep all of it because we've got to do things, and then other things have to be paid, and then there's something left over and that's profit.' It doesn't happen a lot, but he's very aware of what I do and that I'm doing it because there's this goal at the end of it: money. You know, it's not like it's the only thing, but I'm not here just to have fun. I'm running a business and a business means making money.

For Jane, achieving leadership meant achieving independence from her mentor, and making decisions for the business and herself without his help.

The remaining interviewees in this chapter—Miriam, Nancy and Ellen— are like Jane in having started their own firms, orienting them towards their personal strengths and needs. They too built their own stages. They either grew up in family businesses or had a parent with strong corporate experience. However, all three said that they believed family expectations were always against their taking a major role in the family business, or indeed any business. Their families all seemed to have taken seriously the advice: 'Don't put your daughters on the stage'. Miriam is a case in point.

MIRIAM

Miriam is one of four children. Two, a sister and a brother, are older than she. In her view, her male siblings were an important restraining force against her entering the family property development firm. Miriam described her family's approach to who would eventually lead the family firm this way:

> Miriam: It was natural for my brothers to [be expected to] take on that role. One is younger than me and one is older than me, and for whatever reasoning, that was the expectation.

Instead, Miriam started her own marketing consultancy specialising in the finance and education industries. It had a small core staff and Miriam deliberately kept the business lean, using sub-contractors and strategic alliances extensively and avoiding the expense of buying or leasing large, inner-city premises. Miriam's approach to risk was nevertheless relaxed, at least in comparison to some businesswomen she knew who had not grown up in a business family. Even so, she described herself as more reasoned and cautious about risk than her father. Despite working in a 'glamour' industry, she rejected a glamorous, expansionist approach to her business, because it presented unnecessary risk and because it threatened her balanced approach to enjoying life:

> Miriam: There are so many competitors that have huge offices and have glamour staff and account managers and so forth, whereas I choose not to do that because I think that whatever happens, you can get to the point where you can't pay for those overheads, or at the end of the day, can you justify it to your client base? I've watched my own family do that in terms of taking on additional floor space and buildings and for what reason? You really have to tough it out in the tough times, and for very personal reasons I don't want to do that. I work hard but I want to enjoy life as well.

The more modest style of her firm and its premises was not just a matter of business practice, but part of her need to define herself and her business as separate from the firm her father started. She did not draw on this 'original' family firm financially, though she could have if she chose. She had a formal involvement with it as a shareholder, but:

> Miriam: I don't draw on any income from that. I don't need to do it because my own business is working well, and I want to be a distinct identity. I would never want anyone to say that I live off the family business.

However, members of her family had a different view of her. To them she was an invisible—a support person in the business her father started:

Miriam: I'm asked for my opinion a lot, but it's very much as a support role. I think they're surprised that I've done as well in my own business as I have, because I don't think they ever saw me as a businessperson.

Miriam readily adopted the original family firm's spirit and, despite wanting to maintain a separate life as a businessperson, she came close to conflating her own objectives and those of the family firm:

Miriam: One thing I can say about the family business, which I don't actually say about my own, is if I hear that the family business has got a really big project or has lost a bid, it really affects me, more so than my own business... I carry the family business a lot more than my own business. I want my business to be successful and I work hard at it, but if I lose something, it only impacts on me and my staff, whereas in the family business it actually impacts on a lot of people I love.

To her family, Miriam was always 'the different one. I was the one who was qualified, I was a professional'. Her family's view of her as unsuited to taking charge of the family business changed because she proved herself in her own business. However, something still prevented her from wanting to enter the family business: her father looked to her to have children for the family business. Even though Miriam's younger brother took a leading role in the original family business and was its most likely successor, Miriam was aware that her father's hopes for successors included the children she might have in future:

Miriam: I'm getting married soon, and I know my father is looking forward to grandchildren. And of course he'll be a wonderful as a granddad, but also... he looks to the future and thinks of how they [the children Miriam might have] might one day be part of his firm.

This issue also emerged for others in our study, including some for whom it became an important obstacle to business leadership. We now consider Nancy, who was kept from firm leadership by a different set of problems.

NANCY

Nancy was born in Egypt but lived in Canada from the age of eight. Her family situation bears some resemblances to Miriam's: she has two brothers and a sister. The expectations of Nancy's family run even more strongly against her having a business career. In her case, the gender issue was inseparable from how family businesses in the Middle East coped with in-law relationships and the thorny matter of inheritance customs. Both participants in our study whose businesses were based in the Middle East mentioned the frequent practice of alienating daughters from the family business, because of the diversion of assets that could occur when daughters marry. While these customs may have held more sway in past times, they still prevent many daughters from being considered for senior family business roles:

> Nancy: They [family business owners in the Middle East] fear their in-laws, the gender issue and the inheritance issue. The inheritance issue works like this: if you are a Muslim you can inherit half of what the boy will inherit. As for the gender rules, they always think that women are going to get married to men of another family and her children are not going to hold the same family name and it's like she's leaving the family, which is not the case nowadays. But that's what they think, and they think if they want her to inherit it will go to another family.

While these and other aspects of her country's culture obstructed Nancy's chances of seeking a position in the family firm, they also suggested the basis for the service her business offers. In Nancy's view, there was a deficit in so-called 'soft' management skills in the Middle East. Her business, a human resources training and technology consultancy, aimed to fill this gap:

> Nancy: In the Middle East there is still today an unbalanced focus, in my view, on the highly technical at the cost of the team, the soft skills, the human interaction and the interpersonal skills. So I took that on. I said, let's have a formula whereby when they come to learn the technical, I address the optimisation of this through the interaction with team members, and perhaps touch on some of the challenges they have in how to optimise these tools.

Nancy met and married her husband, also an Egyptian citizen, in Canada, but had divorced from him. She made no direct mention of how the business they operated together started. However, it was clear from the beginning that she was unlikely to have a long-term role in that business. It may have been more her husband's business than hers. It only occurred to her during the interview that she had a family business background by virtue of having run that firm with her husband. She credited her husband with being 'very entrepreneurial-minded'. However, in her view, problems in both the marriage and the business stemmed from her husband's expectation that he would be the sole leader and decision-maker. In the long term, Nancy was unable to deal with what she saw as a lack of choice in important matters. She summarises her experience in the earlier business:

> Nancy: It was horrible, because we have such different styles and because he is ten years older than me I thought that he was the wiser. He was always the technical expert and I was just there to fill in the gaps.

This description echoes Brenda's view of her first role as in the business she started with her husband as 'just a support person'. Nancy later mentioned the disagreements with her husband about where the family and the business should be located during the first Gulf War:

Nancy: If anyone knows me they know that if you don't give me a choice you pay the consequences. I must have a choice. The root cause [of their break-up] was just our interaction and how we were dealing with things. It was the unilateral decisions for my own good that I didn't think were for my own good. That was a symptom of the relationship and the business relationship.

Nancy's need for control was an important factor in how she determined both her personal and her business future. She eventually built her own stage to satisfy these needs. Our next interviewee, Ellen, also had a high need for control.

ELLEN

Ellen was our third interviewee to 'build her own stage' against family opposition. She ran a business manufacturing corporate uniforms. Ellen started it after leaving professional practice as a psychologist, then spent several years in the police force, and still did not 'feel happy'. Her parents did not run a family business, but her father was a senior executive with a multinational company in the 1950s and 1960s. So Ellen was always comfortable around businesspeople. Despite this, she experienced direct opposition to her interest in business from her mother, who said that a business career was not for girls. Her mother was 'devastated' when Ellen stopped practising psychology. Ellen's father died just as she started the business, so she could not discuss it with him, or use him as a mentor. However, she recalled that he did not reinforce her mother's advice, or even give much advice at all. He presented as a somewhat remote, stern figure:

Ellen: He never talked to us. All I remember is that his words of wisdom were: 'As long as you can always stand on your own two feet'. 'I can give you whatever you want, but if you can't stand on your own two feet you are nothing.' He was a quite a ruthless, tough man [laughs].

Despite the forbidding image of her father Ellen retained, she recalled the strong message he gave her about the attractions of being independent and doing what you wanted to do. She also felt that she had inherited his business drive:

Ellen: All I really remember from him is... the working ethic, and that you would lead a wonderful life if you did pursue what you wanted to do. And not necessarily just in business life. Because we went to all-girls schools. You had to be a perfectionist.

Entrepreneurs frequently cite family influences and demands as factors behind their starting their own businesses. Ellen presents as a natural entrepreneur, although she still thought of this as something that women, or 'typical wives', did not do.

> Ellen: Just after our son was born—he is now 21—friends in the local area always went to craft. I didn't work for five years and so I went along to the local craft but was kicked out because I... I hate doing things with my hands. And I thought, this is for the birds. I couldn't bear those ribbon roses. [They] were ribbons to me, not roses. So I ended up changing their venue, getting in proper teachers, getting in babysitters, buying bulk cellophane bags and we made money on them and I started doing all that sort of thing, rather than the craft. And so I really loved wheeling and dealing [laughs].

These comments make it clear that, for varying reasons, Miriam, Nancy and Ellen were all aware they were not considered likely candidates for business leadership. Despite having chosen an entrepreneurial path and being enthusiastic about its benefits, all three felt at odds with what even they saw as 'normal' for women. In this respect, our findings are similar to those of Dumas (1989, 1990, 1992), because interviewees' ambivalence about being in business stemmed from their mother, father or another male figure, such as a husband: people important to them and their ideas about what they might become.

LEARNING WHILE BUILDING

Our four learning stages of family business (Moores and Barrett, 2002) show that Jane, Miriam, Nancy and Ellen followed a different, somewhat smoother pathway to family business leadership, compared to Brenda and Deborah.

Learning Business (L1)

All four participants were exposed to business thinking early in life. Even Ellen, whose father was a successful manager, rather than an entrepreneur, had 'lived and breathed' business from an early age. Consequently, they all 'learned business' (L1) through their family backgrounds. Much more than the women who were 'thrust into the spotlight', they gained an early understanding of the business environment, even if they did not learn the routines and skills of a particular business. They also learned the personal discipline needed for business, including the need for personal versatility and flexibility, along with a careful but non-fearful attitude to risk, which resembles Brenda's. At this early stage, the participants looked much like any other group of potential family business leaders.

Learning Our Business (L2)

The participants' families' expectations, which carried the spoken or unspoken message that the business spotlight should not be directed towards women, affected the second learning stage (L2): 'learning our business'. Here, several participants found some important aspects of their 'background' business culture unattractive: often they disapproved of their father's or husband's style of business management. Jane, whose father was not a business person, recalled a disproportionate pressure on her to succeed in life. Nancy rejected her husband's lack of formal processes and what she saw as his unilateral style of decision-making in matters that affected her. Ellen remembered her father as a remote, unsympathetic figure. Yet she had absorbed the lesson of independence he left her, even while this also made it difficult for her to delegate or to share leadership. At an earlier stage in the history of her firm, she found herself unable to work with a partner in the business, because this would have meant taking a lesser role in making decisions about it:

> Ellen: The first four months [of having a partner] were fine, because I still drove things. And then I started being asked why I did this and why I did that, and don't make decisions unless it goes through... I said, the business is successful the way I think. If you stop me from thinking that way, how can it continue to be successful? And I am not egotistical, I just know that I have to be free to a certain extent to do things.

Miriam viewed her father's approach to business rather like Nancy viewed her husband: they both disliked the men's authoritarian approach to management that they regard as outdated and damaging. Miriam was also concerned to see her father passing on his management approach to her younger brother, the likely heir to the 'main' family business:

> Miriam: I often think with my little brother, my father is his role model. Without going out and learning about other acceptable modes of behaviour in corporations that have big HR departments and that have to adhere to certain standards, he's going to perpetuate that through his life.

Learning to Lead Our Business (L3)

The previous section tracked how these four participants gained a strategic view of their businesses, and learned the value of personal and business independence. These skills were important for leading their family businesses, because the circumstances and choices they had already made meant they were unlikely or unwilling to lead the business their father or some other member of their family founded. All discovered that leadership depended not merely on their view of themselves, their activities and results, but how others regarded them and their businesses. The view that family members and the staff in their businesses took of them was particularly important to their being recognised as leaders. Merely having constructed their own stage was insufficient to assure their status as leaders.

Learning to Leave Our Business (L4)

There is a further issue about holding the spotlight, related to how the participants saw their businesses as family businesses 'by intent', and therefore how they thought about eventually handing it on. Each participant in this chapter hoped to pass the business on to her children. But this depended on the children regarding the business as a viable entity—which did not always happen. Nancy, for example, had difficulty getting her children to regard her business as a 'serious' or a 'real' business. They saw it as 'just Mum's business', despite its considerable size and credibility. Miriam did not have children at the time of interview. However, she said that she would want them to consider going into her business. In the meantime, she was aware of a conflict between this view of her children's future and her father's desire to have her children go into his business, the 'main' family business. Miriam's father may not have considered her business as a family business in its own right. One solution, at least in the view taken by Miriam's father, would be for his business, Miriam's business (and indeed other businesses in the family) all to be connected in some way.

> Miriam: I think the interesting thing is my father would ideally like to link up all our businesses. At one point we all had premises inside his building. I think on his part, he would love them all to connect, but I think there's too much emotion, that now it's just easier not to.

Ellen thought along similar lines, and was already canvassing the possibility of diversifying her clothing business to accommodate her children's possible business interests. However, this would have involved major restructuring, because the other potential businesses were in industries very different from hers. While none of these participants had so far dealt with the 'learning to let go' (L4) phase of learning family business, major diversification would have opened up new possibilities for keeping the business in the family.

Ellen had already started to discuss possible diversification strategies to accommodate the businesses her children might start, suggesting that her children had already begun to learn the personal disciplines needed for entrepreneurship and the values her business exemplified. These are phases L1 and L2, respectively, of our four phases of learning family business (Moores and Barrett, 2002). Ellen gave us a copy of a talk that one of her daughters gave at school about growing up in her mother's family business. It described how when she was growing up she resented how much of her mother's time the business took. She particularly took umbrage at her mother's solution to this problem, which was to get her daughter to work in the family business in her spare time. However, she realised that growing up with a family business background also taught her the value of attention to detail, which she learned by doing menial tasks in the business, 'starting at the bottom'. This lesson was as important as seeing that the family firm was the result of determination and the willingness to follow a personal passion, even when, like Ellen, you might lack some basic skills.

DEFINING A DIFFERENT LEARNING COMMUNITY: CHANGING THE SCRIPT

The experiences of this group of participants differ from those of the two leaders which Chapter 1 considers, because this group was either blocked from entering the 'obvious' community of practice (the original family firm) or simply discouraged from considering a business career at all. This had important effects on the belongingness (engagement, imagination or alignment) strategies interviewees adopted when they created their new firms. In some cases, there was also an impact on how interviewees managed their new communities' boundaries and identity. These issues in turn affect the dimensions Wenger (1999) defines as vital for a healthy community of practice: its learning energy, trust and self-awareness.

Engagement

Being cut off at an early stage from the original family business meant there were relatively few opportunities to engage with it. For some, it was a negative learning experience. Rather than learning and endorsing the principles of an original community of practice, Miriam and Nancy learned what not to do, and constructed their new communities of practice along opposing lines. Jane and Ellen, who had even less exposure to an earlier business learning community compared to Miriam, dealt with the knowledge gaps this created by importing expertise from elsewhere. For Jane, the lack of access to a real business learning community meant that her business mentor, Simon, needed to be the 'complete MBA' which, fortunately, he turned out to be. Ellen's husband also served as a substitute for Ellen's lack of engagement with an earlier learning community. He filled gaps in Ellen's expertise by building the necessary systems to allow the firm to expand, something Ellen could not have done on her own. Yet her husband's presence led to problems in the imagination mode of belongingness, as we shall see shortly.

Imagination

When a leader is blocked from entering an earlier learning community and builds a new stage, the new community at first has difficulty imagining itself. Members lack a vision of the community's potential, and find it hard to understand the meanings the community has for other people in it. They also have trouble seeing the community in new ways when this becomes necessary (Wenger, 1999, 2000).

For Jane, the lack of an earlier community at first reduced her capacity to imagine herself as the leader of one, and this might have echoed her life generally. She adopted many early career activities in a haphazard way. Later, in the context of the firm she established, they became part of the way she imagined a new role for herself in the world, as the leader of her own firm. Looking back on a job with the Young Nationals she took on 'because she didn't have anything better to do', and where she was frustrated because the group would never really influence government policy, Jane realised that she had led—'sorted out'—a group of young, strong-minded politicians. Still earlier, she had led at school. But while she was killing time with these and other 'fill-in' activities, she would have had trouble imagining herself as a leader.

In contrast to Jane, Ellen had trouble with the imagination mode of belongingness after (rather than before) she established her community of practice. The problem arose from how the staff viewed the firm's leadership roles: their perceptions were different from Ellen's about what it meant for Ellen's husband to enter and later leave the firm. While this important male figure was present, Ellen's staff imagined that he, rather than she, filled the role of leader: the person who defined the community's norms, codes of behaviour, principles and negotiated commitments. Ellen only realised her staff saw things this way when her husband left the firm after some years spent developing its systems. While she had instigated her husband's departure for the sake of his professional development, she discovered her staff had interpreted it as a sign that the firm must be about to fail. She was not regarded as the face of the business, even though she had founded it. The presence of her husband reduced her significance as its leader.

> Interviewer: Was there ready acceptance of you as the boss in relation to this [systems development activity]?
>
> Ellen: Well I thought there was, which is interesting, because when Martin [name disguised] left the company I got a big surprise from some staff, who saw him leaving and thought that the company was very weakened. But that's why they left... I suppose we did a couple of other things around the time he left. For one thing, we also sold a building because we had actually purchased a factory in a residential area which ended up being quite a windfall. We sold the building and the staff became so much more solid, and yet they saw this as being almost the

demise of the business. But we did have a couple of men working for us, one as a courier and another as an operations training manager and they were ex-army. One had been a major and one a colonel or something and they saw Rob leaving, and so did a couple of ladies, and they saw this as being a weakness in the business.

These staff had come into the business while her husband was there, so had not developed a view of Ellen as the firm's leader. While Ellen always had the final say about what happened in her business, she had avoided making her formal authority obvious to the staff and, in particular, she preferred not to be seen as occupying a position of authority over her husband.

Ellen: Martin and I don't have that sort of relationship. But I suppose people perceive what they think or whatever. That was a surprise for me, yes, it was surprising.

By not insisting on being seen as the most important figure on the stage, Ellen risked not being seen as the true boss. If she had had the experience of an earlier family business learning community, Ellen might have had the chance to learn how to manage the overlap between firm and family relationships in the workplace.

Alignment

Not having had access to an earlier learning community also meant that these four interviewees at first had problems with the alignment mode of belonging: creating a shared purpose and a set of principles and roles which could be transmitted to new generations. As with the other belongingness modes, engagement and imagination, the leaders in this group eventually solved their alignment problems. Miriam, for example, made a point of occupying modest, rather than extravagant business premises as a way of aligning her firm with her modest style of business management. Both Miriam and Nancy created norms that contrasted with the authoritarian approach to management they observed in their original family firms. For a time, while her husband worked in the firm, Ellen neglected to align her firm's leadership role with what her staff saw as normal on the basis of their previous experience. For Jane, Simon's advice about following conventional corporate disciplines such as annual reports and regular audits from the outset was part of aligning her community with the wider world of sound business practices. This in turn provides external legitimacy, vital for pre-profit start-ups (Zimmerman and Zeitz, 2002). Having her mentor inside her own embryonic community of practice from the outset meant that Jane could 'incubate' the necessary goals, norms, traditions and routines within her own community's boundaries. Her firm's norm of fairness, her adherence to the idea that there was trouble if you need to look at the contract, the dedication to 'doing what you say', even her acknowledgement that she was 'in business', rather than in a particular business, are examples of this.

Boundaries

While exclusion from the original family business was painful, some participants turned their enforced isolation to advantage. Miriam reinforced her firm's boundaries by refusing business referred to her from the original family firm. She also declined to have her firm share a building with her father's firm, at least for the time being. For Nancy, establishing her own firm was primarily a matter of establishing its boundaries with respect to another firm—the one her husband had started.

In these cases, establishing clear boundaries was part of negotiating the new community's identity (Wenger, 1999, p. 175). However, in other cases, the leader had to persuade other people that the firm need not be closed to them. For example, Ellen had to change her children's view of her firm's boundaries. They believed the firm could not offer a wide variety of learning experiences for them, and unfairly saw it as 'just Mum's business'—small and insular. While this might not be important for a firm whose founder did not envisage it continuing over a long period, it was a problem for a family business by intent—Ellen's. However, the problem faded as the various members of the family, especially the younger generation, discussed diversifying the firm's activities.

Identity

Despite these participants being blocked from participating in an earlier family firm, they managed to develop their own firm's values. Where being female was the reason for refusing them entry to the family business as a potential leader, they fought back, endorsing what they saw as 'female' approaches to doing business and making these attributes a part of the new firm's identity. For Nancy, recognising the need to go beyond the male norms of doing business prominent in the Middle East actually gave her the founding idea for her business: training people in 'female' or 'soft' management approaches, unusual for that part of the world. Nancy also used 'soft' skills in the general running of her business, but did not solely rely on them. She valued 'follow-through, not just creativity', and contrasted this with her husband's more improvised approach:

> Nancy: He [her husband] is not very organised, and he doesn't follow through with things and he's all over the place, which for me is okay, because that's his creativity and that's fine. But you cannot run a business just that way. You must have both.

ROLES THAT BUILD

In contrast to Brenda, who first occupied an invisible role in the firm she and her husband started, these participants are all 'professionals' in the sense Curimbaba (2002) uses the term. By necessity, Jane, Miriam, Ellen and Nancy always knew that further possibilities existed, other than seeking a career in the original family business, or in business generally. Those with a family business background can never join their family firms and separate themselves from the authoritarian business norms they believe these firms represent. The sibling birth order positions Miriam and Nancy occupy confirm the impediment to female leadership Curimbaba (2002) predicts for women with brothers in their own generation.

As well as confirming these characteristics of Curimbaba's professional role, this group demonstrates a new aspect of the problems 'professionals' experience. Their experiences suggest that when family business women have a relationship with more than one business, the 'original' family business and her own, discrepancies are likely to exist between her own and her family's view of her role in each business. These discrepancies can be difficult or impossible to resolve. For example, Nancy's arguments with her husband arose from differences in their views about her role in the business that he started—'his' business. Later they disagreed about where the family should live during wartime, and his view prevailed. However, as well as being a source of problems, the war finally gave Nancy a business opportunity and created a sphere of operations for her, which took her away from her husband's business:

> Nancy: What happened was this particular client was rolling out an even bigger program right after the terrorist attack in Hatshepsut Temple. All the training stopped from one day to the next and basically I had no work. This was in 1996 and the steady flow of income and work just stopped. That was because it was related to the tourist industry. I had a very good relationship with the managing director of that company at the time and he said there were a lot of frustrated staff in his 25 hotels and we had to do something. We couldn't keep them waiting until the tide turned again... I got Lara [Nancy's business partner, name disguised] to join us and the three women—the consultant, Lara and myself—sat together for three days and ironed out a proposal, which Lara said would never happen, and they bought it. We took this project and that launched our company.

Miriam refused to handle referrals for clients that came from her father's firm, passing them to other firms if they came her way. This was not simply for the sake of being financially independent, but to prevent problems for the main family business which might arise if Miriam were to make a mistake. In this respect, Miriam bears a 'professional' role in relation to the 'original' family business, always trying to separate family from business. Again, typical of a 'professional', Miriam said that she believed merit was something universal, valid and clear in all contexts. She acted as an adviser and sounding board to her younger brother—another instance of her professional role—on the basis of her expertise and the business development resources she offered.

Other members of the original family firm might not have shared these perceptions. Miriam maintained something of a professional stance regarding her own firm, and said that she regarded her 'real self' as separate from her business, 'so that if one is going badly, the other one is probably still okay'. She maintained this perspective even more strongly with respect to her father's firm. Yet her father tended to cast her in an invisible role, or at best, as an anchor. While Miriam regularly discussed with her father what direction the original family business should take, and took its fortunes closely to heart, she knew that she would never be asked to join the original family business.

Nancy and Ellen also found that other members of the family firms they were associated with might have regarded them as invisibles. Nancy had left her husband and the firm he started. But before this, she had shared his view that she was there 'just to fill in any gaps'. It took her some time to define herself and her expertise as including similar creative, leadership and entrepreneurial qualities as her husband had. Describing the differences between what she did in her husband's business and the personal qualities she exercised her new role, Nancy stressed a combination of discipline and creativity:

> Nancy: I have a strict process, but I can also work completely off a blank slate when the time requires and when it serves a purpose… I was finding myself being the office manager, the systems designer, the quality… the person that did everything other than be the creative ideas person. That was a shame, because I am very creative.

Nancy's role as 'everything except the creative ideas person' corresponds to Curimbaba's anchor role, where women are highly visible—indeed essential—for the continuity of the family business. Anchors are never completely unnecessary, despite passing through phases that tend to reduce their significance. Nancy's husband would probably concur with this: in his view, Nancy left just when he and his firm most needed her. Nancy's view was that the anchor role she held in her former husband's firm prevented her from developing her latent entrepreneurial capacities. In her own business, started with a female partner, she had the chance to use these skills. She considered her capacity to remain calm and flexible under stress a major strength. The business she and her friend started came to a crossroads, owing to her partner's changing family circumstances; however, Nancy was not perturbed by this, or even thrown into a frenzy of planning:

> Nancy: I believe it's better to work with energy than against it. I could worry about all the things that could potentially go wrong, but I don't particularly do that. I prefer to handle situations as they arise and maybe beforehand have some kind of

contingency plan in place if it happens. If I'm not prepared then I will problem-solve.

Nancy resembles Miriam in having a relaxed attitude to risk and remaining flexible as a way of coping with the unexpected. Miriam contrasted herself to a friend who recently started her own business. While the friend had always wanted to start a firm of her own, she did not have Miriam's family business background, and so was much more disconcerted when she had to deal with the unknown:

Miriam: Her mother is a psychiatrist and works for a hospital and her father is a corporate. I've been encouraging her to do this [start her own firm] because she's always wanted to do it and she's actually taken a leap of faith to go and do it. Whereas I had the attitude when I started my business, everything will be all right and I'll make it work, she rings me every day in panic. There's massive fear and I think, again, that's what I've learned, not to be fearful. It's the whole 'risk-fear' thing.

When Ellen started her clothing manufacturing business, she resembled Miriam's anxious friend. She found it difficult to delegate tasks and not worry about every kind of problem. She stated that she really loved learning the financial side of being in business, but was 'driven by a fear of failure', and needed to have lots of control:

Ellen: Because... I knew I couldn't sew, I felt I had to have control... But once things started going out to contractors, I suppose when orders were to the point where, yes, they were getting larger and I didn't quite... I used to crucify myself with problems that I felt were mine, that I should have known... You realise you have to go off the rein and manage. Yes, I do. In fact, the first girl I brought on in a capacity to take on any of my work was Nicole [name disguised]. And she came and I thought, what would I do with her now? [laughs] That was very awkward. I didn't really know what to do with her. But she knew because she had been in sales and marketing in a company similar that had gone under, actually. And when I think back, she probably thought I was a dill. She just sort of took over because we had so much sales enquiries, not the financial side. So the first thing that I relinquished was sales, because that was not really my forté.

Like the others, Ellen needed to shake off the fear of risk to be able to delegate. Recognising others' merits finally allowed her to delegate part of her work.

CONCLUSIONS

In many ways, this group's journey to leadership was more straightforward than that of the first participant group. Instead of having to learn to lead in the glare of a spotlight they did not fully choose, they built their own stage. This gave them the chance to set the stage the way they wished. For example, they could establish the new business' culture in keeping with values they considered important. They could maintain or extend the skills they gained during their previous life experience and background. They could delegate or share other aspects of their roles as their businesses grew. Ellen delegated the sales side of her business, which was not her strength. Jane appointed someone to take on much of the operations side of her business, and trained him to think entrepreneurially in the way she did.

Even so, once the entrepreneurs have 'built the stage', and got the business going in the way they want, it is not always easy for them to keep the spotlight where they want it. Sometimes they find other people do not perceive them as running a serious business which is capable of continuing into the future. For example, Ellen's husband was seen by some of her staff as the leader of her firm. Miriam and Nancy also wrestled with the disparities between their own view of their roles and how other people perceived them. Ironically, Jane had the least difficulty with being perceived as her firm's leader, despite having shared firm leadership for many years with her partner and mentor, Simon.

Other complications exist for these stage builders. Some arose because the needs of the original family business clashed with those of the business the interviewee started. Miriam's father saw the firm he founded as taking precedence over Miriam's enterprise, and hoped Miriam would have children who would make their careers in his firm. This was likely to be impossible, given Miriam's ambitions for her own firm, both then and for the future.

Despite the problems created by family expectations, Jane, Miriam, Nancy and Ellen learned a lot from their early exposure to a family business or a general business environment. In the long term it helped them see themselves as business leaders, as at home in the spotlight. Their experiences of the spotlight, considered in relation to those of other participants, yield some more general propositions in Chapter 9. The next chapter considers family business women who deliberately 'risk invisibility', directing the spotlight onto someone other than themselves.

NOTE

[1] Sadly, Simon passed away not long after the interview, and Jane then completed an MBO of the business.

6. Directing the Spotlight Elsewhere

In earlier chapters we considered how some women leaders are pushed into leading a family business and deal with finding themselves in the spotlight. Others build their own firm away from the original family business, where they can do things their way. However, another approach exists to women's family business leadership where, instead of seeking to be in the spotlight themselves, leaders direct it elsewhere. Two cases illustrate this approach: Gloria and Cass.

GLORIA

Gloria's journey, like Brenda's, was a rapid introduction to firm leadership, but it was far less difficult. Even having entered, expanded and left the family business to start her own firm—now a listed company in Hong Kong—Gloria was still only in her early thirties. The first few sentences of the interview summarise her progress through life and business:

> Gloria: I was involved with the [original] family business [a large plastic moulding injection company in Hong Kong], for about 15 years, then I was promoted to a senior managing director position. Later on I felt that my personal vision was slightly different, and I would like to pursue something different than spending the rest of my life running a family business. So I started my own business and now I'm the founder of a listed company as well. I still provide some advice for my father's company. I think I've already passed the stage of leaving the business.

The listed company Gloria founded was also family controlled. She hoped to pass it on to her children, if they showed an aptitude for business. But Gloria's story focuses on the business her father founded. Like many interviewees, Gloria spent time in the family business as a child. This meant spending lots of time with her father—true for many women in our study—but her role in the family firm was even more active than usual. Even as a very young child, she demonstrated the innovative qualities of the family business' products to potential customers:

> Gloria: He [her father] was very advanced and did a lot of things that people didn't do at that time. He used new technology. Everybody thought his machine looked

strange. I have a strong memory about this. When I was four years old my father wanted to show people how safe his machine was, so we—the young children— had to go and do the moulding. We were too young to be scared, but apparently he was very confident. I can remember we were moulding a footplate: a clear plastic footplate. So that's how he started his business. He had a tough time in 1973, but we were too young to really know what he went through.

Gloria remembered tough times in general during her childhood, but claimed that she and her siblings (she was one of seven children) 'grew up with the factory', and that her mother and father 'started it together and grew with it together'. So she acquired her early knowledge of the business against a background of family harmony. She studied mechanical engineering which, though not a business discipline, was clearly related to the industry in which her original family business operated.

Like Brenda, Ellen and Miriam, Gloria, as a middle, female child, was never expected to enter the family business, even though this was discussed with her brothers and also her oldest and youngest sisters. Her older sister worked in the business when Gloria was still quite young, and Gloria remembered the distress her sister felt when sometimes she had to lay people off. Instead of being under pressure to join the family business early, Gloria had the freedom to 'go outside' to acquire the skills necessary for business. She went to the United States, where she studied and worked as an engineer. Later she had a serious accident and decided to return to Hong Kong to spend time with her father.

She also felt that she could make a real contribution to the family firm. However, unlike other participants (such as Ingrid, whose story Chapter 7 discusses), Gloria did not have to try to solve a problem in the family part of the system, a frequent reason Curimbaba's 'professionals' enter the family business.

Gloria avoided drawing attention to herself, preferring to direct it to others, especially her father. Shortly after joining the family firm, she mounted a marketing campaign to increase awareness of the firm's product, by 'packaging' her father's adventurous story as a self-made man, a refugee from the Kuomintang. Throughout, she remained in the background, denying any suggestion that there would be an interest in her own story:

Gloria: Then I started packaging my father. I started having interviews for him—he was very shy at that time. He's a very humble good person. I packaged how he started, how he came from the army, how he was very poor. He became a legend in Hong Kong. He received an OBE from the Queen of England; the Hong Kong Government gave him the Grand Bauhinia Medal.

Interviewer: How did you do this packaging?

Gloria: I started telling people the story, probably twenty per cent made up by me, to make it interesting. I started telling newspapers, customers. I was almost like his spokesman. I will never have a fascinating story like his. What can I tell people about me? Nothing. Nobody would be interested in a young girl. If you want the company to have a legend, you need an older person, some history, something people will think about.

The same applied to Gloria's dealings with the banks from which the family firm sought loans. Gloria was a good negotiator, but her skill lay in deflecting people's gaze away from herself and any authority she might have when arranging the deals. She explained it:

Gloria: I'm a good negotiator. I cut the interest rate with the bank to the lowest the company could ever get. I always tell them that they know my father is very harsh and very tough on us, and if they don't cut the interest rate I don't know what I can do—maybe switch banks.

Interviewer: Do you try to make it sound as if your father will decide whether or not you stay in the business? Do you pretend that you are not the decision-maker?

Gloria: Yes, because that's a very good tool. I always say I have to go back and consult my father and the board.

Gloria made herself invisible as a deliberate strategy, and not because she doubted her own abilities, which she had already tested in the marketplace. Gloria first thought of herself as 'too big, too intelligent and too well-educated' for the family business, although she had long before dismissed this idea as childish. She respected her father's entrepreneurial spirit, saying she 'only has the education'—she felt that she could never do as well as her father and her father's most senior staff member in the business, Dr Lu [name disguised], who had long practical experience in the business and who were both mentors for her.

Despite realising that her father and Dr Lu could always have managed without her, Gloria was also aware of her market value elsewhere. Sharma and Irving (2005) would identify Gloria's choice to work in the family firm as based on 'affective commitment'. According to Sharma and Irving, this choice contrasts with three other bases of commitment to the family firm which potentially Gloria could have had: a sense of obligation (normative commitment), an awareness of what she might lose if she did not work in the firm (calculative commitment), or a lack of confidence in herself or the feeling that she could find other suitable job opportunities elsewhere (imperative commitment). Sharma and Irving (2005, p. 28) propose that, although the different bases of commitment result in similar commitment-focal behaviour relations, they produce varying levels of discretionary behaviour. This in turn leads to varying levels of effectiveness and firm performance.

In Gloria's case, joining the family firm with the knowledge she could easily find satisfying work outside it gave her great belief in herself and allowed her to exercise a high level of discretionary effort on its behalf. Gloria believed she was more able and willing to act as an entrepreneur within the firm, compared to if she was always destined for a role in it. In Sharma and Irving's terms, this would be consistent with joining it out of a sense of obligation. Her boundless confidence was rocked only momentarily when she was preparing for major trade exhibitions. Under her influence, these were on a scale greater than the business had ever contemplated before:

> Gloria: I'm a hardworking person. That's my personality. In the company, although I thought it would do nothing for me [a reference to her early view of herself as 'too big for this business'], I was still hardworking. There was an exhibition and that was the time everybody turned around and looked at me and said, 'Wow!' because I wanted to show three newly designed machines. I was leading a team and nobody believed I could do it because there was only four days before the show when my parts started coming in to make a big machine. I worked in the factory for seven days and nights without going home and probably slept for one hour per night. I even cried in the toilet because of the stress and I was scared. Normally the company spent $10,000 per show and I forced my father to spend $80,000 for the show, but we sold a lot of machines. After I joined the company [she was 21 at the time], the first year the turnover was up to $98 million.

Indirectly, Gloria revealed a lot about her father's role in her development as a business leader and, finally, an entrepreneur. Gloria's account painted him as a modest, even silent figure. Gloria described him as always having had a humble attitude. She had even 'written him a new script' by using his personal story and embellishing it for marketing purposes. However, he was clearly a shrewd individual when managing relationships in his firm, as well as managing his daughter's talent for increasing production levels, which had the potential to—and actually did—create conflict. His talent for managing learning in the family firm became clear when Gloria described a time she had a disagreement with a longstanding staff member:

> Gloria: There was a guy who could only deliver 30 machines a month. I said to my father that if he doesn't fire that guy, he will never increase his production capacity. That guy had worked there for 17 years. He wasn't a bad guy, he just thought I was too young to know anything. I knew that he didn't have the drive. I guess that was the first vote of confidence from my father. He saw what I had done.

> Interviewer: Did he fire the guy?

> Gloria: No. He told the guy to be my assistant. Then he promoted me to Deputy Factory Manager. In three months the production increased from 30 machines to 75 per month.

Gloria's father did not fire the employee Gloria thought should be fired, and instead placed the employee in a position where Gloria had to form a close working relationship with him. Gloria had absorbed her father's tacit lesson about loyalty to longstanding staff. Despite her achievements, Gloria resisted any suggestion that she was more of a driving force in the company, more of an achiever, or more important, than her father or other people in the company:

Interviewer: You were really building the company, much more than your father ever could have. Your father didn't have this way of looking at the company.

Gloria: No, I wouldn't say that. Even if I wasn't with the company, he'd still be okay. It was luck when China opened up.

While she absorbed the family firm's values, Gloria also knew she brought an important maverick influence to the firm. However, mavericks are most useful when the firm already has a firm financial base:

Gloria: I'm different to my family. I've been to Antarctica with the scientific team. I went through the physical training. I think the wild part of me helped the company to 'push out'. I think because of the way they built such a strong foundation for the company, if we made a mistake, it was affordable. If the company had not been very strongly built, any mistake would have caused the company to collapse. No one is too big to fall.

This difference in approach was noticeable in how Gloria and her father approached debt. Gloria described her father as:

Gloria: …very sceptical about asking for a bank loan. He's very cash rich. He's very tight on accounts receivable and he doesn't have bad debts.

Gloria did not try to change him by suggesting that he use more debt. She recognised her lack of knowledge of the company's financial affairs:

Gloria: I'm an engineer. I don't understand finance. As long as I have money to spend and do what I want, I don't really care. That's why we can afford for me to spend $80,000 on an exhibition. I wasn't looking into company accounts.

Gloria knew that the business was bigger than she was, despite her personal ambitions and her ambitions for the firm. So when she decided to leave the family business it was for her own reasons: to allow her younger siblings a chance to work in the business, as well as to start a firm of her own.

Our next interviewee, Cass, also started her own firm. Like Gloria, she entered the family business in a considered way, and with a full set of work options elsewhere.

CASS

The family business, of which Cass was a part, was a large wholesale and retail fruit and vegetable business. Cass and her husband were both from family business backgrounds and studied business together at university. Cass, like Gloria, was an expert in directing the spotlight away from herself. She saw her role as a mentor to the business and to her husband, its CEO. She saw her main job as staying invisible, while professionalising the business and working on its strategic direction through her husband.

Cass and her husband started the business together, but for 27 years or so Cass had very little direct role in it. Her contribution to the family firm's knowledge base was to gain corporate skills in a retailing environment while her husband learned the practical side of fruit and vegetable wholesaling and distribution in another firm, before starting his own.

> Cass: David [Cass' husband, name disguised] was off learning the business so I had to go and work. What we decided was I'd go to [an established retail business] and learn the corporate side. What ended up happening was I never got out of that. David's business went like this [gesture indicating rapid growth] on the entrepreneurial side and I stayed at [Cass' employer], and then had babies. In those days, the minute you had babies you were out of the workforce. As soon as [Cass' employer] found out I was pregnant there was a huge celebration, but the clear assumption was that I would be leaving. So I left. I then had five children very rapidly, but worked the whole time doing various things. I worked in Mum's business.

Cass accumulated considerable business experience in various arenas. As well as working in her mother's business, she started one of her own, in communications and public relations. Both David's and Cass' firms went very well for a while, but then both hit problems around the same time. Cass' husband's business faltered in the currency collapse of the late 1980s, and a major client of Cass' firm went bankrupt. Cass recalled it as a very stressful time, and decided to position herself as the family breadwinner:

> Cass: I realised that I might be the income earner. My business was terrific and very glamorous, but [her main client] was going down, and I suddenly thought that it might be me in charge of the five children and the husband, so I'd better get a real job. I applied for a job at [an Australian university] as head of their alumni section and I was offered that job. So I then had a real job with real money and I felt secure. At least I knew we had enough to feed the kids.

While her husband's business struggles continued, Cass was headhunted for a high-profile government job. Her expertise in managing large corporate organisations, especially guiding them through large-scale change, was becoming increasingly recognised beyond her own organisation. As she said about her increasing public profile: 'I became a bit of a change management guru person'.

Cass finally entered the family business at her husband's invitation to solve a specific business problem in the firm—not because she had no other options. On the contrary, she was aware of her value in the marketplace. When the Australian tax system was overhauled in 2000, the informal, cash basis for running her husband's business was no longer viable. Accordingly, Cass' brief was to introduce formal, transparent transaction systems to the firm.

> Cass: After five years [with the government agency] I had a five-year contract. I was so overworked and I had the situation where the government had offered me a fairly big job in government. Morgan & Banks were talking to me about taking over one of the headhunting things, and David had said to me that he didn't want to make the mistakes he made last time and he needed me in to corporatise [the family firm].

Cass' role as joint CEO with her husband differed from that of Jane with her business partner Simon: Cass, rather than her husband, had the detailed knowledge of how to add the architecture of structure and formal systems to a family firm. However, she did not feel instantly at ease with the task in front of her. On the contrary, because David's firm was very large and she was unfamiliar with the fruit and vegetable industry, she found the task unnerving at first. Cass felt that she could not have moved into the family business and taken on such a large task without a formal invitation. She also needed first to prove her abilities to herself:

> Cass: I also didn't have the confidence. It wasn't until I went out and did my own thing that I had the confidence. I knew how to run my own little business but David's business was so much bigger.

Cass described the family firm as 'a closed book', which nevertheless intrigued her. She was amazed that the business could have worked for as long as it did with so few formal systems. She had a lot to learn about the operations of the fruit and vegetable industry before she could change how it worked in the context of their firm. One problem was the potential for various abuses that arose from the traditional cash basis of the industry:

> Cass: We had accounting systems, but it wasn't just a case of adding your GST [goods and services tax] on. I think that was part of the reason why there was so much secrecy, because everybody dealt in cash. One of the things that we have spent the last five years doing is getting rid of every bit of cash in the business, and it's quite interesting, because in a way it makes us non-competitive, because every other fruit market out there pays everybody $250 a week on the books and $500 in their hand. That is absolutely standard. It's the black economy. That would have been part of the reason, I think. It wasn't about taking home bucket loads of money

to spend yourself. It was just how you got staff. You didn't get staff by employing people on the books. They were all migrants and nobody trusted the government.

Cass' solution was to implement a computerised accounting system. However, to do this, she had to deal with a deeply rooted values system in the family business which opposed the changes she wanted. The informality of the existing cash system was linked to the sense of trust that managers and employees associated with the firm and its industry in general, and her husband's management style in particular:

> Cass: He [her husband] has a real caring for the people who work for [the family firm]. It's not even really paternalistic. He genuinely sees them as his colleagues and workers, and there is a tremendous lack of hierarchy. My husband is not a very outgoing person. He's the strong silent type, and he loves the way his staff come and speak to him and share with him. He's a confidante. That's probably why it worked, having 500 employees and no systems—they felt part of the family. And in this business, of course, you really do rely on trust, because people still pay cash for their fruit and vegetables and it's a huge cash business. We don't touch it [cash] at all now because it just goes into the till and we have people to come and collect it and take it away. But in the [retail] shops it's there every day.

The 'familiness' aspect of the family firm extended to everyone who worked in it. But familiness can have a downside, as Miller and Le Breton-Miller show in their discussion of the 'four Cs' of family business (see Chapter 1). In a similar way, Habbershon et al. (2003) refer to the 'distinctive' (positive) and 'constrictive' (negative) aspects of familiness. Through the informal, even secretive familiness that was part of this family firm's traditions, staff resented Cass' efforts to put in systems which accounted for transactions in a transparent way. They particularly disliked the fact that she had the formal title of executive director when she did this.

> Cass: People absolutely hated it [the title]. In fact, people even said that it used to be a family company before I came in, because I was getting rid of all the cash and making people do things, and sign dockets and so on.

Cass made the most of the family firm's culture. One of her tactics was to work through her husband, the firm's respected 'front person', its operational face, to persuade others to make changes. But this meant changing her husband's way of doing things as much as the way the firm did things, a difficult task.

> Cass: He [her husband] felt threatened. He didn't personally feel threatened, he just felt that it would all fall apart, that it wouldn't work. He was terrified that things would fall apart again. I started getting David to have managers' meetings and at the meetings I'd bring up occupational health and safety and everybody would roll their eyes. It wasn't until David really started hammering people that it changed. I didn't have an influence on changing the firm—I just changed the CEO... I don't

think anybody else could have done what I did, not because I have the skills, but because I have David's trust.

David's management style was also a target for change. According to Cass, her husband was 'a definite person, and a bit of a dictator, and he doesn't like change'. This manifested in his reluctance to consult staff before making changes in the business. David, unlike Cass, had not worked in a range of other organisations before starting his own firm. So he lacked some of the conventional corporate disciplines:

> Cass: Men like David, and other men who haven't been through that external experience, have missed out on consultation... I keep my ties strongly with the university, and there you wouldn't do anything without consultation. Also, in big business you consult on everything, even more so than universities. It's the same in the public sector... So you learn this word 'consultation'. These chaps that have gone out and started their own business, that word 'consultation' never enters their heads.

Cass, like Brenda and Nancy, brought skills from the domestic sphere into the business arena. She regarded her capacity to get things done in an indirect way as a 'female' skill:

> Cass: I'm sure wives bring that to family companies. Because as a mother, you don't get anything with power, you only get the kids to do things by cajoling—that's how you operate. Whereas David just says something and he expects it to be done. I think that somehow women bring that into the workforce so I sort of hold David's hand through these things and at least he appears to be consulting.

Jane and Cass present two contrasting models of leading with a partner. Jane learned to lead the business as a whole through a process of mentorship. She started from an operational perspective, working primarily in the business and gradually expanding her capacity to work on the business. Her leadership role gradually became more prominent as her skills merged with those of her mentor and partner, and the need to rely on him decreased. In contrast, Cass always worked on the business, and did so as invisibly as possible, given the demands created by the scale of change she implemented. She never sought operational roles and insisted that firm strategy was her husband's territory:

> Cass: He's the main strategist. Without him, there wouldn't be a business.

Nevertheless, without Cass, there would not be a business run on professional lines. Cass' influence manifested itself in the 'front stage' and 'back stage' division of labour between her and her husband, which made both effective.

LEARNING WHILE DIRECTING

Gloria and Cass have mastered the first three of our family business learning stages (Moores and Barrett, 2002), though they bring a new flavour to them.

Learning Business (L1)

Gloria undertook the business learning stages in the conventional sequence, though at a very rapid pace. She learned the personal disciplines needed for business, an important part of 'learning business' (L1) outside the firm. This was also true for Cass, who learned corporate disciplines through her exposure to large public and private sector entities. She saw the damaging effect on the firm that resulted from her husband not having learned such skills. Cass was an expert in both the functional and so-called 'soft' skills of business. This meant she knew how the family business' operations need to change to accommodate reforms in the national taxation system, but also appreciated how important it was to consult people when making such major adjustments. In contrast, Gloria described herself as an engineer who stayed away from the background detail of her family business' functions. When she entered the firm she 'didn't understand finance'. Like Brenda, she learned the functional skills of business, especially finance, later and more gradually on the job. However, she understood marketing and customer service, which leaders must acquire in the 'learning business' phase.

Learning our Business (L2)

As both Gloria and Cass discovered, just knowing what the business needed—whether increased production or better compliance with government regulations—did not mean it was easy to bring change. To achieve these things, both needed to 'learn our business (L2). Cass did this almost by stealth. She knew that the real family in the business was the family created through the relationships of her husband and his staff. She had to work through those relationships, rather than through her title of executive director, which, if anything, alienated people from the changes she wanted to make. In her terms, her husband was the leader, even though she directed strategy from behind the scenes. The business' operational staff were as much its family as the CEO's wife.

Gloria had similarly absorbed the values of her father's family business, especially hard work and innovation. She had done this so completely, she could use these values to 'write the script' of her family firm for marketing purposes. In Dumas' terms, this makes Gloria a 'keeper of the king's gold', one of the positive ways fathers and daughters can work together for the good of the firm (Dumas, 1989). Gloria had clearly 'learned our business' (L2), the values of the family firm, as well as the market value of family firm values. She showed this by 'packaging' her father and his achievements as head of the family firm. Just as Cass rejected any suggestion that she had a strategic role to play in changing her husband's firm, Gloria directs the spotlight away from herself. She avoided representing herself as part of a father–daughter team and insisted that anyone in the firm could occupy the place she did:

> Interviewer: Did you stress that it was a family company, that this was a father–daughter relationship?

> Gloria: I just made him a self-made man. I portray the image that it is a professional company. Anyone who is in this company is a family member. You have the same opportunity—no need to carry the same last name.

Learning to Lead Our Business (L3)

The deliberately indirect style of leadership Gloria and Cass adopted created a new approach to 'leading our business' (L3), which contrasts with the leadership approaches adopted by the predominantly male sample in our earlier book (Moores and Barrett, 2002). Neither Gloria nor Cass would describe themselves to us as leaders, in the sense of being more prominent or important than others in the firm. Nevertheless, they functioned as leaders by perceiving the need to introduce new strategies, structures and systems, and took steps to do this.

Learning to Let Go Our Business (L4)

At the time of interviews, neither Gloria nor Cass had retired from a CEO role, while Brenda and Deborah had. However, Gloria's decision to start her own firm, partly in order to allow other members of her generation to gain experience in the family firm, suggests that she had gained some practice at 'letting go' (L4). Like Brenda, Gloria had took advisory role in the original family firm.

DIRECTING THE SPOTLIGHT ELSEWHERE

Cass and Gloria both started their own businesses. However, unlike the participants whose stories Chapter 4 examines, their real drama lay not with that business, but with their relationship with the original family firm— started by Cass' husband and Gloria's father respectively. The most striking aspect of Cass' and Gloria's activities—and the origin of their success—was their ability to direct the spotlight away from themselves and on to someone else. Oddly enough, being deliberately invisible formed part of two belongingness strategies they use: engagement and imagination. Finally,

Gloria and Cass both needed to manage the boundaries of the 'original' family firm.

Engagement

In terms of Wenger's model of a community of practice, Cass and Gloria both had plenty of opportunities for engagement—to negotiate a joint inquiry, ask important questions, identify gaps in their knowledge and work together with others in the community of practice to address them (Wenger, 1999, 2000). Gloria learned the inner workings of the family business from two mentors, her father and Dr Lu, and eventually left to start her own firm. Cass was unfamiliar with the fruit and vegetable industry when she entered the family firm, but she was intrigued by it and her firm's place in it. She disapproved of the 'duct tape' approach to management in the firm, its lack of formal systems, the absence of anything in writing, the absence of any formal governance practices. But she was nonetheless amazed by the way 'familiness' held such a big firm together. Her prime qualification for the task ahead was just as intangible: the trust her husband placed in her.

Imagination

Gloria was embroiled in the firm's most central activities from the time she entered it. Unlike Cass, who came with a firm sense of the mission, Gloria arrived after many years away from the firm studying and working in the United States. She also imagined the firm differently from the way it was when she entered it, but she had a less defined view of its potential than Cass had for her husband's firm. At first, Gloria considered the firm to be beneath her capabilities, but quickly recognised that she had been too cocky, and had acted like an upstart. Gloria's father knew better than Gloria how to direct her considerable energy and knowledge. As with the incident of the employee she considered underproductive, Gloria was at first unwilling to learn from other members of the community of practice, or to respect their competence if their performance was less spectacular than her own. But she changed, and rapidly gained her father's trust by achieving remarkable sales results.

Cass' task—to change the firm so that it would run on professional lines— was also the main obstacle to others developing the trust in her that members of a learning community normally seek from other members. This was because her goal of achieving transparent business practices contravened the established norms of the community. Cass brought a contrasting—even alien—experience, language, artefacts, histories and method to running the family firm. In short, she imagined it differently from the rest of the community. Cass' strategy for dealing with the gap was to direct the spotlight towards her husband, the CEO. Thus, when he began to support her proposed changes, they had some hope of taking hold.

Boundaries

Wenger (1999, 2000) points out that bridging boundaries between communities of practice creates the potential for members who have spent time in another community to enrich their original community with their new learning. However, considerable imagination is required for learning to occur through boundary-spanning experiences. That is, people need enough understanding of their own perspectives to present issues effectively and anticipate misunderstandings on the part of others. They also need the ability to build a picture of another practice, and both sides need to see themselves as members of an overarching community in which they have common interests and needs.

In both cases, but especially for Cass, it was more necessary for the newcomers than the wider community to build this understanding, but for both the newcomers and their communities, building such understanding was not easy. Our interviewees, different from the other members of their communities, stood to lose if they did not gain other members' understanding, trust and perception of common interests. Cass had previously built up a repertoire of corporate skills that the family firm needed, and she had no difficulty understanding which of these skills and practices the family firm needed. Gloria also knew what the family firm had to do to 'think big' and transcend its small-time level of operations. For both, the boundaries between the two communities were permeable, but for their family firm communities, they were not. Neither could bridge the boundaries between the family firm community and the world of larger corporate enterprise if it brought attention to them as individuals. So both adopted the practice of shining the spotlight elsewhere.

In both cases, this meant shining the spotlight in places where it created discomfort—in Cass' case, onto the financial abuses in the firm, and in Gloria's, onto areas of underperformance. However, they made more progress when they directed the spotlight not into these dark corners, but onto another person—the visible firm leader. Gloria's and Cass' leadership was based on leading without appearing to lead. While conventional family business leaders need to learn 'formal informality' to be leaders, leading without appearing to lead requires even more skill. Both Cass and Gloria actually wrote the script for the CEO. When Cass talked about occupational health and safety in meetings, people rolled their eyes—she needed to get her husband to take this role. Gloria did not even get her father to play the part of the hero—she both developed the script of his leadership and read it for him at the training presentations which were her stage.

INVISIBLE STAGE MANAGEMENT ROLES

Gloria and Cass are clearly professionals in Curimbaba's terms, because they maintained a clear view of their market value when they entered the firm and afterwards. Both entered the firm because they believed they had something to bring to it, and both entered to solve a business problem or improve business performance, rather than solve a family problem. According to Curimbaba (2002), fixing problems in the family system is a frequent feature of professionals' entry to the firm. However, it tends to create constraints for the professional, since the family problem may be out of line with their professional expertise, or might simply take up a great deal of the professional's time and energy, diverting her from other tasks. When we consider Ingrid's experience in a later chapter, we see more of the difficulties professionals face when they enter the firm primarily to manage family issues.

Gloria's position as a middle child, with brothers who could take senior roles in the firm, could make her an 'invisible' in Curimbaba's sense of the term. At the outset, this seemed likely, because she was not considered part of the firm's succession arrangements. Later, Gloria's father appreciated the way she had developed the firm and saw her, even more than her brothers, as a potential leader after his retirement. So Gloria was never an 'invisible' in Curimbaba's sense of having no effect on the firm's strategies or performance: she chose to be invisible to produce her best results. Cass also used her husband's role as CEO to legitimate large changes to the firm's information systems and decision-making processes. Like Gloria, she did not resent this—during the interview, we could not persuade her even to acknowledge, let alone describe, any of her activities as falling into the realm of firm leadership.

CONCLUSIONS

Gloria and Cass devised an unusual approach to firm leadership. Their strategic use of invisibility—turning the spotlight in the direction of others—allowed them to learn business (L1), learn our business (L2) and learn family firm leadership (L3) in unobtrusive, yet highly strategic ways. They dealt creatively with the belongingness modes of their respective learning communities using engagement and imagination strategies, and managed their communities' boundaries to enhance learning. They transformed Curimbaba's invisible role into a tool for strategic action as professionals. Both shared the rewards of professionals because they were prepared to assert their market value in the business, and both spent many years in other activities before joining the firm. Gloria did leave the firm, on her own terms and without resentment. Their special approach to invisibility and its advantages becomes clearer in Chapter 9, which compares their approach to that of other participants.

The next chapter, Coping with Shadows, considers the experiences of two participants who are just moving from the wings towards centre stage.

7. Coping with Shadows

The leadership journeys considered so far show how women in family business learn to manage the spotlight of leadership. Some interviewees were thrust into the leadership spotlight and learned to deal with its glare. Others, blocked from entering an original family business, established their own firm with its own spotlight. Still other participants took a more subtle approach to leadership, deliberately pointing the leadership spotlight away from themselves onto someone else. This chapter considers Ingrid and Robyn, whose journeys towards leadership we are less complete than those of our other interviewees. In Ingrid's case in particular, shadows cast by others, especially her father, still hampered her capacity to move to centre stage. We met Robyn before, as the daughter of Deborah, whose story we encounter in Chapter 5.

INGRID

Ingrid is the second-generation CEO of a large agricultural machinery and real estate business in the United States. Despite her title, when we interviewed her we detected a certain fragility about her role, which led us to wonder if she was still on trial as leader. Her journey to her current position took many years, with frequent exits and re-entries to the family business. There was a period of over seven years between her final re-entry to the family firm for good, and her move to the top job. Like many family business leaders, Ingrid recalled spending time on the business premises as a child. Like so many interviewees who became interested in some aspect of the family firm as children, Ingrid was entranced by the farm machinery the firm dealt in. But she also associated this time with seeing little of her father:

> Ingrid: In 1956 I was born, the first of five children. Five children in five years and my mother basically stayed at home raising the children. My father went to work. In the mornings he was still sleeping when we went to school and in the evenings he wouldn't come home until after we were in bed. Sometimes we saw him on the weekends. If we did he often brought us down to the family business and we would go through the parts department, try the typewriters, telephones, whatever, and he was back in his office working. Sometimes he'd drop us off at a rock pit and let us play for a while. We didn't have much interaction... I loved the equipment and I

wanted to ride on the tractors when I was a little girl. I wanted to operate it and drive it, but my dad wouldn't let me. All that pretty well continued until 1967 when I was about 11 or 12 years old.

Ingrid's family experienced a great deal of conflict. Her parents divorced when she was about eleven (she was in her late forties at the time of interview). Both her parents found new partners. Until very recently, and for close to 40 years, there was major conflict between Ingrid's father, the founder of the family firm, and each of his children, as well as between the siblings themselves, between them and their step-siblings, and between them and their step-parents. The family history was also scarred by alcohol and drug abuse as well as serious illness. Ingrid's path to leadership of the family firm was marked by her efforts to cope with and try to resolve this conflict—often through the courts. She blamed her father's way of dealing with people for much of the difficulty in the family and in the management of the business:

Ingrid: He [her father] was brilliant in the business sense, but when it came to people and family relationships, very bad, very destructive, very hurtful. But his visions of what he wanted to create business-wise were brilliant.

At first this family conflict and Ingrid's perception that her father would frustrate her ambitions meant Ingrid was determined not to enter the family business, despite the attraction the machines always held for her:

Ingrid: My mother said that I needed to find a job because when I was at the company I would say to her that there's got to be a better career than this. I did not want to be in the family company... It was, in my opinion, a very conservative, staid company.

Although Ingrid found formal learning easy, she argued with her father over whether she should focus on studying business as he wished her to, or even continue with formal study at all. She finally enrolled in a computer systems degree, but soon dropped out. Her way of explaining what happened next indicated she wanted to find her own direction, rather than follow a conventional course of study:

Ingrid: When I was 18 I went to university. Learning was easy for me at school and I made straight As. I went to the University of Kansas and I kind of felt a little footloose and fancy free. By the end of three years I had a very low GPA and I went to my parents and told them I needed to stop going to school, that it wasn't working for me. I needed to go and work.

Ingrid eventually completed a business degree, but only much later, following one of her several exits from the family business in the early years of her working life. She found a job in the hotel industry, which was relatively easy for women to enter, and a good source of experience for running an enterprise. Ingrid found the hotel business exciting and a quick way forward:

> Ingrid: I worked my way up in the hotel business. I was having fun and loving it. I went from a front desk clerk to a front desk assistant manager and was responsible for training the front desk cashiers and clerks. I then became a night auditor, then I was in charge of payroll. Then I was promoted to personnel payroll the first time the two positions had been combined, so I wrote my own job description. We had about 700 employees.

Later, Ingrid was not sure that staying in the hotel business was better than entering the family firm. She was alienated and worn down by the constant family quarrels. Her father, who was fast running out of options for possible successors because he fought with so many people, had to offer her large financial incentives before she would even consider joining the firm. This suggests that for Ingrid, the decision to enter the family firm entailed a measure of calculative commitment: paying financial incentives to family members to get them to work for the family business is consistent with recognising that there would be losses if one did not join the firm (Sharma and Irving, 2005, p. 19). Whatever the basis of her commitment, Ingrid knew choosing to enter the family firm would not mean a settled career path because of how her father dealt with people:

> Ingrid: It's his [her father's] dynamic: I'm going to lure you in and as soon as you get too close I'm going to push you away. Then I'm going to lure you back in again. That's his dynamic.

Ingrid's move—or series of moves—into the family business caused—rather than solved—conflict with both her brothers and father, as well as between the brothers themselves, between them and their father, and virtually every possible combination of the other family members. Ingrid's entry into the family business was also difficult because she carried the family name. She commented on the time she first entered the firm:

> Ingrid: It was hard for me when I was there for the first time because I got treated differently. My last name was [family name]. So I would walk into rooms and conversations would stop. I couldn't really form friendships with anybody because they were all afraid that I was going to run and tell Dad things.

It also meant Ingrid had few opportunities just to listen to the staff and other family members, talk with them, and find out about how the firm worked. Once she was inside the business, her father made life in the firm 'impossible' by setting her and one or more of her brothers in competition with each other for rewards such as a better-paid role. This further discouraged Ingrid from wanting to learn more about the firm. Ironically, the network distributor organisation, of which Ingrid's family business was a part, had always tried to have its individual businesses family run, precisely because it believed family-run businesses have higher market value. As Ingrid explained the network dealer's perspective:

> Ingrid: Statistically, the average length of relationship between [C, the network dealer] and its dealers is three-and-a-half generations, meaning C is very unusual in its business model. It wants those businesses to stay within the family. Its belief is that the business and the family build the business within the community. It has its established name and they don't want to disrupt that. Their distribution model is through their dealer network. That means the only way you can buy a piece of C equipment is through the dealer network, which is worldwide. So C does not want to see those businesses go out of the family. It's very rare when they do. They will work and go to extraordinary lengths to help those businesses.

Because of the constant family conflict and Ingrid's attempts to manage it, it was very costly for her to try to keep the family-based 'community continuity' the network dealer valued so highly. Consequently, Ingrid always maintained the possibility of working elsewhere. At one point, she returned to the hotel business, even though her father offered her a much better paid job in the family business:

> Ingrid: He kept asking me if I was sure I wanted to leave and literally started trying to lure me back in again. None of my brothers and sisters were around yet. My dad and I left it with what he called the swinging door. He wanted to know what I was going to do and I said I would go back into the hotel business.

Even when she or others in the family responded to the incentives and entered the business, Ingrid's father was ambivalent about their presence:

> Ingrid: My father's dynamic was such that he always had to have a scapegoat around, somebody to blame for everything. It was always one person he focused on; we called it 'being in the slot'. You could tell who was in the slot because that person couldn't breathe right. If my dad said he wanted XYZ and you showed up with XYZ, he was mad because you didn't bring ABC, and why didn't you know to bring ABC?

When it finally became clear that Ingrid might have the support of the dealer network to lead the firm's machinery division, she adopted a 'stewardship' mindset more typical of leaders of much longer established family firms. In so doing Ingrid allowed a long-term perspective to dictate how she approached her leadership of the firm:

> Ingrid: I was going to have big battles. Could I heal the past? My father had pushed away everybody: my brothers and sisters and me. Would I ever get to a point that something could be more harmonious within the businesses? How would I get the support I needed to go forward? I was not married. I had my own home. I loved my house and my life, but how was I going to get my batteries recharged? I had good friends and my life and I thought it would okay because for me recharging my

batteries was kind of being alone anyway, so I decided that I would do it, but I was really going to be more of a steward to the next generation.

Ingrid had a mentor at one point, but he was a consultant to the business, rather than a family member or a permanent member of staff. Regardless, he was only employed for a short time. At the time of interview, he was no longer associated with the business. Ingrid saw the mentor's main value as insulating her from the unpleasant aspects of the business, rather than helping her learn how it worked, but this in turn limited how much she could learn it. As well as protecting her, the mentor made sure she was properly paid.

> Ingrid: The consultant actually helped me a lot. He made sure that I had market rate compensation, that I was not underpaid. They [her father and his advisers] baulked at the rate that he [the consultant] wanted to put forward, that he suggested I be paid. He told them he couldn't find anybody who could do what I could do for any less than that. So he made sure from day one I was on a market rate salary.

While Ingrid always dreamt of running the machinery side of the family firm, the unhealthy ways family members and the business were entwined sapped her energy and made it difficult for her to figure out how best to structure it. Unlike Deborah in Chapter 4, who encouraged both family involvement and a family atmosphere in her firm—to the extent of 'mollycoddling' the staff—Ingrid aimed to reduce what she saw as excess familiness in the firm.

> Ingrid: From an ongoing perspective [the main issue is] how am I going to set up the structure that is linking the family in a healthier way so that the businesses can continue? We have all these unhealthy family dynamics playing out within the business and we have too much of a mingling between family and business, so the first thing I am working on is separating the family from the business and putting a structure in place that allows the family to do its job, which is a very different job than what the business has to do.

However, the strain of this reduced her belief in herself as a leader. This in turn delayed the task of thinking through the long-term direction of the business, one of the classic tasks of leadership:

> Interviewer: What would you say it's taught you about leading? Is it all 'how not to'?

> Ingrid: That's what it started out as, very much so. Part of it was also where I was emotionally in terms of my self-confidence level. As long as my confidence level was lower then it was more what not to do. The more my confidence level builds, then the more I become proactive in setting systems in business and I can set the future course because I now have the belief in myself that I can do this and I'm actually good at it. But I didn't know that for a long time.

In contrast, and as we glimpsed when considering Deborah's story, Robyn developed new strategic directions for her mother's firm for years before she formally led the firm, as well as dealing with the operational side, gradually taking more of this from her mother's shoulders.

Ingrid developed a genuine vision for the family firm she grew up with. She wanted to expand it and divide its various sub-businesses between herself and the one brother who remained in the business, according to their interests and skills. However, her ideas for the future of the firm were not yet piloted, let alone implemented thoroughly, so it was impossible to be sure they would work. The changes she planned were enough to win the approval of the network dealer, but they were only just beginning to take shape at the time of interview. The process took a long time:

> Ingrid: I was running things more and more on the business end and I was seeing big changes that needed to occur, so I started literally thinking about what I was going to do for those changes and what was going to be right for the business. I met with C in 2002. They were beginning to see that maybe I wasn't so bad after all. In 2003 I started making the changes. It took me a good year and half to two years to figure out what I wanted to do and once I got all the side stuff settled and was able to focus more on the machinery side, I then realised what I needed to do to make the changes. So I started making the changes in 2003. I'm making the last change as we speak. It will be announced on January 1. It's the final change. I've put a whole new leadership team in place, a new vision statement, and a new mission statement, and we've started the changes. [The network dealer] are liking what they see and I now have completed their approval process and I am approved. So... it has been a seven-and-a-half-year struggle to finally have the approval.

ROBYN

Robyn's apprenticeship for leadership was the longest of all. Deborah described Robyn's learning for the CEO role as slow—it took 17 years. However, it was steady and comprehensive, encompassing the learning stages (Moores and Barrett, 2002) in a logical way:

> Deborah: She [Robyn] learned about business and management outside, then she came in and she started to understand more about the family business. Then she worked alongside me for 17 years and learned to lead the business in the direction she wanted to go.

Robyn worked in the firm directly delivering the firm's service, and enjoyed this. Ingrid, in contrast, never got to operate and drive the machines which fascinated her as a child. Despite Robyn's long apprenticeship and her mother's earlier reluctance to hand over the leadership, when we talked to Robyn she appeared more confident than Ingrid that members of he firm acknowledged her as being in charge. As with Deborah's story, this was because the founder was confident in Robyn's leadership, and because Robyn exercised patience by waiting for her mother to hand over leadership of the firm.

Robyn learned the family business in an orderly way, even though she had not seen herself as destined to run it. Like Ingrid, early in life, Robyn did not want to enter the family business, a nationwide house-cleaning and general help service her mother had established. This was not for negative reasons, but simply because she had already spent so many afternoons and school vacations there, absorbing what went on. As Deborah relates it:

> Deborah: She [Robyn] said, 'I am going to be the only one of your daughters that is not involved in the business.' So I said, 'Great, who cares?' I mean, I didn't care. I wasn't building an empire. I was doing what I had to do. I was not building an… an empire to hand on to my children. It was my own thing. I was doing it on my own. If my kids were interested, that was fine. If they weren't interested, that was fine too.

So Robyn's journey was straightforward, if slow, because there was no pressure to enter the family business and no pressure to solve problems in the family part of the system. This contrasts with Ingrid—for her, entering the family firm was never a restful prospect, but a question of how much conflict she could cope with.

Robyn did not have Gloria's high levels of self-confidence. Robyn's mother said that she had to encourage her daughter's belief in herself. However, Robyn had more self-knowledge and quiet confidence in her abilities as a manager than her mother gave her credit for. Like Ingrid, formal education was less useful to her than her talent for sport. She had a realistic view of where her skills lay:

> Robyn: I did very averagely at school, very average. But I… was very sporty, so I focused very much on my sport and… I always thought I was very average.

> Deborah: She thought she was dumb.

> Robyn: No, I thought I'd scrape through. I just got through and I didn't really want to go on to university. I wasn't that keen a student and I thought, I'm not going to push myself that way if I'm not that way inclined. I don't want to fail. No, I've got through and I'll just see where I am heading. I knew I was good with people and I knew I could manage things.

Like Ingrid, she began working in the hotel business and found it developed her capacity for solving management problems. Both she and Ingrid used their hotel experience to prove to themselves and others their capacity for hard work, discipline and initiative. Robyn always knew that she was organised and a good listener:

Robyn: I would think about problems and get feedback from people about whatever didn't work as well as it should. I was then able to pass that up to the managers in the hotel industry and they were like, 'Wow, that's a great idea'. Cos what I did, I listened, I took a problem but I also took a solution to them. I didn't just bring problems all the time to people. I would think it through.

It also prompted her to think about starting a business of her own:

Robyn: It was a big responsibility for an 18-year-old to be running a hotel of that size. But... they pushed me. They said, 'You can do it', and I was working in the bar, behind the bar, I was doing waitressing in the restaurant, I was in the kitchen, I was in housekeeping, I was in maintenance, I did every section of the hotel. And I enjoyed the various aspects of the hotel, but I also realised that I could see holes in the staffing issues and things like that, and thought I should run my own hotel. You know, maybe get a little B&B and do it myself the way I think it should be done.

Later, during what she thought would be a temporary stint in her mother's firm while she figured out what to do with her life, Robyn took the time to listen to the staff, develop rapport with them and think about and develop solutions to their problems:

Robyn: As I said, I'm a good listener and I listened to what the coordinators were saying. [I thought] 'Gee that doesn't sound quite right.' And I would go and sit with them and I would talk to them about their procedures, and they're trying to streamline... There was a lot of paperwork and I mean, we were used to a manual system then anyway. It was a card system and there were things that they were doing that were going round in circles. And I thought, if they could cut out a few procedures, yet get the information that they needed...

Consistent with being a good listener who works problems by developing rapport with people, Robyn's journey was a slow, patient emergence into visibility, rather than a rush to the top like Gloria. While she worked in her mother's shadow for 17 years, she did not have to struggle with the shadow of the founder in the way Ingrid had. Robyn started at the bottom and worked for a while in the operations side of the business. As well as learning the business product from the inside, she enjoyed the freedom that earning an income from the business gave her, and this was another quiet lesson in the benefits of business leadership. Deborah made it clear that Robyn's job was never going to be a sinecure:

Deborah: She [Robyn] needed money too. She knew I wouldn't give it to her; I'm not the sort of parent that gives money to my children because they look pretty. [But] if they're prepared to roll their sleeves up and show me that they're serious, they can ask me for anything.

While Robyn's job meant she worked hard, unlike Ingrid, she did not have to work through an intermediary to be sure she would be paid a fair salary.

In contrast to the fraught communication patterns in Ingrid's situation, Deborah and Robyn shared a closeness, which they said 'borders on the eerie'. They each often knew what the other was thinking, and finished each other's sentences. In this, and in the way they appreciated the 'familiness' qualities of the firm, they contrasted themselves with another of Deborah's daughters. This daughter 'had wanted to be the boss very quickly', and had a superior—even tough—attitude in her dealings with the staff. Deborah soon felt this daughter would not be suited to running the business long term.

While Robyn spent many years in the shadows, she finally enjoyed a smooth entrance onto centre stage. Deborah, as we already saw, planned for the event carefully, and this accorded with her general propensity for long-term planning. One of the mainstays of her firm's philosophy was the acceptance that no one, even the founder, was there forever. Deborah's high level of planning might have been at the heart of why Robyn's journey to leadership resembled the grooming process we found in our earlier study, which was more typical for family business men. In addition, the female image of the business could have contributed to Deborah's 'macho' son not being interested in it. Deborah announced the handover in a ceremony with all the most long-serving staff present. Robyn spoke to us later in private, and mentioned that by the time of the handover, she had been managing the operations side of the business for ten years, knowing her mother would eventually recognise she was frustrated by needing to deal with all the fine detail that came with managing the operations side of the firm. However, Robyn left it to her mother to decide when to leave the CEO role. Robyn, like Deborah, had the patience needed to manage a slowly emerging visibility. This, combined with how she learned her role in a regular learning sequence, made the handover much smoother for both parties than could ever have been the case for Ingrid.

LEARNING FROM THE SHADOWS

Ingrid and Robyn both entered their family businesses after a period of not being sure what they would do with their lives, and they learned their family businesses slowly, in the conventional sequence of phases described in our previous book (Moores and Barrett, 2002). They both learned them in the shadow of a founder. However, beyond that, their experiences have few resemblances—clear when we consider how Ingrid and Robyn dealt with the paradoxes that go with each learning phase.

Learning Business (L1)

Going outside, during the 'learning business' (L1) phase, means dealing with the risk that the potential heir to family firm leadership may not ever come back. Ingrid's case takes this paradox one level further. It took Ingrid's father a great deal of effort to persuade her even to consider entering the firm, and she finally did so with the attitude of a temporary caretaker. We put it to her that perhaps she had sought half-consciously to avoid joining the firm by doing poorly at her university studies in computer systems: a degree in that discipline would have pointed too directly towards a career in the family business. Ingrid agreed. Later, when she made up her mind to study business whole-heartedly, she passed with ease. For Robyn, in contrast, her mother's firm was a refuge. She used it as a way of 'parking' her ambitions while she figured out what she wanted to do long term. She had left it before, and could do so again, because she had previously been a little bored with the kind of jobs she performed there. However, working there as an adult gave her a new perspective on the firm: it became an outlet for her creativity, especially when she devised systems to solve business problems.

Learning Our Business (L2)

Ingrid's early experience of the family business had many negative associations, so later, she found few of the firm's special qualities attractive. Even the machinery, which she loved as a child, became associated with her difficult relationship with her father. Robyn knew and respected the 'familiness' ethos of the firm her mother started. She contrasted Deborah's and her own view of the firm with her sister's criticisms of its 'mollycoddling' management style. So while both Ingrid and Robyn needed to 'continue differently', working out how to manage differently was virtually Ingrid's entire task. In contrast, Robyn quickly got to work implementing systems which responded to and extended the 'family' approach to management her mother instigated.

Learning to Lead Our Business (L3)

Learning to lead our business (L3) entails the 'formal informality' paradox: family business leaders balance the growing firm's need for formality and systems with the fact that the business was run by a family. Ingrid also had more problems than Robyn with this phase. She had to put so much effort for so long into trying to 'heal the past', manage the family's relationships or at least minimise the damage they caused, that her attempts to put the firm's management on a more professional footing seemed hurried and a little forced.

Developing mission and vision statements, convincing outside stakeholders of her competence, devising new systems, structures and strategies... all these occupied her in the year before interview. Because each development was produced against a backdrop of conflict and after much delay, a question remained about how stable the new arrangements were.

Robyn, in comparison, quietly assumed more and more of the firm leadership by introducing systems which made the operations side of the firm run more smoothly. Neither she nor her mother discussed the matter much; when two people can complete each other's sentences, there is little need for talk.

Learning to Let Go Our Business (L4)

The final learning phase of family business leadership, learning to let go our business, requires the leader to plan for the time when they would no longer be there. In a practical sense, neither Robyn nor Ingrid developed a retirement plan; both had moved into their current CEO roles relatively recently. So we would not expect them to have figured out the detail of their eventual relationship with the firm in retirement. However, in yet another reversal of the usual paradox, Ingrid worked out a kind of mental stepping back from the firm even before she entered it: she decided she would be there as a steward for the next generation.

AILING AND HEALTHY LEARNING COMMUNITIES

Robyn's family firm was a healthy learning community, but Ingrid often mentioned the 'unhealthy dynamic' of the firm she took on. Against a background of lawsuits, secret deals—even embezzlement by firm members—it was extraordinarily difficult for members of Ingrid's firm to do the work of engagement: negotiating a joint inquiry and working on important questions about how the firm should function (Wenger, 1999, 2000). Members (including Ingrid) found it just as difficult to address gaps in their knowledge. However, in Robyn's firm, a quiet undercurrent of lively problem-solving energy emanated from Robyn, made easy by the trust between Robyn and her mother. Robyn and the staff had a similar tradition of working together. In Ingrid's firm, shared interactions had produced strange, negative forms of self-awareness, or 'repertoire': practices which arise from the firm's conscious or unconscious view of itself (Wenger, 1999, 2000). An example is the term 'being in the slot'—family-speak for being the scapegoat for anything that went wrong. In contrast, members of Robyn's firm trusted each other to such an extent there was sometimes no need for language at all.

The contrast in the two communities' histories is reflected in how Ingrid and Robyn used the belongingness modes (engagement, imagination and alignment) to try to create or preserve a healthy learning community.

Imagination Rather than Engagement

Because members of Ingrid's community of practice lacked a history of working together to solve problems, Ingrid tried to bypass this stage. She focused instead on 'imagination': ways of inspiring participation and defining a learning agenda for the community. This partly explains why she spent so much time developing mission and vision statements: these were new ways for this community to represent itself and its future to its members, as well as to outside stakeholders, such as the network dealer. Earlier leaders in Ingrid's community disqualified themselves for the task of 'imagination': representing the community to itself, for example, by becoming ill, by squandering the resources of the firm so that they attracted unfavourable attention from the network dealer and so on. Consequently, the firm's leadership was not widely distributed: Ingrid did the work of thought leader, networker, the person who documented the practice, took on pioneering roles and so on, by herself.

Engagement then Alignment

We saw how Robyn used engagement, listening to the staff and working out solutions to streamline work processes. She did this both before and after taking on the CEO role. By the time of interview, she was well into the task of alignment: articulating a shared purpose for the community in line with practices in the wider world. This was a major aspect of how she took the business forward, before and after her formal succession. Deborah could not have done this task. Robyn's capacity to introduce and codify systems that acted as 'traditions, methods, standards, routines, and frameworks' (Wenger, 1999), meant she increased the firm's self-awareness dimension. The way the firm knew its methods of operations and could share them with others meant it could be franchised.

> Robyn: Then I saw the need for our services to be standard. We were doing more in the western suburbs here and more around Penrith. Brisbane opened and we've got all the offices opening gradually. And so you know in 18 years we went from two branch offices and two franchised offices to seven branch offices and five franchises.

ROLES IN THE SHADOWS

Like Gloria and Cass, Ingrid and Robyn initially exemplify Curimbaba's notion of the female professional in the family business. Like them, Ingrid and Robyn worked outside the family firm, and both knew they could go back to working outside it if necessary. However, beyond this basic similarity they had a different experience of the professional role. Ingrid struggled with the political side of the business, a typical problem for professionals. Like Miriam and the other interviewees in Chapter 5, she always tried to separate family from business, and tried to work out the most meritorious solution for the business problems that developed from multiple family conflicts. This was an exhausting task. In Ingrid's view, her brothers regarded the business as a source of wealth available to draw on at will, and they came and went from the firm as they pleased. In Curimbaba's terms, this makes them 'invisibles', supposedly a female role. One of Ingrid's brothers even embezzled from the firm, which gave rise to one of the many lawsuits Ingrid tried to settle.

Both Ingrid and Robyn were working on renewing and expanding the firms they led. However, in Ingrid's case, the plans were still in the early, untested stages, and they focused mainly on internal restructuring. In contrast, Robyn had begun expanding the firm while her mother was still in charge, and soon after she joined it. Quite quickly, even the possibility of Robyn leaving made Deborah nervous because the business, though it expanded slowly after Robyn joined it, became larger than Deborah could have managed on her own.

CONCLUSIONS

Ingrid needed to change the firm's culture radically and struggled to do this; Robyn was instantly able to understand and endorse the firm's existing culture. This included the 'familiness' manifested in the approach Robyn's mother took with staff, which was also why she chose Robyn as her successor. Being at ease with the firm's culture was a mark of Robyn's likely success. Where Ingrid struggled to be heard and to make others 'hear reality', as she put it, Robyn could quietly listen to other people's problems and use what she found as a basis for putting in new systems to make the business run more smoothly. In terms of how they learned the family business, Robyn's learning was slow, but basically smooth and steady—she took the learning stages in the standard order. Robyn, though a professional, had something of the anchor about her. Like Gloria and Cass, she took a business approach to the firm and, despite the long period she spent working in the shadow of the founder, she had no need to find an ideal separate from the family business. In comparison, Ingrid joined the family firm almost against her better judgement, and under emotional pressure from her father. Her way of dealing with the pressure was to adopt a long-term 'stewardship' relationship with the firm. To be there 'just as a steward for the next generation' meant that she could retain some emotional detachment and not tie her destiny irrevocably to the family business.

Both Robyn's and Ingrid's apprenticeships were long, and for Ingrid in particular, difficult. However, both seemed likely to find and manage the spotlight of leadership, although Ingrid had some way to go. Chapter 9 considers more general propositions arising from these findings about 'learning from the shadows' by comparing Ingrid's and Robyn's learning experiences with those of participants who spent more time in the spotlight or, alternatively, were pushed into the shadows. The next chapter considers interviewees who were pushed towards invisibility and so lost the possibility of leadership altogether.

8. Becoming Invisible

This chapter considers three women who, for one reason or another, lost the leadership spotlight in the family business or, worse, turn out never to have had it in the first place. They were pushed towards invisibility, despite their efforts to achieve some prominence in the family firm, despite the respect people outside the firm had for their expertise, and often despite having helped it make important innovations. To start with, each had looked much like many other family business women who became leaders: they often brought similar skills to the firm. Just as important, all three brought a high level of affective commitment (Sharma and Irving, 2005) to the firm: a real enthusiasm for it because of how it linked their identity and career ambitions. This chapter tries to fathom why, in the face of these qualifications, leadership eluded them.

HANNAH

Hannah is the daughter of a successful supermarket entrepreneur whose business interests were based in Lebanon. Like Nancy, her role in the family firm was strongly influenced by decisions her family made earlier: they wished to avoid claims on family assets they thought her future husband might make. She has two brothers, but their future wives cannot make such claims under the inheritance customs of the Middle East. As Hannah explained it:

> Hannah: The inheritance issue was like this: if you (as a woman) are a Muslim you can inherit half of what the boy will inherit. As for the gender rules, they always think that women are going to get married to men of another family and her children are not going to hold the same family name, and it's like she's leaving the family, which is not the case nowadays. But that's what they think. They think if they let her inherit it will go to another family.

According to Hannah, this fear was powerful enough to prevent many daughters of business-owning families from being considered for senior family business roles. However, at first, Hannah's father ensured that Hannah got some business experience. For Hannah, these inheritance norms did not at first mean less access to business experience. This was unusual, because her father was an authoritarian person with traditional views of women's roles. However, he had frequent conflicts with his sons, and Hannah had to mediate between them:

> Hannah: He [her father] is kind of an authoritarian businessman. My brothers discuss things together and they're very smart, but I think there's still the influence of my father on them, although they try to make decisions without letting him know. But any time they're having conflict with my father I am the adjudicator.

Oddly enough, the political instability of the Middle East region released Hannah from some of the gender-based constraints that would normally have operated in that part of the world. The 1990–91 Gulf War meant her father allowed her to leave her home in Lebanon to study in France. When she graduated, she kept working in France because of the shelling in Lebanon and was eventually offered a position in a French university. She met her husband, also a Lebanese citizen, in France. Fearing she might never return home, Hannah's father encouraged her to start and build a smaller business in France, a subsidiary of the family firm. Starting and working in a subsidiary business was an excellent way of learning leadership and entrepreneurial skills. As the Carlson, Packer and Murdoch families demonstrate, giving the potential heirs to the family firm a fair-sized business to manage that is somewhat separated from the core family business is a time-honoured and effective way of grooming the eventual successor.

Hannah eventually returned home from France, and the demands arising from the traditional role of women in the Middle Eastern business setting reasserted themselves. She was expected to live at home and fit in with whatever decisions were made on her behalf. But she managed to accommodate the situation and even use it to increase her flexibility at a personal level:

> Hannah: When I came back from Paris to live in Lebanon, I first stayed with my parents, and my son had this special relationship with my father, and then my father didn't want us to move. When we decided to move, he talked to my husband and they made the decision—without asking me—to stay in the same building, or buy an apartment in the same building. I didn't want that at first, but it turned out to be very practical. It's given me some flexibility, living near my mother. But at the beginning I didn't like it, the fact that the decision had been made without asking me. At the same time, I didn't want to live next to my husband's parents or on my own just to have some independence, especially as I'd come from Paris with a certain mentality and I didn't want anyone to interfere.

Hannah was an academic specialising in family business. She also created her own consultancy firm and advised many family firms worldwide. Despite this, her family only asked her opinion about family matters in their firm, never business problems. So while she acted as an entrepreneur in her own spheres of activity, academia and business consultancy, her own family did not recognise or draw on her expertise in a professional sense. This was a problem for her, because, like Miriam in Chapter 5, she felt a strong emotional pull towards the original family business:

> Hannah: You have your challenges at work, and sometimes I say, 'Why am I here? I should be managing my own business'. If I'm doing something I enjoy, like giving my courses or organising conferences, I don't think of that. But when you have certain challenges that you have to pass, then this comes to my mind. What I think mostly is that if I had to manage my own business, I think I would have made that grow. The growth that I'm doing for the centre at the university—that effort would have been good in our own business.

This lack of internal legitimacy in the family business was a pattern throughout Hannah's whole career. Before starting and managing the subsidiary firm, she had briefly returned to Lebanon after completing her studies. However, the senior managers in the family business 'did not make [her] any offers', because of the cultural barriers discussed earlier. She was effectively invisible to the family business:

> Hannah: But let me make one point. I was never consulted, never asked, to give my opinion on any issue, and I would say that many of the females in the Arab world are rarely consulted on issues to do with family businesses.

Later, she noticed a softening in her father's attitude, prompted by her externally recognised expertise in managing family businesses:

> Hannah: I know for sure that in our family my two brothers and my father make the big decisions and I'm always alienated from those big decisions. I'm still disappointed, but now I think that my father wants to involve me much more and he wants me to be involved much more in what's happening... He would never have expected that his daughter could play such a role. I think he's proud of me because when I'm not here he brags about me, but at the same time he's surprised.

Reconciled to not having a larger part in the original family firm, Hannah stated that she was reasonably happy as she was. However, she would have liked to advise her male siblings about how to manage aspects of the firm in which they all grew up. As well as acting as the adjudicator in family disputes between her brothers and between them and her father, like Miriam, she was concerned that her brothers replicated some features of her father's authoritarian management style. This, and the hostile attitude of her brothers' wives, who were concerned that Hannah might try to reduce their claims on the family business assets, combined to make a larger role in the family business impossible for her.

> Hannah: Now I have no problems with my brothers, but I don't know how much they would want to involve me because there's now also the influence of the wives.

Maybe they think that if I had more than a minor ownership that wouldn't be beneficial for them. As simple as that.

Hannah said that she would be happy if her children made their careers in the context of a family firm. However, she thought that her husband's business was the most likely place for this to happen, and not her firm, or the firm her father started.[1] It was more important to Hannah that her children should develop the personal qualities of independence and responsibility that would allow them to be business people in their own right, than that they set their sights on inheriting any other business.

> Hannah: Ideally, that's how we see it, but I never say to my children that their parents' business is their business. I tell them that when they grow up they'll start their own business, and I say that whatever the options will be in the future, they will be very independent and responsible individuals. I don't want them to rely on that [going into her husband's firm].

By partly transferring her emotional allegiance from her father's to her husband's firm, Hannah allowed her husband's business to become a family business 'by intent'. Hannah hoped this approach would help create a new generation of entrepreneurs: that her children would learn the necessary personal qualities for business leadership by being exposed to her husband's firm, and not depend on any pre-existing firm as a future source of wealth. While Hannah may have been resigned to being invisible so far as her original family firm was concerned, this did not prevent her from setting the next generation on a path where they could develop their own leadership stage.

SUE

Until shortly before interview, Sue was a third-generation member of an Australian roofing manufacturing business that was started by her maternal grandfather in 1947. To Sue's profound disappointment, the business had just been sold to a New Zealand competitor. The founder of the business had four daughters; Sue's mother was the founder's second daughter. The founder, an engineer, was an extremely idiosyncratic and authoritarian person. From the outset, Sue's father, also an engineer 'by inclination if not by formal training', was very much the subordinate of the founder:

> Sue: My grandfather was the owner. He was very much the patriarch in the family—a strong charismatic type. Very erratic—one of those people you would either love or not. He used to ring Dad up at all hours totally obsessed about the business. He used to write down his inventions on the backs of envelopes. My

father was complementary in that he was much more of a 'working on the inside' person, rather than a person who worked on the outside as my grandfather did.

To add to the problems created by this difficult relationship, there was always conflict between Sue's father and her uncle, the husband of the founder's eldest daughter. This conflict arose partly because of the different personalities and values of the men in the first and second generations: while Sue's grandfather was sentimental and charming, Sue said that she believed her uncle was underhanded in his dealings with people. Her father, on the other hand, was both too 'straight' and too unassertive for his own good. Sue described the three:

> Sue: My father is very over-honest, and that uncle was probably the person who would take the spoons or the towels from a hotel, you know what I mean? Whereas Dad would be standing at the back of the bus queue waiting for everyone else to get on, [my uncle] would have pushed on first. [My grandfather] probably would have charmed the conductor to let him on first too.

At one point, Sue's uncle struck problems in a separate business he had established, and wanted to start a new venture in the UK that would be linked to the family business. While both Sue's father and her uncle were involved, in Sue's opinion, the arrangements for the UK move were not handled equitably, because Sue's father could not defend the interests of his side of the family:

> Sue: Dad would never be assertive about it. We had to pay our own airfares to go overseas. The other [her uncle's] family moved to a very smart part of England. They went to Hertfordshire, [the children] went to the best schools and we were in dodgy Miningsville at the top of the world. So those issues, while it didn't impact on me, I think built up resentment...

Later, Sue's father had a dispute with an American firm over the patent rights to a new roofing product the firm had developed. Sue's father lost, and Sue suspects this was because her uncle gave information to the other side. While Sue's uncle was no longer part of the firm, and Sue's father was its CEO until its sale, this history naturally led to continuing strains between the two sides of the family. There were also other disputes, especially with the remaining second-generation daughters, who did not take an active role in the business, but wanted financial returns from it.

Sue's father's failure to acknowledge he was at the head of a family firm helps explain Sue's problems in gaining internal legitimacy: a formal role that could be construed as long-term, and as preparing the way for a position in the spotlight as CEO. Sue had been a teacher, run medium-sized community organisations and gained marketing and professional writing experience via her husband's commercial photography business. So her skill base was adequate; she was at least as well prepared for business as most of the interviewees in earlier chapters who eventually gained leadership roles. She entered the family business as a marketing consultant, but encountered major resistance to her having even this tenuous involvement in the firm.

> Sue: There was a huge resistance to me working in the business towards my dad from my mum. My uncle didn't want me there either. As for Dad, he just said the aunts didn't want... I found out afterwards he said no whenever anyone else's children wanted to come into the business to do anything, and so he actually said no to my brother-in-law, my sister's husband who had needed work and wanted to come and do something. He said no to everyone. But I came in as a consultant. [On this basis] Dad would have said, 'Oh we're not a family business'. Yet he had inherited the business and he had his sisters-in-law as shareholders...

Being employed 'just as a consultant', rather than being a member of the firm who might one day run it made Sue's role in the firm highly ambiguous. It also meant Sue never gained enough legitimacy for her future in the business to be secure and her ideas taken seriously.

Chapter 4 points to research on corporate legitimacy—specifically, how entrepreneurs manage the period after they establish new firms and before these firms become profitable. Such firms need markers of legitimacy in the form of endorsements, testimonials, membership of industry bodies and so on. The same principle applies to Sue, who wanted to bring a stronger marketing orientation to a firm which had already been in business for more than 40 years when she entered it. However, she lacked the legitimacy she would have had if the firm's present leader had strongly endorsed her work. Without this, it was always an uphill job to get her father and others to recognise that the business needed more attention to marketing to support its traditional focus on engineering innovation and quality manufacturing. Sue's father was 'not strong on communication' and this extended to a lack of strategic thinking:

> Sue: He probably didn't think like that [strategically]. At a management meeting he would get real excited when we started to talk about the front-end extruder, and then the whole meeting would go on to the detail of the machinery, whereas 'What are we going to do—we've got a major new competitor!' was just not interesting at all.

Consistent with his lack of a strategic plan for the firm, and his general lack of assertiveness, Sue's father was vague and inconsistent about how rewards and responsibilities in the business were allocated. Sue recalled how things gradually changed after she moved physically into the main office and worked there practically full time:

> Sue: He [her father] is gradually giving me more responsibility without ever clearly giving it... which is very much his style. He wasn't a 'group meeting, group process' person. He's a person who [has] a one-to-one talk to you. You feel very

intimate, feel very good and you think you've made a decision. And then he'll come and talk to you—very intimate, very good—and changes the decision! So a lot of things would be run in that way.

Sue had a mentor—briefly—in Keith [name disguised], an external CEO whom her father brought in to the firm after he bought out the remaining aunts and stepped back from the leadership role and its endless family conflicts. Blumentritt et al. (2007) researched the difficulties of non-family CEOs in family businesses. Their chances of succeeding in their task tend to be small, since they need unusually strong business and interpersonal competencies as well as the support of family business boards and councils to strengthen family members' acceptance of them in positions traditionally held by a family member. Keith had interpersonal and business skills, but the many ambiguities of the family firm environment reduced the support he enjoyed from many longstanding employees in the firm. Unsurprisingly, Keith did not stay employed in the firm for long. However, while he was there, Sue felt she made progress in getting her ideas for better marketing accepted. In all, working with him was a pleasurable, exciting and formative experience for her:

> Sue: We really worked very closely together. He was CEO, but we co-led if you like. You know, the opposite to Damon [her father, name disguised], who would never share where things were. We worked through a lot of things together.

Despite being the same age as Sue, Keith was effectively a mentor 'because he was very personable, very good at building the rest of the team, very outward-going'. Sue was not strong at small talk:

> Sue: I love talking about the ideas and I love doing that but I'm not [good at small talk]... While he, Keith, was. He was always hanging around chatting, 'How's your mother?' and I... have to force myself to do that. Frankly, it's not my natural thing.

In that way, Sue resembled her father, who did not communicate easily or clearly. So Keith's management approach would have created a clash with her father's style. Sue said that it was symbolically very important in a business marked by secrecy and lack of direction that during Keith's time several buildings were refurbished in a modern style with lots of glass and open space. One objective of the style chosen for the refurbishment was to reflect in the business premises the change of culture Sue and Keith were trying to produce:

> Sue: We changed the structure of the office so everything was all visible. Took all the walls down, lots of glass—as a symbolic thing.

Sue learned from Keith's team building skills. She and Keith also worked on systems, structure and strategy with good effect:

Sue: I was really fortunate to build a very good team, and one key person was my export manager. She was a 'she' too. She and I basically restructured a lot of what we had been doing as a business... When Keith and I came on board the return was about 5.5 per cent. The return is now, as a result of some of the structural changes, 24 per cent. What we did was we restructured. I changed the distribution in Australia so that we got rid of our master distributor in Australia and we set up a distribution business. I did that... we set that up in 2003. Keith left in January 2003, and so from that point it was just Damon and I until the business was sold in December 2004. And then I also set up a distribution business in the UK. Again, because over time we'd sold that, that really has given us a huge additional profit...

Sue was not surprised that Keith only lasted a few years in the firm. He and many other highly productive staff who tried to change the firm were driven out by their inability to penetrate what Sue referred to as 'the bastion': her father and several longstanding employees who held tightly to old approaches. Her father had supposedly stepped back from the firm because the high level of conflict he had to manage affected his health. However, he could not truly let go:

Sue: Where the whole thing faltered was the fact that Damon was still basically the operations manager. That's always what he was and always what he would be. And what really came through was that he couldn't let go. We got a very good operations manager and he lasted six months. He's now running an automotive factory and he's highly competent... If we couldn't get into the bastion and all those people that were there we really couldn't do a lot and Damon could not cope [with so much change].

Sue did not take this personally, citing the forces of conservatism of people already in the firm. She was finally forced out when a different new arrival successfully courted favour with her father, and usurped her hopes of getting a senior role in the firm:

Sue: I'd obviously shown my interest and commitment to the business and my passion for it and had been succeeding in this very difficult situation we had in the Australian market, and then... this chap Richard [name disguised]... Damon said... 'Richard is going to be the general manager' and I just nearly fell over. It was just so... I just felt completely outside the loop, not respected. And I just thought, 'Right, I'm off.'

The only resolution Sue's parents found to the many family conflicts was to sell the firm so Sue's father could retire. Before the firm was sold, Sue organised a group of people, including her brother, who had strong business experience (though he had never held or sought a role in the family firm) or could offer capital backing to make an offer to buy the firm or part of it. Sue only wanted to buy *part* of the firm—a proportion she could handle using her expertise. Her parents rejected her offer as too risky. Another issue which deterred her parents from selling the firm to Sue was that they saw a potential conflict between Sue and her sister, who tried to persuade her parents not to sell the business to Sue. For Sue's mother, this brought to mind her own problems with her sisters (Sue's aunts). This in turn gave Sue's sister leverage to argue that the business should not be passed to Sue. In trying to maintain the status quo, Sue's mother actually prevented anyone finding a solution to the existing problems which threatened the continuity of the family firm—as a family firm.

FELICITY

Of the three women in this chapter, Felicity had the least ability to attain the leadership spotlight, the most firmly enclosed in a mantle of invisibility. She was a third-generation member of the family firm, a prominent funeral business. Her job title—her name featured in the organisation chart as head of a major division of the firm—suggested she had a highly visible and strategic role. However, her apparent prominence masked an invisibility which would likely only deepen with time. At the time of interview, Felicity had become resigned to the situation, despite the fact that her early experiences in the firm closely resembled those of several participants who eventually occupied leadership positions.

Like so many others in our study, Felicity recalled having a special interest in the family firm—it was part of the close relationship she had with her father. Felicity told us that many people did not understand what went on in the funeral business, and at an early age Felicity became a sort of spokesperson for the firm:

> Felicity: I got asked lots of questions from lots of people. You know, like kids at school and that sort of thing. And I would always feel like I had to come back home and get the right answer and go back to school the next day and tell them what the answer was.

Like Robyn, after leaving school, Felicity went through a period of not knowing what she wanted to do with her life. She had a couple of false starts, which her father, the CEO, at first left her to deal with, believing she should 'find her own direction'. He finally sent her to business college, which meant that, when she finally entered the family firm, she could make a genuine contribution to it. Felicity's first task was to be part of a new business unit, self-funded funerals, for which the chief market was elderly people who wanted the satisfaction of knowing that they had taken care of their own funeral and would not inconvenience anyone else or put them to expense.

While the role was basically to sell self-funded funerals, and to act as an assistant to another, male manager who was responsible for the new business' revenues, Felicity also saw herself as offering a counselling role to customers:

> Felicity: I was brought in to assist Gerard [the other manager, name disguised] initially, in an administrative role, but very quickly I moved from that, and that was what the job offer was: administration, a secretarial role. But I very quickly moved into face-to-face dealing with people...

It soon became clear that Felicity's value in this role depended on her gender and her family name—not her strategic input. It was the first serious inkling of her eventual invisibility. Despite Felicity's early interest in the firm, her parents literally never saw her taking a role in it.

> Felicity: I was really not encouraged... No, you know, Mum and Dad were sort of saying... They thought that teaching would be something I would be good at... They thought more in terms of my brother...

> Interviewer: Despite your early interest in what the family firm did, and despite the fact that you probably knew most about it?

> Felicity: Yeah, that's right.

At the time Felicity was chosen to head a division, other firms in the funeral industry were starting to emphasise in their marketing efforts the special qualities of empathy a female funeral director could offer a bereaved family. So from Felicity's father's standpoint, a daughter who held the family name would be useful as the visible face of a business expansion. The way Felicity was selected for the role put her in a position of prominence, but was actually emblematic of how she was slipping from view. As Felicity told it, she was present behind a screen, while possible names of the new division were being discussed in customer focus groups:

> Felicity: Dad scribbled down on a bit of paper, 'What about [daughter's first name + family name] and Associates'? ...and ran that in and people were saying, 'Well, you know, is she a real person?' And they said, 'Well, yes, that makes sense. That's a good idea.' We wanted to link the name... we wanted the family name in there somewhere, because it's such a well-known name in the funeral industry.

> Interviewer: So were you then subsequently appointed to head that division?

> Felicity: Yes, they had already made the decision that I was going to be, at that point... Look, I was too young at that time and too inexperienced to realise the... I suppose, the ramifications of having my name above the door... I really had no say in the matter, the decision was made. I wasn't actually asked to think it through and I never... I just sort of got swept up in it all basically.

Felicity agreed that in this matter and others, she was basically a resource to the firm, rather than a real influence within it. Others were selected for career development over her—her brother and her husband (from whom she later separated). Most woundingly, even an old school friend whom she introduced to her father when he was looking for a new personal assistant, eventually moved into what Felicity had hoped might be her role. In a telling metaphor, her father looked on this person as his eyes in the business. Felicity envied the learning Kath [name disguised] achieved through her exposure to all areas of the firm while she was upstaged, quite literally. Like Felicity, Kath had no formal training for such a prominent role. However, as a person of natural competence, it was not long before she moved into the spotlight. In contrast, Felicity was a reticent, unassertive individual.

The issue of children became a difficulty for Felicity. In the light of how often the management literature mentions women's motherhood roles as an obstacle to their reaching leadership roles, it is remarkable that, while several of the participants in our sample had children, until Felicity, none suggested motherhood hindered their ascendancy in the family firm. In contrast to Felicity, Gloria incorporated her children, aged five, three and one, easily into her hectic schedule:

> Gloria: I normally get up early in the morning and have breakfast with the kids, send them to school, and spend about four nights a week with them for dinner; also a half day on Saturday and a full day on Sunday. The rest of the time is business or public service. Sometimes I go on business trips and take one of the children to spend some quality time with them. When you go on a business trip your time is much more free after your business meeting. All my colleagues know that I always bring my children along.

Felicity found being a mother demanding, and said that it was definitely an obstacle to her advancement in the business. Her work commitments were rearranged while she was on maternity leave, and she felt the new set-up left her at a disadvantage when she returned. Furthermore, Felicity felt her previous importance as her father's confidante gave way so that her value in the firm became primarily because she was the mother of her children. They were a potential resource for the business, and Felicity was seen primarily as the provider of that resource:

> Felicity: I just felt that, like... he saw me as just James' mother now, and not as you know, not as...

> Interviewer: And James is the grandson who might ultimately be a CEO of [the family firm]?

> Felicity: He could be.

Felicity was not included in the inner circle of family firm management, and this continued in the long term. The interest Felicity's father took in his family's business projects depended on his changing interests. This meant that whether one was 'in' or 'out' depended on the mood, whim or passing interest of the incumbent leader. While Felicity's father was not angry or hostile in the way Ingrid's father was, Felicity's problems in trying to hold on to a position of prominence look similar to the way people in Ingrid's family were periodically 'put in the slot': blamed for whatever was going wrong. But in some ways, Felicity's fate was even worse, especially when she looked back on her childhood when she identified so strongly with her father. At least when Ingrid was 'in the slot', others were there to lean on for support—others who had shared the experience. And in the end, regardless of being 'in the slot', the leader was still interested in you. Unlike the participants who directed the spotlight onto others as part of their strategy for the firm, invisibility was not something Felicity chose.

MISSED LEARNING

Hannah, Sue and Felicity share some characteristics and some differences to other participants in our study who became leaders of their family firm, in terms of how they passed through the learning phases our previous study (Moores and Barrett, 2002) discerns:

Learning Business (L1)

All were outside the firm long enough to have acquired some business-oriented skills. Hannah was an acknowledged business expert. Sue had the personal discipline and several functional business skills, as demonstrated by the organisational and leadership roles she held before entering the family firm. Felicity had the least developed skill set, but even so, she would have disdained entering the family firm without bringing some relevant skills to it. All had learned business at least to the same extent as several others in our sample who succeeded in attaining leadership.

Learning our Business (L2)

All three had a strong emotional attachment, even a passion, for the family business. Hannah regretted her inability to put her energies towards the family firm instead of towards her university or even her own consultancy activities. In Sue's case, the strength of this passion surprised even her:

Sue: I spoke to my mother about it [her wish to take over the business] on Saturday, because it sort of came up in another context. She said, 'Oh darling, I couldn't imagine anyone could feel that passionate about a business.' And I said,

'But I do, Mum. You know that's how I have always felt about this. And you know I didn't want to feel passionate about it. I don't know why I felt passionate about it—an industrial business. But that's how I felt.'

Felicity's passion for the family firm went back furthest of all: she recalled explaining the obscurities of the funeral business to her peers at school.

Learning to Lead Our Business (L3)

Hannah helped other family firms to develop their strategy, but was not allowed to do this in her own family's business. Sue also knew her family firm's strengths and where and how it needed to change. Under Keith's tutelage, she made considerable progress in developing the skills needed to build a team of people who could help her make these changes. Both Hannah and Sue were ready or close to ready for the spotlight, if they could only manage to direct it towards themselves and keep it there. Felicity's is a contrasting case: by the time of interview, she no longer sought a leadership role. Given the increasing demand in family firms for formal, tertiary-level qualifications in business, she would have needed more skills before being considered for a more senior position in the firm. Nevertheless, she was reasonably content with her present role:

> Felicity: I think that I've found my niche, I think I enjoy what I do most of the time and I really enjoy just being able to assist the family. So my general day-to-day role would be meeting with families to arrange funerals and then following them through, so I do all the organisational side of it. Then I follow through on the day of the funeral... I believe I've got the ability to do it very well and over a 20-year period now, I've built up those skills. It's a sort of counselling role in some ways, but we don't refer to ourselves as formal counsellors, but you get to see the human dynamics, the family dynamics that go on. It's always interesting and I get a lot of satisfaction from that.

Letting Go the Family Business (L4)

Like most women in our sample, Hannah and Sue would have liked to see their children eventually enter the family business if they had shown the necessary interest and aptitude. Hannah transferred her allegiance in terms of her children's future to her husband's firm. For Sue and Felicity, the relationship between their children's future and the future of the family firm was still a sore point. Felicity resented being seen as important to the firm primarily as the mother of her children, a potential resource to the firm. Sue's situation was more complex. Because in the end she did not take over the family business, she did not have the opportunity to discuss with her children—whether or not they would have liked to have entered the firm in their turn. So she had special regrets when she told her son the firm was sold, because he would have liked to have worked there when he grew up. In her mind, the firm was a family firm 'by intent' as well as in other ways. Sue's daughter, in comparison, said that she was happy the family firm was sold because now her mother would be home more often. The upside and the downside of a succession dilemma that Sue never had the opportunity to resolve are neatly summarised in her children's opposing attitudes.

LIMITING LEARNING: RIGID BOUNDARIES AND FIXED IDENTITIES

The three family firms in this chapter suffer from a problem that reduces a learning community's capacity to learn from interchange with others: the boundaries of all three were either uncertain or too rigid. Reducing a firm's capacity to learn reduces the resources available to it. Consistent with wider gender relations in the Middle East, Hannah's family firm limited her involvement in it, and Hannah did not think this would change once her father stepped down from the CEO role. Hannah found this difficult to accept:

> Hannah: I felt that I was alienated from the business, and that part I do not like personally, because for me it means maybe a lack of trust and for me it goes deeper than that. It's not only trust. What bothers me in all of this is that they wouldn't take you as your own personality and they would think all the time that your husband is going to influence you, which is not the case for me personally.

Like Cass, Hannah could have brought sophisticated human capital resources based on her recognised expertise in the academic and corporate worlds, and this would probably have improved her family firm's functioning. However, the family firm's boundaries were too impermeable to allow this.

Sue exercised a high level of entrepreneurial skill on behalf of her father's firm: she had the capacity to boost its marketing efforts, and while she was there managed to overhaul its research and development activities. But she did this from the ambiguous, 'neither in nor out' position of a consultant. Outsiders such as Richard managed to penetrate the family firm's boundaries far more easily and displace Sue's leadership hopes. The ambiguity of Sue's position meant that she finally left the firm, taking her expertise with her. Like Hannah, Sue tended to believe her gender had something to do with her problems in gaining legitimacy:

> Sue: If I had been a Sam, not a Sue, would a different door have opened? And would the way Damon took Richard down to the factory: 'Come on, I'll show you. You're going to be my general manager' ever have been available to me? I doubt it. Yet I've resuscitated the whole R&D part of the business...

Only Felicity was at ease with her situation; she regarded herself as having found her niche. But even Felicity wondered whether she would have been offered better opportunities if she were male. She recognised that she was not a natural leader:

> Felicity: I... lack the leadership skills to be able to come up with the ideas and the innovations and that sort of thing. Once the concept is presented to me and I get on board with it, I can run with the ball. But I couldn't dream something up and do it.

Felicity therefore acknowledged she could never have measured up to her father, who was a very charismatic person. On the other hand, in her opinion, her brother Matthew [name disguised] was also not as talented a leader as her father. He lacked their father's effortless capacity to inspire and motivate people, and his capacity for clear strategic thinking. Nevertheless, despite being less talented as a leader than their father, Matthew received career development opportunities which cemented the legitimacy of his position in the succession arrangements of the firm. These opportunities never came Felicity's way:

> Felicity: Now he [Matthew] came into the business a couple of years after me, and he's a couple of years younger than me. He's been given all those opportunities, and I could have been all bitter and twisted about all of that and said, 'Well, why did you pick him and not me?' ...but his training for that role... he's a lawyer... he worked as a lawyer. But then he... he really did have... a career path mapped out. It was part of the whole succession planning thing... So Matthew was given a lot more... I suppose Matthew has been given more opportunities than me... in that respect.

When Ingrid's firm found someone to run it, the business as a family firm was crucial, because, from the network supplier's point of view, the firm lost value if it was not family run. Given the dearth of eligible and available family members who could succeed Ingrid's father following years of conflict, the situation was becoming critical before Ingrid took over. Ingrid believed this was one reason she was eventually supported by the network supplier to take a leadership role.

The situation was not so acute in the three firms we consider in this chapter. The firm Hannah's father ran was successful, according to the norms of family firms in the Middle East. Felicity's firm was also successful, at least from the point of view of most people in it. Hannah's and Felicity's roles were not so crucial in their family business structures that, without them, their continuity as family firms was threatened. Hannah and Felicity felt as individuals that their ambitions were thwarted, but this did not influence the future of the firm from the perspective of those who ran it. Those making the decisions were also unaware of the feelings of firm members who believed they were being overlooked.

Only in Sue's case would it have made a real difference to the future of the firm if Sue had had her leadership ambitions rewarded. Because Sue was always kept somewhere outside the rigid (and yet ambiguous) boundaries of firm membership, she was never considered as a potential CEO. Consequently, the firm was sold and lost its family nature. No one, including her parents, was happy about the situation. Sue's was the only family firm in this chapter (and indeed in our sample as a whole) not to have continued in more or less its present form. From a resource perspective, none of the three firms in this chapter used the human capital and skills of their female members as fully as it could have.

ROLES THAT LEAD TO TRUE INVISIBILITY

Earlier chapters note that participants' families sometimes regarded a participant's role in the family firm differently from how the participant saw it. This gap occurred for Hannah, Sue and Felicity and pushed them towards Curimbaba's invisible role, even though they always saw themselves as anchors or professionals. Felicity sounded like a typical professional when she vehemently rejected the idea that a family firm should 'just give people a job':

Felicity: I just cringe when I heard some of the stories... that guy talking about his children that just come in and expect the business to provide for them... it's never been in my mentality...

Felicity held that a job in the family firm should not be a sinecure, and she made a real contribution to the family firm she worked in. She saw herself as at least an anchor, someone who was highly visible, and while this may have changed from time to time, never entirely unnecessary. However, the major decision-makers, especially her father, did not see her as moving into a strategic role. After establishing the new 'funerals by women' division which Felicity only appeared to lead, her father rapidly moved on to new projects and took little further interest in her division. Things were different for her brother. Since the interview, Felicity's brother succeeded to the CEO position, having completed his MBA, which was paid for by the firm. This might have confirmed Felicity's view that her brother received special advantages.

Hannah had an experience similar to Felicity's, and had a more developed set of skills, which she believed the firm failed to utilise. She had special expertise in family business that was recognised through her consultancy work, and she had acted as an entrepreneur by establishing both new academic courses in the university she worked for as well as founding the consultancy. Yet Hannah was only allowed to contribute to the family firm she grew up in by adjudicating disputes between her father and her brothers. Sue regarded herself as a professional by virtue of her specialised marketing expertise and her long contribution to the family firm in marketing and research and development. However, this turned out not to count when a new potential managing director caught her father's eye.

Two main clues foreshadowed the inexorable shift for these participants from an anchor or professional role towards invisibility: their formal educational qualifications and the reasons they entered the family firm. None of the three participants in this chapter had formal qualifications in areas closely related to the firm's product or service, and the firm did not fully utilise the qualifications they did have. Hannah was an academic expert in family business, and Sue had marketing skills, but no formal training in marketing. Felicity was in the most difficult position of all. Before entering the firm she needed a job, and after entering the firm, she strengthened its relationships with its potential customers. Nevertheless, she lacked formal training in business and was excluded from discussions about the overall directions of the firm. Consequently, she lacked confidence: she was always a little worried about being asked a question about the strategic direction of her division, because she might be unable to answer it.

The reason these participants entered the firm and their role in it after coming in was mainly to solve problems in the family part of the system or to offer a 'female presence'. Hannah adjudicated disputes between the male members of her family. Sue's position as a consultant was left undefined, so as not to upset other family members. Felicity's presence as head of the 'funerals by women' division of her firm presented a resource of 'femaleness', but did not require strategic input from Felicity. This reason for entering the family firm is not unusual for professionals. Curimbaba (2002) points out that women are often brought into the family business specifically to solve a business or family problem, but that it may be hazardous for their careers. The experiences of Hannah, Sue and Felicity suggest that personal costs are attached for professionals who deal with problems in the family, rather than the business part of the system, or who do jobs where the main requirement is 'femaleness'.

Hannah, Sue and Felicity were the only participants in the sample who suggested that their invisibility might have been due to discrimination. Hannah saw it as inevitable that male family members would be more likely to be selected for management positions in her firm. Sue told us about her previously unspoken suspicions that her prospects in the firm would have been different for her if she were male. Felicity was aware that her brother was offered better formal educational opportunities than she had—an MBA at the firm's expense. For Felicity, her brother's subsidised degree studies coincided with her maternity leave and her father's changed view of her once she became a mother, pointed to her growing invisibility:

Felicity: I think at that point too, the other thing is, when Matthew joined the business, it coincided with me having my first child. And if we are going to get into all the nitty-gritties, I suppose I had a difficult time feeling... Because then, when I came back from maternity leave, Matthew was sort-of fully engrossed in the company, and then I came back part-time. I found it quite difficult in those twelve months after I had James, because Dad then, I felt like he didn't see me... Because I wasn't working in the business any more, for that period of time, he didn't talk to me about business any more. He just, you know, talked to me about the baby, and in a way it was almost as like I didn't exist. But I was still wanting to have that relationship.

Ingrid was also offered, and finally undertook, a business degree paid for by her father's firm when her father had exhausted all other 'lures' to bring her into the firm.

In discussing the ways men are often 'anointed' to leadership positions, Curimbaba (2002) cites Marceau (1989), Scott and Griff (1984) and Villette (1975), who discuss merit systems based on 'reconversion strategies'. These are the ways positions to be inherited in top companies are defined and favoured by the very social and economic structures from which the heirs already come. According to Curimbaba (2002), the same happens in the family business setting: the family and the company 'construct' the heir's ability as a leader through educational qualifications, as if it is unimportant that the heir is the owner's son. This could be said about Felicity's situation, and may be even more marked in Hannah's, where she had educational qualifications superior to her brothers'. However, Felicity also declared that she would not have wanted to pursue an MBA. She had, at least to some extent, chosen her own path.

Trying to be a professional or an anchor, when your role is to solve problems that are seen as 'personal' or 'female', rather than business matters, means risking invisibility. Even some invisibles who aim to keep the family firm on a level emotional keel can end up defeating their own purpose by staying out of sight. Sue's mother is an example. She never took a professional or even an anchor role in the firm that her father founded. She was hurt by family quarrels in her own generation, and saw the toll that the business took on her husband's health. She had often tried to sort out problems of sibling rivalry between Sue and her sister. So she warned Sue that owning and actively running a family business can disrupt family harmony. She also refused to consider using help from outside the family in an effort to develop a succession process which could have included Sue as an eventual CEO. Sue commented about her mother:

Sue: Mum didn't want anyone to know what was happening with her business and her life. She didn't want to have any accountability, she didn't want any generational involvement.

The result was that when the business was sold, both Sue's mother and Sue lost even their positions as anchors in the family business. Their experiences echo Curimbaba's warnings about the difficulties for anchors, who are:

> ...a group more exposed to change, yet unaware that unpredictable things could happen to them due to shifts in the family. [They] were subject to losing their positioning—a process triggered by either the appearance of a competitor, for example, a brother-in-law, or an unexpected interest... Throughout this process the Anchors become more or less significant in the family business system (Curimbaba, 2002, p. 250).

CONCLUSIONS

Hannah, Felicity and Sue differ in terms of how they dealt with being passed over for a leadership role in the family firm. In varying ways, they found new niches inside or outside the family firm. However, as a group, they exemplify the hazards of invisibility when it is imposed, rather than freely chosen for strategic purposes, as Gloria and Cass had done. They also illustrate Wenger's contention that knowledge in a community of practice is essentially a social act: what you know is a function of what the relevant community is prepared to agree that you know. These findings have particular importance for the next chapter, which draws together the findings of the analysis and generates some general propositions.

NOTE

[1]   Hannah's husband, like her, is both an academic and a businessperson.

9. Lessons of the Spotlight

The previous chapters closely examine women's experiences as leaders in family businesses, how they found and then managed the leadership spotlight. We drew on the phases of family business learning we described in our previous book (Moores and Barrett, 2002) and Curimbaba's (2002) typology of women's roles in family firms. Because family firms have been characterised as adopting clan-like behaviours, we also drew on the community of practice literature, especially Wenger (1999, 2000) to discern patterns in what learning in family business means. This chapter summarises the experiences of the whole sample, underlining how the distinctive aspects of family business influenced interviewees' approach to leadership and entrepreneurship, sometimes helping, sometimes hindering their aspirations.

SAME LEARNING PHASES, NEW LEARNING JOURNEYS

Chapter 1 outlines how the present study was prompted by our interest in revisiting our earlier findings about the phases of learning family business, findings based on a sample mainly of male family firm leaders. Chapter 2 examines empirical evidence from countries worldwide that suggest that men's and women's entrepreneurship activities and profile vary according to factors in the entrepreneurial environment. We speculated that, because of the ways family businesses serve as training grounds for future entrepreneurs, and the ways the special characteristics of family businesses can lead to sustainable competitive advantage, having a family business background could further influence these environmental factors. We know that these factors, though universal, can affect female and male entrepreneurs differently, so we wanted to look closely at how a family business perspective could inform issues in women's entrepreneurship and leadership generally.

The family business leaders we spoke to during that earlier study—and many more afterwards—said that they felt our sequence of learning phases was 'a good model'. They meant both that the 'learning phases' model aptly described what was important for them in achieving leadership, and also that the learning phases represented what they thought would be a suitably direct path for a person being groomed for family firm leadership. They agreed, for example, that future family firm leaders needed to 'go outside' to learn business, especially the personal disciplines, despite the risk to family business continuity. They then needed to 'learn our business', by returning to the family firm to learn what was distinctive about their family firm in particular, and the 'value of family business values' in general. They agreed that leading the family firm meant achieving insights into self, family and business, so that the leader could develop the family enterprise. Finally, leaders had to learn to let go the family firm. The question arose: would these ideas still hold up when we considered women's experiences?

At one level, our earlier findings did hold up. Interviews with family business women confirmed our original view that there were four broad tasks involved in learning family business. Participants readily recognised their attempts at managing the paradoxes inherent in each learning phase, and often pointed to how they were trying to help members of the next generation cope with them. Nevertheless, participants varied in the extent to which they thought they had achieved the phases, especially as a planned sequence, or thought they were likely to complete them. This led us to discern five broad groups of family business learners, whose experiences each formed the subject of one chapter.

Stumbling into the Spotlight: Brenda and Deborah (Chapter 4)

Brenda and Deborah managed, led and exited from a major family firm. They both then handed on its leadership to a successor, the only participants in our sample to have done this. Thus they completed all four family business learning phases (L1–L4). However, they did not necessarily pass through each phase in the order predicted by our original model. They did not seek the leadership spotlight; rather, the spotlight found them. We labelled this journey 'disordered learning'.

Building Their Own Stage: Jane, Miriam, Nancy and Ellen (Chapter 5)

These four all had some previous exposure to a business background. They all started and successfully managed their own new venture—each of which was a family firm by intent. So they completed the learning phases L1–L3. However, they had not yet needed to deal with the practical detail of family business succession. They built their own stage and sought out the leadership spotlight, but then sometimes had trouble learning to manage and control it. We labelled this journey 'learning while building'.

Directing the Spotlight Elsewhere: Gloria and Cass (Chapter 6)

Gloria and Cass, both from family business backgrounds, learned business (L1) and also mastered the intricacies of an existing, successful family firm. They also started and led separate new ventures. Thus, like the 'stage builders' of Chapter 5, they completed the L1–L3 learning phases. However, they differ from the stage builders by exercising leadership and entrepreneurship skills in a firm started by a close family member (father and husband, respectively). Their approach to managing the leadership spotlight could hardly be more different from the first two groups: they deliberately directed it away from themselves and towards other people. We labelled this journey 'learning while directing'.

Table 9.1 Participants' Completed Family Business Learning Stages

Participant	Learning Business (L1)	Learning Our Business (L2)	Learning to Lead Our Business (L3)	Learning to Let Go Our Business (L4)
Brenda	✓	✓	✓	✓
Deborah	✓	✓	✓	✓
Jane	✓	✓	✓	
Miriam	✓	✓	✓	
Nancy	✓	✓	✓	
Ellen	✓	✓	✓	
Gloria	✓	✓	✓	
Cass	✓	✓	✓	
Ingrid	✓	✓	[✓]	
Robyn	✓	✓	[✓]	
Hannah	✓	✓		
Sue	✓	✓		
Felicity	✓	[✓]		

Note: A ✓ indicates that the family business learning phase had been successfully completed and acknowledged as such within the firm which was the main topic of discussion in the interview. Brackets [ ] indicate that the particular learning phase was not yet complete.

Coping with Shadows: Ingrid and Robyn (Chapter 7)

These two participants succeeded to CEO roles in firms started by their father and mother, respectively. They completed the L1 and L2 learning stages (learning business and learning our business), but both were still coping with the shadows of their predecessors. While they were well on the way to learning to lead (L3); particularly Robyn, they were yet to prove themselves as leaders and entrepreneurs over the long term. With greater or lesser confidence, they were emerging from the wings and finding their way to centre stage. We labelled this journey 'learning from the shadows'.

Becoming Invisible: Hannah, Sue and Felicity (Chapter 8)

These three participants were united by their experience of working in the family firm, yet were blocked from its leadership. At most, they completed the L1 and L2 family business learning phases. While once they might have hoped to occupy the spotlight, they were increasingly pushed back into the shadows. We labelled this journey 'missed learning'.

Table 9.1 summarises our findings about the phases of learning our participants completed.

FEATURES OF THE NEW LEARNING JOURNEYS

Our participants' experiences echoed the original four phases of family business learning and suggested variations on them. The next section considers the variations more closely, to see what propositions they suggest about women's learning for family business leadership.

Learning Business (L1)

Proposition 1: Women May Have to Go 'Further Outside' than Men

According to the learning phases model, family firm leaders first have to go outside to learn business. For men, 'going outside' typically means working in a firm in the same or a similar industry to the family firm. Occasionally, if the family firm is large, this might mean working in and developing a new division of the family firm. In our earlier study of male leaders, only one interviewee had worked in a markedly different industry to that of the family firm he eventually came to lead.

This aspect of the L1 learning phase was frequently different for women in our sample. While women in our sample also 'go outside' the family business, none had gained experience in an industry similar to the one in which she eventually led a firm or hoped to lead one. The hotel business, academic studies in history and politics, a psychology practice, the police service, working as a sewing demonstrator in a department store, were among the places interviewees gained 'outside' experience. Consequently, our sample suggests women may have less opportunity than men to learn business in an 'outside' firm or organisation which is similar enough to the family firm for it to function as a close learning community.

Proposition 2: Women Still 'Swim Upstream'

The value of the non-family learning environment for learning business is that it is often a more forgiving context, where the learner can experiment and make mistakes, compared to the family firm. Learners go outside the family firm so they will be well equipped to come back and lead it.

Women in our sample also differed on this aspect of the original model. Several female interviewees who started their own firms, such as Miriam, Sue, Hannah and Nancy, did so at least partly because they were discouraged from envisaging a long-term future as a leader in their original family firms. Others, such as Ellen, had absorbed a general message that business was not suitable for women. Ingrid had still other reasons to be reluctant to join the family firm. Despite being fed up with working in the hotel industry where she learned fundamental personal and functional business disciplines, Ingrid disliked the prospect of having to deal with family conflict in the business setting. For all these interviewees, going outside to learn business felt like swimming upstream.

Learning Our Business (L2)

Proposition 3: Women May Continue the Family Firm 'Even More Differently'

The second (L2) learning phase in our original model requires the potential leader to come back to the family firm to learn what makes their business special, even unique. This entails the paradox of 'continuing the family firm differently': developing it in new directions while respecting and reinforcing its fundamental values.

Some women in our sample took the task of 'continuing differently' much further than men. Rather than simply reinforcing an existing firm's fundamental values and philosophies with some variations in its practices, Jane, Miriam, Nancy, Ellen, Gloria, Cass and Ingrid either tried to create and bed down a new set of firm values in an entirely new firm, or else tried to change the existing family firm's values and practices radically. They often tried to create businesses whose values and practices they would like to have learned, rather than recreate the family businesses they observed as they were growing up.

Were the new values participants tried to create prompted by their intention to create or continue a 'family' business? The answer may be yes, but 'familiness' manifested itself in varying ways in our sample. It sometimes meant interviewees' new ventures were run on 'softer', ostensibly 'female' management lines compared to the interviewees' original family firms or others they observed. Brenda and Deborah were committed to this softer approach. Brenda asked her staff to help her develop solutions to business problems, and Deborah treated her staff like family, to the point of 'mollycoddling' them, according to one of her daughters. In the terms of Miller and Le Breton-Miller's (2005) model of 'enduring family firm characteristics', Brenda and Deborah tried to develop the priority of community in their firms, creating a nurturing ambience which supported people to take initiative and collaborate on solving problems. However, our sample also contained other approaches which do not suggest a 'softer' approach. Cass and Sue strove to create more transparent and systematic approaches to managing their firms. Gloria wanted to lift the performance of her father's firm and tried to remove people she considered an obstacle to this goal. In their view, the family firms they joined suffer from an excess of community, which produced the downside of family firms: insularity, lack of transparency and nepotism. These contrasting approaches tend to confirm the yet-to-be-defined status of the global construct, familiness.

While Brenda and Deborah tried to increase the positive aspects of community in their firm, and Cass and Sue tried to reduce its negative aspects, all insisted that their management approaches differed from those exercised by powerful men in their firms. Cass pointed to how she encouraged consultation, compared to her husband's unilateral decision-making; Sue fought to increase the level of transparency in a firm run by a cabal of male leaders, some of whom who were in the firm for more than thirty years. These women, by 'continuing the firm differently', sought to incorporate their experience in other business or public sector organisations with established corporate disciplines, rather than necessarily adhering to a 'soft', so-called 'female' management style.

Proposition 4: Managing Risk and Legitimacy are Part of 'Continuing the Firm Differently'

Our participants often saw managing risk and legitimacy as part of how they continued the family firm differently, sometimes very differently, from how they saw an earlier firm being managed.

Members' approach to risk is also linked to how they deal with familiness. Two examples, Gloria and Miriam, illustrate this. Gloria was never very concerned about risk during her time with her father's firm; she was prepared to spend much larger sums on marketing exhibitions than her father was. To her, being a risk-taker was part of a certain 'wildness' in her personality, the same quality that led her to leave her Hong Kong and go to the US alone at an early age, play extreme sports and so on. In her father's firm, this wildness helped 'continue the family firm differently'. She believed she had to transcend her father's naturally modest and retiring nature to develop the firm he started. Regardless, Gloria also appreciated and respected the family firm's core competencies in engineering and innovation. These are an equally important aspect of many family firms' continuity (Miller and Le Breton-

Miller, 2005, p. 520). Gloria saw her high-risk, expensive marketing efforts as complementing, rather than replacing, these capacities.

Outwardly, Gloria's approach to risk looks different from Miriam's, who deliberately kept a low-profile firm. But Miriam's approach is also consistent with a resource building approach. Miller and Le Breton-Miller (2005) point out that great family firms focus on decades-long time horizons and avoid elaborate offices, expense account luxuries and so on. Miriam exemplified this approach in her firm, avoiding flashy spending on glamour events or luxurious premises, even though this was normal for the industry. She preferred to justify expenditure in terms of value offered to customers. Ironically, since she was unlikely ever to run the original family firm, Miriam was more committed than her father to this aspect of building familiness resources. Despite her aversion to unnecessary spending, she was still 'fundamentally relaxed' about taking risks, and attributed this to her family business background, where she became accustomed to living with changing business cycles.

New firms need to establish legitimacy in the external world during their early stages of operation before they achieve the 'natural' legitimacy that comes with profitability (Zimmerman and Zeitz, 2002). So the problem of achieving institutional legitimacy is not peculiar to women. Nevertheless, the women in our sample often suffered from insufficient internal, personal legitimacy. This occurred for several reasons. Women in our sample were less likely than men in our earlier study to have gained outside experience in a firm based in the same or a similar industry as the family firm (for example, Brenda, Deborah, Cass and Robyn). Sometimes, as with Miriam, they were subtly (or not-so-subtly) removed from the list of possible successors to the family firm. Ingrid left getting a formal qualification in business until her mid-forties. As well as the usual problems of external legitimacy at firm level, women frequently have difficulty representing themselves inside their present firm as people qualified to lead it.

Even women with the 'right' qualifications from an external perspective may be denied personal legitimacy inside it. Cass, for example, found her substantial corporate experience reduced her internal legitimacy instead of enhancing it. It ran too far against the culture of informality that characterised the firm, and which many employees saw as part of its family nature. Some interviewees, such as Ingrid, Sue and Felicity, had more than one personal legitimacy deficit, as well as a simple lack of personal confidence in their capacity to run a large firm.

Women in our sample often tried to achieve institutional and personal legitimacy simultaneously. Jane developed a business plan for her new publishing firm. While it later seemed embarrassingly amateurish, the plan reminded Jane that she was a business person, which gave her confidence and a sense of her place in the firm as its leader. Simultaneously, her mentor

Simon introduced her to important industry players and firms outside the firm. This allowed Jane to learn the process of publishing a book as quickly as possible and gave her some external legitimacy in the industry. Brenda and Ingrid also demonstrated their personal seriousness (and their firms') by getting certifications for their firm and endorsement of their personal achievements from outside entities such as network dealers.

Proposition 5: Mentors Present Special Issues for Family Business Women

The value of mentors for women with corporate leadership aspirations is well established in the literature on women's career development in business (see for example, Donaldson et al., 2000; Ensher and Murphy, 2005; Ensher et al., 2000; Noe, 1988). Because women may have fewer opportunities than men to gain business experience outside the family firm, mentors inside the firm may be even more important for them. However, mentors may present dangers. The academic and popular business advice literature indicate both advantages and disadvantages to women of having a mentor of the same or the other sex, who works in the same or a different firm, whose own corporate fortunes may decline, with the result that their association with the person they mentor becomes a political hazard (Berfield, 2007; Ensher and Murphy, 2005). A major requirement for a good mentor is that they have both adequate distance and objectivity from their protégé and her firm, as well as a capacity to understand the detail of the protégé's situation.

Along with these general mentoring problems, there are some special ones for family business women who aspire to leadership. The better mentors for women in family business are people who work in the firm, rather than outside it. Jane's mentor, Simon, was a kind of one-person MBA. He steered Jane quickly, yet methodically, through the practicalities of learning business, and also pushed her towards the contacts she needed to establish the firm. He then stayed on in the firm for years to help her as new issues arose. Such a mentor is rare, as Jane knew. For Gloria, Dr Lu was almost as good a source of information and guidance as her father. He was not threatened by Jane's rapid advancement and flamboyant approach—rare in family firms where insiders and outsiders often feel they each have much to lose from the presence of the other (Blumentritt et al., 2007).

Both Simon and Dr Lu guided their protégés through the first three learning stages of family business. Jane and Gloria were successful leaders of their own ventures by time we met them, and both acknowledged their mentor's role in getting them to that point. Their experience contrasts with Brenda's, who never had a mentor, either inside or outside the firm. Consequently, she never felt confident enough to 'tell those bastards she was on top of this', even when her firm was profitable for many years.

The special qualities of Jane's and Gloria's mentors may have arisen because they were 'in' but not 'of' the family firm. They were firmly entrenched inside it (Simon was Jane's business partner and Dr Lu was Gloria's father's most trusted employee), and yet they had no personal career stake in the business, which might have interfered with the protégé's personal ambitions. Simon had already achieved prominence over a long business career, and did not need to make his name through the firm he started with Jane. Dr Lu entered the firm many years before Gloria did, and was content to help her. This made Simon and Dr Lu both able and trustworthy mentors.

Importantly, these exemplary mentors were not family members. In our participants' experience, family members presented problems as well as solutions when they mentored someone in the next generation. Only Robyn's mother, Deborah, and Gloria's father, were both senior enough in the firm and close enough to their protégés to know what learning experiences their daughters needed, and to give them the leeway they needed to develop. Gloria's father let her learn how to manage risk. In refusing to sack someone Gloria thought was an underperformer, he also gave her a short, sharp lesson in building familiness. Robyn was mentored by her mother over a period of 17 years. While Deborah took a long time to hand on the leadership, she and Robyn were both confident in Robyn's abilities when she finally did so. Even Brenda, who had an excellent way of working with staff, knew she had not passed on this skill to her son.

Less helpful founders can present as many problems and dangers to women in family firms as some mentors in non-family business settings. Ingrid's father was capricious and created rivalries among the members of the next generation in order to play them off against each other. Felicity's father set up Felicity as head of a division, but rapidly shifted his attention to new projects. As Dumas (1989) found, these types of fathers are often unaware of their daughters' ambitions and do not use enough of their talents.

Outside advisers or consultants may also act as mentors to family business women. However, this usually only lasts a short time: an outsider's position in the firm is often not secure enough for their advice to be available for long. Keith, the consultant Sue persuaded her father to hire, is an example. He and Sue made considerable headway in improving the firm's systems, research and development and marketing, but Sue's father could not finally deal with these changes. Ingrid also found one of her father's consultants helpful at both a personal and professional level, but he, like the others, left within a few months.

Another way to 'learn our business' (L2) is to be your own mentor, to take charge of your own learning of the business. One aspect of this is simply to accept, like Jane, that one is in business. While this may be obvious, several women in our sample avoided the issue. Deborah, for example, established a nationwide business, but referred to it as 'this thing I'm creating', even while she was planning its succession process. Deborah was unwilling to accept that she created, if not an empire, then a major corporate entity. Perhaps this reticence is a way some women manage their own and others' doubts about whether they are equal to the task. Other participants, for example, Jane, Miriam and Gloria, recognised early that they were business people, not hobbyists or minor players. By acting as serious players they convinced themselves, other industry players and even their families, who sometimes saw the firms as 'just Mum's business', to take them and their enterprises seriously. Still others, such as Cass and Robyn, managed their own initial lack of confidence by waiting for an invitation from the acknowledged leader to be active in the firm. This led them to more senior leadership roles.

Learning to Lead Our Business (L3)

Proposition 6: Developing Insights Means Grasping 'Familiness'

The third phase of learning family business is learning to lead it; that is, take a helicopter view of the firm, especially its stage of development in the business life-cycle, in order to plan its strategy. In a family business, leadership requires 'informal formality': the capacity to combine the attributes of familiness, especially informality, with the increased formality of systems and processes usually needed to expand and professionalise the firm.

Women, no less than men, need to deal with the formal informality of leadership in the family firm—the special demands created by the firm's qualities of 'familiness'. Managing 'familiness' includes dealing with the firm's sense of its mission, developing its caring culture, its outside connections and its capacity for adaptive courageous decisions—and where necessary, curtailing the downsides of these same priorities (Miller and Le Breton-Miller, 2005). The interviewees who completed the first three learning phases typically focused on at least one or more of these priorities, even if they could not always further them in the way they wanted.

Some interviewees, especially if their leadership was still being tested or was frustrated, had to cope with the downsides of familiness. For example, Nancy, Gloria, Ingrid and Sue were impressed by the sense of a 'mission that matters' when they joined the family firm, especially its reputation for quality, innovation and service. Such a sense of mission is a typical part of a family firm's strength through continuity (Miller and Le Breton-Miller, 2005). Sue, who saw her father's firm focus on quality and innovation at the expense of marketing, worried about this and tried to counter the firm's tendency to stagnate. Brenda, Deborah, Robyn and Cass each maintained their firm's caring culture, but Cass needed to avoid the secretiveness and nepotism—with their accompanying agency costs—which come with too much or the wrong kind of caring. Robyn went beyond caring, focusing on streamlining the firm's systems as much as looking after the staff. Brenda, Jane, Miriam and Ellen (via her husband) cultivated outside connections to legitimise the firm in its industry, but Miriam insisted these connections not be through the original family firm. Jane, Nancy and Ingrid wrestled with their firms' need to change, Jane because her partner was ill and the industry was changing, Nancy because her business partner was about to leave.

These 'familiness' concerns are the same as they would be for men. However, because interviewees usually took a circuitous path to leadership, they did not find it easy to take a helicopter view immediately. They first needed to establish their position in the firm, sometimes against a hostile environment. For them, leading the firm first meant fathoming and then managing its more inscrutable aspects, such as its history and its political undercurrents.

Proposition 7: Women Use Visibility and Tactical Invisibility to Lead

Women leaders in our sample either made important issues visible to everyone in the firm: opening up issues, pointing to problems, and producing, measuring and sharing results. We saw this 'make it visible' approach with Brenda, Deborah, Jane, Gloria, Cass, Miriam and Ellen. Some combined this approach with a participative style of problem-solving or a nurturing approach to staff. Such leaders usually place themselves in the leadership spotlight to do this, inviting scrutiny of themselves as leaders as well as the firm's performance. However, this does not work—or is extremely difficult— if the culture of the family firm is not receptive to such openness. If people in the firm prefer not to read the evidence or, to use Ingrid's terms, 'hear the reality', the would-be leader put forward, then she was unlikely to succeed. The experiences of Ingrid and Sue point to this. Ingrid spent years disentangling the firm's structure from its family issues, and was still engaged with this task when we interviewed her. Her success was still hanging in the balance. Sue tried to create a new openness in the firm's decision-making processes, and indicated this symbolically by refurbishing the premises using lots of glass and open spaces where before there were dark corridors and small rooms. But her efforts were ultimately unsuccessful.

An alternative approach is its opposite, 'tactical invisibility': working behind the scenes using intangible aspects of the firm, such as stories, ideas— and even family history—to bring about change. Cass and Robyn are examples. Both worked themselves quietly into positions of leadership before they were recognised as such. Cass never allowed herself to be named as a leader. Others, like Gloria, worked with both approaches. Inside the family firm, Gloria was aware of the need to get her father to notice her performance. The strategy worked: she created record-breaking sales and neglected no possible avenue to promote the firm to potential customers. In turn she was promoted and was allocated staff to help her keep producing results. However, in other respects, and especially to the external world, she remained deliberately invisible, promoting her father as a self-made man. In many cases, where the firm founder is a close relative, such as a father or a husband, aspiring leaders prefer not to stress their achievements or their leadership role, believing this only leads to problems.

Learning to Let Go Our Business (L4)

Proposition 8: Succeeding with Succession is Similar for Women and Men

'Letting go our business' means dealing with the classic family business dilemma: succession. The leader must manage the paradox of leading with a view to no longer being a leader, and working out how to manage a relationship with the family firm after their retirement.

Few interviewees had to deal with this stage: only Brenda and Deborah had truly moved through it. They had long since overcome their early internal legitimacy problems and did not hesitate to use their authority to dictate how firm ownership would be transferred to the next generation. Their experience of succession, good and bad, most closely resembles the learning experience of men in our earlier study: they experienced similar problems and reached for much the same solutions as they worked out how to manage their relationship with the firm after retirement. Brenda, for example, adopted an ambassadorial role in the business her son took over and kept it in the public eye. This is typical of the strategies we observed in our earlier sample of male leaders, and is yet another variation on a 'make it visible' strategy.

Others in our sample gave 'letting go' a lot of thought. They wanted their businesses to continue in the family, provided their children showed the appropriate aptitude and interest. Our participants sometimes started working out how this interest might be encouraged. The intention to continue the firm as a family firm is at the heart of the 'essence' approach to defining family business. Direct evidence of how our participants would handle this final leadership stage is necessarily limited. Nevertheless, however circuitous women's route through the learning stages may prove, provided they pass through enough phases successfully, women and men are likely to handle succession in similar ways.

LEARNING PHASES AND LEARNING COMMUNITY STRATEGIES

Analysing the four phases of learning family business shows that family business women who get to the top follow a tortuous route. Following the phases of our original model in sequence was a rarity, not the norm. Wenger's communities of practice framework complements the learning phases framework, bypassing its sequential aspects—the *when* of learning—in favour of the *how*: the belongingness, boundary or identity management strategies with which leaders develop and sustain their family businesses as learning communities.

Table 9.2 Managing Interviewees' Family Firms as Learning Communities

Name	Learning Phases	Defining Events, Projects or Principles	Learning Strategy
Brenda	1 2 3 4	Catastrophic entry into firm leadership; success through sharing problems with staff	Engagement
Deborah	1 2 3 4	'Visionary' start-up, recent handover of her creation	Imagination
Jane	1 2 3	Mentoring, preparing first business plan as a sign of growing professionalism; fears responsibility when hiring first employee	Alignment
Miriam	1 2 3	Creating a separate firm from original family business	Defines boundaries
Nancy	1 2 3	Commitment to combining creativity and professionalism	Imagination, alignment
Ellen	1 2 3	Hiring first employee teaches her the need to delegate; husband's presence decreases her visible leadership	Alignment
Gloria	1 2 3	Stages an expensive exhibition of new machines, marketing strategy based on 'packaging Dad'	Imagination
Cass	1 2 3	Entering the firm at her husband's invitation, introduces external corporate disciplines	Identity, alignment
Ingrid	1 2 (3)	Launches new vision statement, strategic plans, revises job descriptions	Imagination, alignment
Robyn	1 2 (3)	Solves problems together with staff, implements new systems, develops franchising operations	Engagement, alignment

continued overleaf...

Table 9.2 continued...

Name	Learning Phases	Defining Events, Projects or Principles	Learning Strategy
Hannah	1 2	Barred from succession despite special expertise in family business	Maintains boundaries
Sue	1 2	Refurbishes family business premises to reflect the firm's new 'open' culture	Maintains identity and boundaries
Felicity	1 (2)	Naming of the new division; counselling role with potential customers	Identity

All learning communities need input from all three basic belongingness strategies: engagement, imagination and alignment (Wenger, 1999, 2002). However, one of these three may dominate in a particular learning community, producing a characteristic style of belonging to it. In addition, or alternatively, strategies for managing a particular community of practice may focus on the community's boundaries or how knowledge is defined through the community's identity. The next section draws together our observations about the strategies which dominated participants' learning communities, and compares them with the family business learning phases they completed.

Table 9.2 summarises our findings and links what we discovered about interviewees' learning phases (column 2) with one (or occasionally more than one) defining learning event, project or principle each interviewee mentioned in her interview (column 3). Taken together, these reflect her main approach to managing learning in the family firm (column 4). For Hannah, Sue and Felicity, who did not attain firm leadership, the firm's learning strategy is the one they saw as dominant in the family firm they belonged to, not necessarily the one they would have chosen themselves. Sue, for example, sought to create a shared sense of purpose and introduce conventional marketing practices to the firm, a typical alignment strategy. However, she was thwarted by the firm's strong sense of its identity and capacity to maintain its current boundaries.

The distinctive aspects of the five groups of family business women we discerned earlier are also evident when we consider how the phases of learning they have completed relate to the learning community strategies they adopted, or in some cases, were subject to.

Stumbling into the Spotlight

Brenda and Deborah, who handed on their firms to a successor, completed all four family business learning stages (Moores and Barrett, 2002). However, the way they arrived in their firms—stumbling into the spotlight—influenced the learning processes in them.

Brenda's willingness to work on problems with staff (learning strategy: engagement) increased her staff's learning. Her greatest pleasure, she told us, was when a former staff member let her know that something he learned while he was employed with her stood him in good stead later in his career. In contrast, Deborah focused mainly on imagination: developing a vision of 'this thing' she created, and what it might mean for her children's futures.

Building Their Own Stage

Jane, Miriam, Nancy and Ellen each learned leadership in the firms they started themselves, but had not yet dealt with succession.

All four kept their community of practice small, as a way of maintaining control and containing costs. Some, like Miriam, worked with associates, rather than dealing with the expense and potential loss of flexibility that comes with adding more members to the learning community proper. Miriam's major learning strategy, from a community of practice perspective, was to manage the community's boundaries. She kept her firm strictly separate from the original family firm, but maintained boundaries permeable enough to allow learning associations with other firms.

Jane, Nancy and Ellen recalled the excitement and sense of opportunity they felt when they first started their own firms. However, at other times, such as when they hired their first employees or wrote their first business plan, they had mixed feelings. Jane worried whether she might not be seen as up to the leadership task of looking after someone else's future. Ellen was concerned that staff's perceptions of her husband's role might mean they believed she did not really control the firm. Jane's and Nancy's strategies focused on alignment from the outset, creating a shared purpose and presenting a professional face to the world. Nancy was contemplating solo leadership after a long period with a partner. She would need to devise a new view of her firm and its profile; in Wenger's terms, she would need to imagine it differently. Ellen, like Jane and Nancy, also adopted an alignment learning strategy, albeit somewhat later, when her husband entered the firm.

Directing the Spotlight Elsewhere

Gloria and Cass are linked by the way they pointed the spotlight at others, instead of themselves. Gloria achieved record sales figures, but this personal achievement was not as important to her as creating a corporate romance focused on someone else: her father and his early days of struggle. In Wenger's terms, Gloria uses a classic imagination strategy.

Cass' defining event was her husband inviting her to join the family firm, which she did in order to bring its management into line with more contemporary corporate practices. In Wenger's terms, she wanted to align the family firm with the practices of the outside world. However, her commitment to corporate practices ran counter to the identity of the firm, so Cass sought to identify her strategies with the main figure on whom this identity rested: her husband. Hence, Cass combined alignment and identity strategies.

Coping with Shadows

Ingrid and Robyn both formally took over the leadership of their existing family firms, but their leadership results were still untested over the long term. As the new CEO, Ingrid focused on figuring out new job descriptions as well as launching a new mission statement and strategic plan, all of which gave the firm a chance to imagine itself more formally as a business entity, rather than as a firm riven by family conflict. She achieved certification by the firm's network dealer, a typical alignment strategy. After such extended family conflicts, she hoped these imagination and alignment activities would create a sense of a shared purpose and a commitment to accountability among members of the firm. Robyn had always found ways for people to work together on problems, an engagement strategy. Following the handover from her mother, Robyn took on alignment projects: implementing systems, expanding the number of offices and franchising the firm.

Becoming Invisible

Hannah, Sue and Felicity found that leadership eluded them. Even though they were more or less resigned to this, the events and projects they remembered most strongly invoked how they were blocked from a role which would match their aspirations to contribute to their learning communities. The dominant strategies for learning in their firms were put in place by someone else, usually the CEO.

Hannah's father maintained the boundaries of his firm to resist possible incursions from in-laws: outsiders who might have gained undue influence in the firm after marrying the CEO's daughter. In Sue's family firm, knowledge was defined by the firm's identity with its engineering history and its reputation for quality. The overriding strength of this identity, which focused on the current CEO, scuppered Sue's plans to shift the firm's attention towards better marketing and more transparent decision-making. Felicity's family firm was likewise built on its identity, as evidenced by how much the family name figured in its marketing strategies. Felicity headed a division based on the family name but, ironically, this meant she was absorbed into the family firm's identity to the detriment of her own learning.

Healthy Learning Communities By and For Women

Linking our participants' learning phases with the learning strategies that predominated in their family firms suggests that no single way of managing a learning community, its belongingness modes, its boundaries or its identity, is the key to managing its learning. Belongingness strategies were important for many in our sample. They included engagement, or working on projects together to further firm learning, as for Brenda and Robyn. Deborah and Nancy preferred to create belongingness through imagination: projecting their idea of how their firms might be, and using this to unify the firm's members. Gloria, who packaged her father's story, actually imagined a new vision of the past. Alignment approaches were also prominent for Jane, Cass, Nancy and Ingrid, who tried to create both an internal sense of shared purpose and a professional approach to management which would bring their family firm into line with the wider corporate world.

A community's boundaries and its identity also matter. Miriam led less by creating belongingness than by managing the firm's boundaries. This meant keeping them sufficiently closed to maintain the firm's separate identity, but also permeable enough to allow members to come and go as the firm's skill requirements demanded. Cass also could not create real belongingness only by aligning the firm with standard business practices in the external corporate world, or at least she could not do so directly. Her plans for running the firm along more contemporary corporate lines created alienation among the staff, rather than a sense of belonging. She needed to work through her husband, the focus of the firm's identity.

Despite how these examples show the breadth of ways that family business women can nurture and be nurtured by their family business communities, we can posit some things that are likely to make both tasks easier. As before, we put these forward as a series of propositions.

Proposition 9: Healthy Learning Communities Give Women a Home Base

Wenger (2000, p. 241) points out that members of learning communities need a clearly defined home base if they are to experience knowing as a form of social competence. Our results suggest that this applies equally to women in family businesses. Several interviewees made sure they established a home base for their firm which separated it from their original family business. This was partly to prove that their own business, with its different values, style and knowledge, had a viable separate existence. It also countered their disappointment at being excluded from a senior role in the original firm.

Proposition 10: Healthy Learning Communities Remind Women Where They Have Been

As well as a home base, women need to understand how they have come to be where they are, if they are to be assured of their own competence. In Wenger's terms, they need a sense of their 'learning trajectory' (Wenger, 2000, p. 241). Rather than something static, a healthy identity in a community of practice allows its members to bring the past and the future into the experience of the present. Like the business plan Jane kept in a desk drawer and looked at occasionally, a learning trajectory shows how much you and the community have learned together. Women in family business often lack this evidence, due to their more haphazard path into the firm and the uncertainties about their competence being recognised.

Proposition 11: Healthy Learning Communities Back Women's Learning (Experience) with Legitimacy (Competence)

Most women in our sample were adept at using skills that were not closely linked to the service or product their firm offered. These included domestic skills and skills learned in unrelated industries. However, in social learning terms (Wenger, 1999, 2000), these are the skills of experience, rather than the skills of competence. As such, they leave women vulnerable: others in the community are likely to see them as insufficiently knowledgeable to lead it. Some family business women even take this view themselves. For their skills to be acknowledged as sufficient for membership, even leadership of the community of practice requires them to back their learning with some form of legitimacy.

Proposition 12: Healthy Learning Communities Have Front and Back Doors

The previous proposition suggests that women need to know where the 'front door' to leadership is located—the formal skills that serve as indicators of competence—and whether less formal skills might be substituted. For example, is formal or informal learning valued in the family firm? How might women acquire informal but valued skills by networking with other learning communities? Are membership or leadership criteria valued differently in the firm for men and women, and if so, how might women overcome these differences? As actual or potential leaders, how might they change the informal membership criteria for future members or leaders?

Proposition 13: Healthy Learning Communities Support Women's Multiple Identities

Wenger makes the point that healthy learning communities support their members' various identities: 'one ought to be able to sustain one's identity as a waitress, a theatre fan and a parent as well as a member of a learning community' (Wenger, 2000, p. 242). Interviewees' experiences indicate that family firms also need to support women's multiple identities. Many commentators reflect on the 'double burden' of women's domestic responsibilities, which they carry in addition to their professional responsibilities. However, something even more complex and difficult happens for some family business women who are mothers. The meaning of their role in the family business may change when they have children, and this creates special problems. As Felicity discovered, and as Nancy, Hannah and even Miriam feared to some extent, they may be perceived as important primarily because they have produced the next generation, rather than because they contribute to the family business in their own right. Healthy family firms allow women to sustain their role in the firm independently of their role as mothers. Real flexibility should facilitate the development of multiple identities for family business women. Nevertheless, as Dugan et al. (2008) point out, even flexibility must be handled with care and wisdom. While it 'sounds like the perfect solution to so many issues of work/life balance it is not always the answer family businesses look for. In fact it's pretty complicated... it can raise some thorny issues...' (Dugan et al., 2008, p. 49). Marilyn Carlson Nelson, writing in her mid-60s, said: 'What I know now is that women can actually come pretty close to having it all, but you just can't have it all every day. It may need to be sequenced' (Dugan et al., 2008, p. 57).

EXTENDING WOMEN'S FAMILY FIRM ROLES

Chapter 3 outlines Curimbaba's findings about how the various roles women ('heiresses') occupy in family firms affect their visibility as family business managers. In a study in which she implicitly used a 'components of involvement' definition of family business, Curimbaba (2002) found that women occupied three roles: the anchor, the professional and the invisible. These roles are largely determined by structural factors, such as birth order and number of males in the family. Women do not necessarily stay in one role, but may move between them.

In the light of our 'essence' approach to family business, where the intention to continue the family firm is the defining factor, we needed a way of incorporating the experiences of first-generation female leaders of family firms, women who created new entities—not only women who were managers in second or later generation firms started and run by a male forebear. By definition, this meant we needed to go beyond Curimbaba's structural factors, such as birth order or number of males present in a particular generation. Because we included women who had started new firms (independent entrepreneurship), and also because some women in our sample had moved into roles where they undertook innovation in an existing firm (corporate entrepreneurship), we added another role to Curimbaba's original three: the entrepreneur role.

Table 9.3 links our participants' completed phases of family business learning (column 2), with the dominant approach to managing learning in their family firms (column 3). It also links these results with our findings about participants' firm roles. With our extension of Curimbaba's model, these roles can include that of entrepreneur (column 4). Column 4 also indicates whether entrepreneurs often function as independent entrepreneurs, corporate entrepreneurs or both.

Using Table 9.3 we can suggest some linkages between family business women's completed learning phases, their strategies for managing their learning communities and their roles in their firms.

Table 9.3 Participants' Learning Phases, Learning Strategies and Role

Name	Learning Phases	Learning Strategy	Family Firm Role: Anchor, Professional, Invisible or Entrepreneur
Brenda	1 2 3 4	Engagement	Anchor → independent entrepreneur following her husband's death
Deborah	1 2 3 4	Imagination	Independent entrepreneur
Jane	1 2 3	Alignment	Independent entrepreneur
Miriam	1 2 3	Defines boundaries	Independent entrepreneur (risks being seen as anchor in father's firm)
Nancy	1 2 3	Imagination, alignment	Independent entrepreneur
Ellen	1 2 3	Alignment	Independent entrepreneur (risks being seen as anchor while her husband is in the firm)
Gloria	1 2 3	Imagination	Professional → corporate entrepreneur (in her father's firm) → independent entrepreneur (starts her own firm)
Cass	1 2 3	Identity, alignment	Independent entrepreneur → professional → corporate entrepreneur (in husband's firm)
Ingrid	1 2 (3)	Imagination, alignment	Professional (aspiring to corporate entrepreneurship in father's firm)
Robyn	1 2 (3)	Engagement, alignment	Anchor → corporate entrepreneur (in mother's firm)

Hannah	1 2	Maintains identity and boundaries	Professional → invisible
Sue	1 2	Identity	Professional → invisible
Felicity	1 (2)	Identity	Anchor → invisible

Proposition 14: An 'Essence' Approach to Family Firms Makes Women's Entrepreneurship More Evident

Table 9.3 indicates that, if we take an 'essence' approach to family business; that is, if we allow for the possibility that new ventures may be family businesses 'by intent', the entrepreneur role figures very strongly in our sample. Many of our 13 participants occupied one or more of Curimbaba's anchor, invisible or professional roles at various times, but no less than ten also acted as entrepreneurs, whether starting new ventures or renewing existing firms. Comparing Table 9.3 with Table 3.2, we see that this finding partly reflects our sampling approach, where we selected both cases where we expected to find leadership and entrepreneurship, and 'stretch' cases which allowed us to see leadership and entrepreneurship in less obvious guises. Family business women who served as corporate entrepreneurs, introducing important innovations to an existing family firm and working to ensure its continuity, were among the corporate entrepreneurs. Some participants served both as independent and corporate entrepreneurs. However, not all firms our participants created were family firms by intent. Gloria and Cass both started their own firms either before they helped develop an existing family firm (as Cass did) or after this (as Gloria did). Yet neither Cass nor Gloria started these firms with the intention they would continue as family firms.

Proposition 15: Learning to Lead a Family Firm Enables Entrepreneurship

Table 9.3 suggests the more phases of learning family business a woman completes, the more likely she is to emerge as an entrepreneur. Specifically, all the participants in our sample who undertook either independent or corporate entrepreneurship completed at least the first three phases of family business learning. This includes the important phase of learning to lead a family firm, which provides a potential platform for a woman to act entrepreneurially. Such entrepreneurial functions can be undertaken within an existing family business (such as for Brenda or Robyn), by starting a new venture (Deborah, Miriam, Ellen or Nancy), or even both (Gloria or Cass). However, we offer a note of caution: as discussed earlier, women who learned to lead family businesses may have done so in a non-sequential, unpredictable way. This means they may have learned to lead and undertake other learning phases simultaneously. So, while they passed through the same learning phases, their learning journey may look different from one undertaken by a man. Consequently, women may be readier for entrepreneurship roles than they are given credit for by other members of the firm, particularly founders.

Proposition 16: Alignment Helps External Legitimacy

From column 3 and column 4 in Table 9.3, which summarise participants' learning strategies and family firm roles respectively, we see that no one learning community management strategy of the family business community would be sufficient to generate future entrepreneurial action. However, Table 9.3 shows that many entrepreneurs paid special attention to alignment. Alignment concerns ensuring that members of a community of practice feel a sense of shared purpose within the community, and also that the community's practices are commensurate with those of the wider world (Wenger, 1999, 2000). Focusing on alignment at an early stage of any entrepreneurial process might help both new ventures and existing corporate entities undergoing renewal to achieve greater external legitimacy.

Proposition 17: Anchors and Professionals may Become Entrepreneurs

Table 9.3 suggests that being an anchor creates no greater obstacle to becoming an entrepreneur than being a professional. This is clear if we compare the journeys of Brenda and Robyn, who both spent a long period as anchors, with the experience of Gloria, Cass and even Ingrid, who all took a professional view of their role in the family firm before taking on entrepreneurial tasks. At first this is a surprising result. Curimbaba (2002) suggests that professionals are more connected with the 'real world' of business. They enter the family firm in a deliberate way to pursue a personal opportunity and, having entered it, keep a close eye on their value in the marketplace. Finally, they are always concerned to find the 'right' or 'most meritorious' solutions to problems, without regard to organisational politics. In contrast, anchors appear less alert to their personal value to the family firm. They tend to 'just be there', never completely overlooked, but sometimes taken for granted. However, this is less surprising when we consider the reason some professionals in our sample originally entered the family firm.

We proposed just now that learning leadership in a family firm is a strong antecedent for entrepreneurship. Achieving recognition as a leader may be a smooth process (as it was for Robyn), or fraught with conflict (Ingrid). The difference depends largely on why the professional enters the firm in the first place. A professional such as Ingrid may enter the firm's management to solve a problem within the firm's family system, rather than its business system. Consequently, her leadership agenda—to create a smoothly functioning firm with a strategic plan and a viable vision for the future—was repeatedly postponed. In contrast, Robyn entered her mother's firm to work out her own life direction—and found it by working out new solutions to the firm's business problems. As a typical anchor, she was quietly working on this while her sisters were being assessed for their leadership potential and found wanting. Robyn achieved a considerable grasp of the family firm and its business issues. However, because she had to spend so much time and energy dealing with the family part of the system, Ingrid was still coming to grips with its business side.

Proposition 18: Invisibility Inhibits Entrepreneurship

Women who are pushed towards invisibility do not emerge as having the capacity to influence the family firm's general strategy or other aspects of its management. The final three participants, Hannah, Sue and Felicity, who were being pushed towards invisibility in the family firm, also had the lowest capacity to shift into an actual or potential position of leadership, and from there, towards entrepreneurial action. However, we should not confuse these three participants' involuntary and unwanted invisibility with the kind of deliberate way Gloria and Cass strategically deflect the leadership spotlight onto others in order to implement their entrepreneurial strategies.

CONCLUDING PROPOSITIONS

This study first aimed to understand whether and how family firms nurture and mobilise women's human capital resources within the business—to enhance women's leadership skills, but also to engender an entrepreneurial orientation in the firm. We also wanted to understand how women in a diverse sample of family firms promoted a learning orientation in the community to foster these outcomes. Figure 9.1 shows how we used and adapted the learning phases framework (Moores and Barrett, 2000), Wenger's (1999, 2000) community of practice framework and Curimbaba's typology of second and later-generation women's roles in family firms to explore the 'why', 'when' and 'how' of women's experiences of leadership and entrepreneurship in family firms.

Using Figure 9.1, we can draw the following concluding propositions:

- Women's family business learning reveals itself in how learning builds 'familiness', which in turn contributes to the family firm's sustainable competitive advantage.
- Women in family firms—like men—learn at various stages (when), and through the operation of community of practice dimensions (how), as they fulfil roles as entrepreneurs, anchors, professionals or invisibles, depending on the timing and content of their learning.

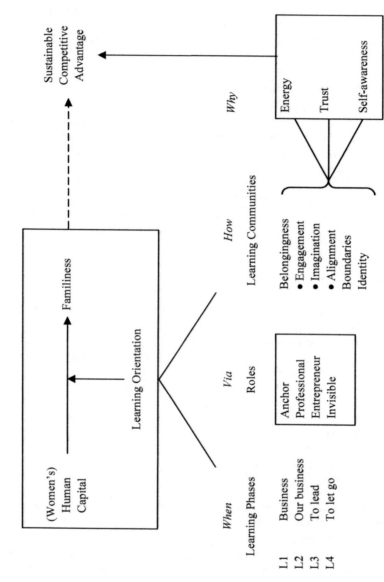

Figure 9.1 The Centrality of Learning Orientation to Building Familiness Resources

- Women of the controlling family in family firms nurture members' learning—and their own learning—when the family business encourages belongingness dimensions (engagement, imagination and alignment), and also when the firm achieves a healthy sense of its boundaries and its identity. These dimensions contribute to the firm's levels of energy, trust and self-awareness.

Recurring Themes and Future Research

Earlier parts of this book examine participants' individual stories in the context of their particular firms, and how those stories reveal the participants' experiences, philosophies and practices of leadership and entrepreneurship in family firms. This chapter summarises the wider themes emerging from the analysis and offers some propositions about how the family firm context shapes women's leadership and entrepreneurship. Future researchers may want to test these propositions using a larger sample, comparing women's firms with men's, firms in different industries, firms with greater or lesser degrees of 'familiness' and so on. Such research should yield valuable insights and provoke new debates. In anticipation of this, it is useful to draw together some themes that recurred in our propositions.

First, our propositions reinforce the growing conviction in the research community that there are more useful and valid research tasks than pursuing a quest to identify inherently 'male' or 'female' approaches to leadership and entrepreneurship. Some family business women in our sample used so-called 'female' management styles to deal with their firm's issues; others tackled similar problems using more conventional, apparently 'male' approaches. Dugan et al. (2008, pp. 19–40) list the following ways they have seen women can participate in their family businesses:

- financier
- innovator
- emergency leader
- back-room support
- nurturer of the next generation of leaders
- co-president
- a groomed CEO or senior executive
- business founder
- board chair
- family business board member
- owner/shareholder
- family leader

- family foundation leader
- individual philanthropist
- ambassador
- employee
- mentor.

They point out that their list is deliberately random because they 'want to avoid implying that one role is more important than another. Each is of value in its own way' (Dugan et al., 2008, p. 20). The list also supports our findings, in that it includes traditionally male as well as female roles. Other studies of entrepreneurial women and men, not focused on family business, are making similar findings. This suggests that there are more genuine, complex and interesting gender-related problems than attempting to find innate differences between women and men—and that these problems demand contextual explanations and solutions.

Second, our analytical approach, which explores social aspects of women's learning in family firms but avoids predetermined viewpoints about whether women and men are inherently different, allowed women's personal experience of leadership and entrepreneurship to emerge. Sometimes women's experiences were consistent with encountering and trying to overcome well-known structural barriers to individual advancement within an organisation. However, just as often, getting to leadership meant devising a personal way of doing things which brought the participant and other members of her organisation into a closer, more communal relationship. This result suggests it will continue to be important to investigate how leadership and entrepreneurship play out within organisational communities—not just how these roles present themselves as the personal dramas of individual women and men.

Finally, we saw how women dealt with the 'familiness' of family business: the 'except' in the phrase 'just like any other business, except…' This expression resonated with the women we talked with as much as with men in our previous sample. Familiness presents some special problems for women, and many women in our sample developed special solutions to it. These problems and solutions, though developed by women, may not be limited to them and their firms.

This is not to suggest that strategies women develop are always or even usually better than those men develop, but simply that considering a wide range of ideas is likely to yield good results. Several theorists suggest that non-family firms should cultivate family firms' familiness as a source of competitive advantage. So the solutions women in our sample devised to meet the demands of their leadership and entrepreneurship roles and the demands of the firms as learning communities may present new insights for male-led firms as well.

Responding creatively to the constraints, demands and possibilities of family firms, sometimes in accordance with 'female' approaches to management and sometimes in other ways, gave our participants their heartaches and headaches, their moments of elation and their periods of quiet satisfaction.

We examined and sought to explain how and why family business works the way it did for our participants as leaders and entrepreneurs, but much is left to discover. Watching family business women—daughters on the stage—promises many absorbing dramas to come.

Appendix: Further Notes on Method

STEPS

Chapter 3 discusses how case studies can contribute to knowledge and how we used the case method for the research in this book. For those interested in knowing more about what we did, here is some additional detail, presented using the series of steps for doing a case study explained in Eisenhardt (1989).

Getting Started

Eisenhardt's first step is to define the research question or research questions the case study seeks to answer. In their simplest form, our research questions were first: 'What is it like for women to attain leadership and entrepreneurship roles in family firms?' and then: 'How does the family business context inform our understanding of women's learning of leadership and entrepreneurship in family firms?' and 'How might women's learning contribute to the unique resources of "familiness", which help the family firm sustain competitive advantage?'

These questions were deliberately framed in a broad way, for two reasons. First, we desired a fresh approach to understanding women's learning for leadership and entrepreneurship in family firms. Specifically, we needed an approach that did not assume that women's ways of leading and acting as entrepreneurs would be either the same as or different from men's. Second, while women are claimed to be increasingly reaching positions of leadership in family firms, we do not yet understand much about how women undertake and actually experience such roles. Consequently, it is difficult to know how women contribute to the special strengths of family firms, and how family firms help to 'incubate' women entrepreneurs—sources of future wealth creation. For all these reasons, our basic research questions are framed to allow us to use—but not be unduly tied to—previous theories and hypotheses.

Because our research questions were broad, they prompted several sub-questions: 'Will women experience the family business learning stages and their paradoxes in similar or different ways compared to men?', 'Will they have the same or different ideas as men about what it means to act entrepreneurially?', 'Will there be differences among women themselves about such issues, for example, will they see their roles as a leader and entrepreneur differently depending on whether they started a firm themselves, or continued one that was started by a relative?' and so on. Also—and this is typical with case study work—we needed to point to and use variables which the existing literature suggested would probably be important. The ideas of 'family', 'leadership' and 'entrepreneurship' recur frequently in the literature on entrepreneurship generally, and family business entrepreneurship in particular. Again, we tried to avoid pre-empting specific relationships between them, and to retain a flexible view of how they might relate to each other and to other parts of the data.

Selecting Cases

Chapter 2 describes how two principles guided us in selecting cases: purposive sampling and selecting 'stretch' cases. Purposive sampling refers to looking for cases which we expected to exemplify the phenomenon under study. According to Eisenhardt (1989), this approach constrains extraneous variation: we avoided the problem of selecting all kinds of women and then trying to decide which among them are leaders. Our purposive sampling led us to choose women who were acknowledged by their peers or in other forums to be established leaders in family firms, who appeared to have completed the four stages of learning in our original model, or who hold (or held) the title of CEO in a family firm and so on. In short, they appeared to be 'unambiguous' leaders.

However, this approach meant we might overlook less obvious leaders, such as women who undertook leadership roles without achieving some of the formal markers of leadership. This is why including 'stretch' cases was important. Because women may act as leaders or entrepreneurs when they occupy roles which do not suggest such activities are likely for them, examining their cases allows us to see whether existing ideas about leadership and entrepreneurship should be extended, because we found some unexpected manifestations of these phenomena. As another kind of 'stretch' case, we wanted to include examples of women who in their own view had not achieved leadership roles in the family firm, despite having wanted to do so, and despite having what are some of the necessary attributes. In short, both our purposive sampling and our 'stretch' cases meant we focused on 'theoretically useful' cases.

Crafting Instruments and Protocols

We developed multiple approaches to collecting data, including both structured and unstructured interview formats. We also collected archival data about the history of the firm, its position in its industry and so on. Where possible, for example, when the interview took place at the interviewee's firm, we also used on-site observations and spoke with others in the firm about the person we interviewed. In some cases, we went back to the interviewee to ask her further questions or to seek additional data about the firm. This process enabled us to triangulate our evidence, to allow a stronger grounding for emerging theories, and admit divergent perspectives.

Entering the Field

For each case, we made one or more visits to a place of the interviewee's choosing. This was usually her workplace, although we did not always visit on a working day. With the interviewees' permission, we taped and later transcribed the interviews. We also took notes during the interviews and during tours of worksites. It was important to be both flexible and opportunistic—as well as use informal networks—to include women occupying family firm leadership roles in overseas countries. We took advantage of the fact that there were two researchers by comparing notes, testing our initial impressions of a situation with each other and so on.

We began analysing our material as soon as we had a reasonably sized body of data. However, because we gathered more data from women leaders internationally, it was not possible to undertake a step-by-step, overlapping process of data collection and analysis, as some theorists recommend. However, our approach had sufficient flexibility to allow us to take advantage of emergent themes and the special features of some cases. For example, how women leaders dealt with visibility turned out to be a common theme among our sample; it emerged early in the interviews as important in the experiences of both successful and unsuccessful leaders. However, it is not as dominant a theme in the leadership or entrepreneurship literature. We were careful to probe this issue in subsequent interviews, and this led to our finding some important new links, for example, between visibility and flexibility, and between visibility and legitimacy.

Analysing Data

We looked for patterns of similarity and difference both within our cases and across them as our main data analysis techniques. Thus, we transcribed the interviews and entered the data into NVivo, a computer program for analysing qualitative data. We coded the case histories and other material in detail according to the issues participants raised, making links between the various coded text segments within individual cases, across cases and across groups of cases as these started to emerge. We used these links to test or 'theorise' about the ideas which emerged by constantly comparing segments of text—sometimes on a small scale—with each other. We also coded the interviews and other data in terms of previous findings in the literature which related to the participants' concerns and preoccupations.

Our within-case analyses began with our spending time to become as familiar as possible with the fine details of each case on its own. Having two researchers was also important during this phase, since our within-case analysis required us to work as alternating 'devil's advocates': comparing our tentative categorisations of each interviewee's standing as a leader and as an entrepreneur, which other family firm role(s) she occupied, which stages of family business learning she had successfully completed and so on. Then we moved to searching for patterns across cases, comparing and contrasting what interviewees said about which aspects of family firm leadership they found most difficult, what plans remained unfulfilled and so on.

The within-case analysis led us to generate some preliminary theories which were later modified in the light of comparing patterns across cases. For example, after comparing women's experience of various roles in family firms, we tried to generate some theories about what 'visibility' meant in terms of these roles and hence to women's leadership in family firms. This required us to revisit Curimbaba's 'invisible' role in the light of what some interviewees said about how they worked to achieve change through others, or from 'behind the scenes'. We had hypothesised that 'maintaining high visibility' was important to attaining and retaining leadership. Women who lost visibility seemed to condemn themselves to losing leadership as well. However, when we undertook the second stage of our analysis, looking for patterns across our cases, we saw the issue was more complicated. For example, we found that instead of trying to stay visible, some leaders deliberately cultivated invisibility. For some, staying invisible was part of how they achieved results in the firm and even beyond it. This required us in turn to look again at our initial ideas and modify them to allow for this variation in how some family business women achieve their leadership goals.

Ending the Analysis

Although we interviewed 16 women and analysed findings progressively from the beginning of the data collection phase, we found after 13 cases that we had reached data saturation—that is, a point when no new patterns or themes seemed to be emerging from the data. Accordingly, the analysis of these 13 formed the focus of our study.

Shaping Hypotheses

Our two broad research tasks—to examine what it is like for women to learn successfully and attain leadership in family firms, and how women's learning can enhance the resources available to the family firm—led us to classify and re-classify interviewees' experiences in various ways to produce comparisons and quasi 'rankings' of their self-described success as leaders and entrepreneurs. The three frameworks that Chapter 3 outlines aided this classification task. Several advantages ensued from working this way. First, after we posed initial research questions and explored them using our case data, we used the frameworks to tabulate the evidence for our developing propositions. This made our workings visible to the reader, which in turn increased their internal validity. Comparing the results across first one, then two, then all three major frameworks (as Chapter 9 shows) shows the reader no less than ourselves how we developed some specific propositions about how, when and, finally, why family business women's experiences were the way they were.

Enfolding Literature

We folded in literature on women's entrepreneurship and leadership as we went. By comparing and contrasting what we had found with earlier studies, we could suggest how these earlier findings might need to be modified, as well as what further research it would make sense to carry out in the light of our findings. We included literature which seemed to confirm our findings along with literature which seemed to disconfirm our findings. For example, we found echoes of our 'visibility' issue in the institutional theory literature on how entrepreneurs manage lack of legitimacy when their firms have not yet achieved a profit. This enabled us to link our findings with other work unrelated to gender issues about the difficulties all firm leaders face. Literature that seemed to throw doubt on our findings included studies suggesting that women's leadership is inherently different from men's or that women are increasingly laying claim to positions at the head of family firms. While our case study approach did not aim either to refute or to confirm earlier empirical findings, it allowed us to sharpen our own and other theorists' ideas about the special issues attaining leadership presents for women.

Reaching Closure

We stopped adding and analysing cases when we judged we had reached theoretical saturation; that is, when adding more cases, and doing more coding, linking and tabulating of the data was not adding anything substantial to our understanding of women's leadership in family firms.

References

Ahl, H. (2004), *The Scientific Reproduction of Gender Inequality: A Discourse Analysis of Research Texts on Women's Entrepreneurship*, Liber: Copenhagen Business School Press.

Allen, I.E. and N. Langowitz (2003), *Women in Family-Owned Businesses*, Wellesley, MA: Center for Women's Leadership, Babson College/ MassMutual Financial Group.

Allen, I.E., A. Elam, N. Langowitz and M. Dean (2008), *The GEM 2007 Report on Women and Entrepreneurship*, available from the Global Entrepreneurship Monitor at: www.gemconsortium.org/files.aspx?Ca_ ID=224, retrieved 30 May 2008.

Allen, I.E., N. Langowitz and M. Minniti (2007), *The GEM 2006 Report on Women and Entrepreneurship*, available from the Global Entrepreneurship Monitor at: www.gemconsortium.org/document.aspx?id=580, retrieved 30 May 2008.

Alvarez, S.A. and L.W. Busenitz (2001), 'The entrepreneurship of resource-based theory', *Journal of Management*, **27**, 755–75.

Anderson, R.C. and D.M. Reeb (2003), 'Founding-Family Ownership and Firm Performance: Evidence from the S&P 500', *Journal of Finance*, **58**(3), 1301–28.

Asia-Pacific Economic Cooperation (APEC) (1998), *A Study of Women Entrepreneurs in SMEs in the APEC Region*, International Cooperation Division, Small & Medium Business Administration (SMBA), Taejon City, Republic of Korea (APEC Project SME 01/98).

Astrachan, J.H. and M.C. Shanker (1996), 'Myths and Realities: Family Businesses' Contribution to the US Economy—A Framework for Assessing Family Business Statistics', *Family Business Review*, **9**(2), 107–23.

Australian Bureau of Statistics (ABS) (2000), *Business Longitudinal Survey, Australia, 1994–95 to 1997–98*, available from: www.abs.gov.au, retrieved 6 July 2008.

Baker, T., H.E. Aldrich and L. Nina (1997), 'Invisible entrepreneurs: the neglect of women business owners by mass media and scholarly journals', *Entrepreneurship and Regional Development*, **9**(3), 221–38.

Barney, J. (1991), 'Firm resources and sustained competitive advantage', *Journal of Management*, **17**, 99–120.

Barrett, M.A. (1995), 'Feminist Perspectives on Learning for Entrepreneurship: The View from Small Business', in J.A. Hornaday, J.A. Timmons and K.H. Vesper (eds), *Frontiers of Entrepreneurial Research*, Babson College, Babson Park, MA, 323–37.

Barrett, M.A. (1998), 'Feminist Theoretical Perspectives on Women's Business Ownership: Some Insights from a Queensland Study', *International Journal of Women and Leadership*, **4**(1), 13–39.

Barrett, M.A. and M. Davidson (2006), *Gender and Communication at Work*, Aldershot: Ashgate Publishing.

Barry, B. (1975), 'The development of organization structure in the family firm', *Journal of General Management*, Autumn, 42–60.

Bartholomeusz, S. and G.A. Tanewski (2006), 'The relationship between family firms and corporate governance', *Journal of Small Business Management*, **44**(2), 245–67.

Belcourt, M. (1987), 'Sociological Factors Associated with Female Entrepreneurship', *Journal of Small Business and Entrepreneurship*, **21**(3), 22–31.

Belcourt, M. (1990), 'A Family Portrait of Canada's Most Successful Female Entrepreneurs', *Journal of Business Ethics*, **9**(4/5), 34–44.

Berfield, S. (2007), 'Mentoring Can Be Messy; Companies love it, but what if that colleague just wants your job?' *Business Week*, 29 January, p. 80.

Billing, Y.D. and M. Alvesson (1994), *Gender, managers, and organizations*, Berlin, New York: De Gruyter.

Bird, B. and C.G. Brush (2002), 'A gendered perspective on organizational creation', *Entrepreneurship Theory and Practice*, **26**(3), 41–65.

Birley, S. (1989), 'Female entrepreneurs: are they really any different?' *Journal of Small Business Management*, **27**(1), 32–7.

Blanco-Mazagatos, V., E. Esther de Quevedo-Puente and L.A. Castrillo (2007), 'The Trade-Off Between Financial Resources and Agency Costs in the Family Business: An Exploratory Study', *Family Business Review*, **21**(3), 199–214.

Blumentritt, T.P., A.D. Keyt and J.H. Astrachan (2007), 'Creating an Environment for Successful Nonfamily CEOs: An Exploratory Study of Good Principals', *Family Business Review*, **20**(4), 321–35.

Brown, J.S. and P. Duguid (2000), *The Social Life of Information*, Boston, MA: Harvard Business School Press.

Brown, S.M. (1979), 'Male versus female leaders: A comparison of empirical studies', *Sex Roles*, **5**, 595–611.

Bruni, A., S. Gherardi and B. Poggio (2004), 'Doing Gender, Doing Entrepreneurship: An Ethnographic Account of Intertwined Practices', *Gender, Work & Organization*, **11**, 406–29.

Brush, C.G. (2006), 'Women entrepreneurs: A research overview', in M. Casson, B. Yeung, A. Basu and N. Wadeson (eds), *The Oxford Handbook of Entrepreneurship*, Oxford: Oxford University Press, 611–28.

Brush, C.G., N.M. Carter, E.J. Gatewood, P.G. Greene and M.M. Hart (eds) (2006), *Growth-oriented Women Entrepreneurs and Their Businesses: A Global Research Perspective*, Cheltenham, UK and Northampton, MA, USA: Edward Elgar.

Bull, I. and G.E. Willard, (1993), 'Towards a theory of entrepreneurship', *Journal of Business Venturing*, **8**(3), 183–95.

Carland, J.A.C. and J.W. Carland (1991), 'An Empirical Investigation into the Distinctions between Male and Female Entrepreneurs and Managers', *International Small Business Journal*, **9**(3), 62–72.

Carland, J.W. and J.A.C. Carland (1992), 'Managers, small business owners and entrepreneurs: the cognitive dimension', *Journal of Business and Entrepreneurship*, **4**(2), 55–62.

Carney, M. (2005), 'Corporate governance and competitive advantage in family-controlled firms', *Entrepreneurship Theory and Practice*, **29**(3), 249–65.

Carr, J.C. and J.M. Sequeira (2007), 'Prior family business exposure as intergenerational influence and entrepreneurial intent: a theory of planned behavior approach', *Journal of Business Research*, **60**(10), 1090–98.

Carsrud, A.L. (1994), 'Meanderings of a resurrected psychologist or, lessons learned in creating a family business program', *Entrepreneurship Theory and Practice*, **19**(1), 39–48.

Carter, N.M. and M.L. Williams (2003), 'Comparing social feminism and liberal feminism: The case of new firm growth', in J.E. Butler (ed.), *New Perspectives on Women Entrepreneurs*, Greenwich, CT: Information Age Publishing, 25–50.

Carter, S. (1989), 'The Dynamics and Performance of Female-owned Entrepreneurial Firms in London, Glasgow and Nottingham', *Journal of Organizational Change Management*, **2**(3), 54–64.

Center for Women's Business Research (2006), *Myth-buster: women entrepreneurs prepare as well as men—and care more about employees—when selling businesses*, available from: www.womensbusinessresearch. org/press/details.php?id=141, retrieved 21 November 2007.

Chaganti, R. (1986), 'Management in Women-owned Enterprises', *Journal of Small Business Management*, **24**(4), 18–29.

Chandler, A.D. (1990), *Scale and scope: The dynamics of industrial capitalism*, Boston, MA: Harvard University Press.

Channon, D.F. (1971), *Strategy and Structure of British Enterprise*, doctoral dissertation, Harvard Business School.

Chen, C., P. Greene and A. Crick (1998), 'Does entrepreneurial self-efficacy distinguish entrepreneurs from managers?' *Journal of Business Venturing*, **13**(4), 295–316.

Chrisman, J.J. and P. Sharma (1999), 'Toward a Reconciliation of the Definitional Issues in the Field of Corporate Entrepreneurship', *Entrepreneurship Theory and Practice*, **23** (Spring), 11–27.

Chrisman, J.J., J.H. Chua and P. Sharma (1999), 'Defining the Family Business by Behavior', *Entrepreneurship Theory and Practice*, **23**(4), 19–39.

Chrisman, J.J., J.H. Chua and P. Sharma (2003), *Current trends and future directions in family business management studies: toward a theory of the family firm*, Coleman White Paper Series, Coleman Foundation.

Chrisman, J.J., J.H. Chua and P. Sharma (2005), 'Trends and directions in the development of a strategic management theory of the family firm', *Entrepreneurship Theory and Practice*, **29**(5), 555–75.

Christensen, C.M. (1997), *The Innovator's Dilemma: When New Technologies Cause Great Firms to Fail*. Boston, MA: Harvard Business School Press.

Church, R.A. (1969), *Kenricks in Hardware: A Family Business, 1791–1966*. New York: David & Charles, Newton Abbott.

CNN Talk Asia (2007), Cheung Yan interview with Anjali Rao, 3 June 2007, available from: ww.cnn.com/2007/WORLD/asiapcf/06/03/talkasia.cheung yan/index.html?eref=rss_latest, retrieved 3 June 2008.

Cole, P. (1997) 'Women in family business', *Family Business Review*, **10**(4), 353–71.

Collins, O.F. and D.G. Moore (1970), *The organization makers*, New York: Appleton.

Collins, O.F. and D.G. Moore (1964), *The Enterprising Man*, East Lansing, MI: Michigan State University Press.

Collins, P., J. Hage and F. Hull (1988), 'Organizational and technological predictors of change in automaticity', *Academy of Management Journal*, **31**(3), 512–43.

Collinson, D.L. (2003), 'Identities and Insecurities: Selves at Work', *Organization*, **10**(3), 527–47.

Collinson, D.L. and J. Hearn (1996), *Men as Managers, Managers as Men: Critical Perspectives on Masculinity*, London: Sage.

Cooper, R.G. (1999), 'The invisible success factors in product innovation', *Journal of Product Innovation Management*, **33**(3), 41–54.

Corbetta, G. and C. Salvato (2004), 'Self-serving or self-actualizing? Models of man and agency costs in different types of family firms: a commentary on "Comparing the agency costs of family and non-family firms: conceptual issues and exploratory evidence"', *Entrepreneurship Theory and Practice*, **28**(4), 355–62.

Craig, J.B.L. and N. Lindsay (2002), 'Incorporating the family dynamic into the entrepreneurship process', *Journal of Small Business and Enterprise Development*, **9**(4), 416–30.

Craig, J.B.L., G. Cassar and K. Moores (2006), 'A 10-Year Longitudinal Investigation of Strategy, Systems, and Environment on Innovation in Family Firms', *Family Business Review*, **19**(1), 1–10.

Cromie, S. (1987a), 'Motivations of Aspiring Male and Female Entrepreneurs', *Journal of Organizational Behavior*, **8**, 251–61.

Cromie, S. (1987b), 'Similarities and Differences between Women and Men Who Choose Business Proprietorship', *International Small Business Journal*, **5**(3), 43–60.

Curimbaba, F. (2002), 'The Dynamics of Women's Roles as Family Business Managers', *Family Business Review*, **15**(3), 239–52.

Curran, J. and R. Blackburn (2001), *Researching the Small Enterprise*, London: Thousand Oaks, CA, New Delhi: Sage.

Curthoys, A. and J. Docker (2006), *Is History Fiction?* Sydney: UNSW Press.

Daily, C.M. and M.J. Dollinger (1992), 'An empirical examination of ownership structure and family and professionally managed firms', *Family Business Review*, **5**(2), 117–36.

Daily, C.M. and M.J. Dollinger (1993), 'Alternative methodologies for identifying family-versus nonfamily-managed businesses', *Journal of Small Business Management*, **31**(2), 79–91.

Davis, J.H., F.D. Schoorman and L. Donaldson, (1997), 'Toward a stewardship theory of management', *Academy of Management Review*, **22**, 20–47.

Davis, P. (1983), 'Realizing the potential of the family business', *Organizational Dynamics*, **12**(1), 47–56.

De Bruin, A., C.G. Brush and F. Welter (2007), 'Advancing a Framework for Coherent Research on Women's Entrepreneurship', *Entrepreneurship Theory and Practice*, **31**(3), 323–39.

De Tienne, D.R. and G. Chandler (2007), 'The role of gender in opportunity identification', *Entrepreneurship Theory and Practice*, **31**(3), 365–86.

Delmar, F. and P. Davidsson (2000), 'Where do they come from? Prevalence and characteristics of nascent entrepreneurs', *Entrepreneurship and Regional Development*, **12**(1), 1–23.

Denis, D., D. Denis and A. Sarin (1997), 'Agency problems, equity ownership and corporate diversification', *Journal of Finance*, **52**, 135–60.

Dewing, C. (2008), 'Out of Pfizer and into the frying pan', available from: www.realbusiness.co.uk/news/business-woman/5245696/out-of-pfizer-and -into-the-fryingpan.thtml, retrieved 9 May 2008.

Dibrell, C. and J.B.L. Craig (2006), 'The natural environment, innovation, and firm performance: A comparative study of family and non-family firms', *Family Business Review*, **31**(4), 275–87.

Dobbins, G.H. and S.J. Platz (1986), 'Sex Differences in Leadership: How Real Are They?' *Academy of Management Review*, **11**(1), 118–27.

Donaldson, S.I., E.A. Ensher and E.J. Grant-Vallone (2000), 'A longitudinal examination of mentoring relationships on organizational commitment and citizenship behavior', *Journal of Career Development*, **26**, 233–49.

Donckels, R. and E. Fröhlich (1991), 'Are family businesses really different? European experiences from STRATOS', *Family Business Review*, **4**(2), 149–60.

Donnelley, R.G. (1964), 'The Family Business', *Harvard Business Review*, **42**(4), 93–105.

Dugan, A.M., S.P. Krone, K. LeCouvie, J.M. Pendergast, D.H. Kenyon-Rouvinez, A.M. and Schuman (2008), *A Woman's Role: The Crucial Roles of Women in Family Business*, Marietta, GA: The Family Business Consulting Group.

Dumas, C.A. (1989), 'Understanding of father–daughter and father–son dyads in family-owned businesses', *Family Business Review*, **2**(1), 31–46.

Dumas, C.A. (1990), 'Preparing the new CEO: Managing the father–daughter succession process in family businesses', *Family Business Review*, **2**(2), 169–81.

Dumas, C.A. (1992), 'Integrating the daughter into family business management', *Entrepreneurship Theory and Practice*, **16**(4), 41.

Dumas, C.A. (1998), 'Women's Pathways to Participation and Leadership in the Family-Owned Firm', *Family Business Review*, **11**(3), 219–28.

Dyer, W.G. Jr (1986), *Cultural change in family firms: anticipating and managing family business transitions*, San Francisco: Jossey-Bass.

Eisenhardt, K. (1989), 'Building theories from case study research', *Academy of Management Journal*, **14**(4), 532–50.

Ensher, E. and S. Murphy (2005), *Power Mentoring: How Successful Mentors and Protégés Get the Most Out of Their Relationships*, San Francisco: Jossey-Bass.

Ensher, E.A., S.E. Murphy and C.M. Vance (2000), 'The application of career strategies from mentoring, self-management, and self-leadership for entrepreneurs', *International Journal of Entrepreneurship*, **1**(2), 99–108.

Evans, M. (2005), *Coutts 2005 Family Business Survey*, available at: www.directorbank.com/graphics_uploaded/coutts2005_family_business_s urvey.pdf, retrieved 19 July 2008.

Fagenson, E.A. (1993), 'Personal Value Systems of Men and Women Entrepreneurs Versus Managers', *Journal of Business Venturing*, **8**(5), 409–30.

Fama, E.E. and M.C. Jensen, (1983), 'Separation of ownership and control', *Journal of Law and Economics*, **26**, 301–25.

Fama, E.F. (1980), 'Agency problems and the theory of the firm', *Journal of Political Economy*, **88**, 288–307.

Ferber, M.A. and J.A. Nelson (1993), *Beyond Economic Man: Feminist Theory and Economics*, Chicago: University of Chicago Press.

Fischer, E. (1992), 'Sex Differences and Small-Business Performance Among Canadian Retailers and Service Providers', *Journal of Small Business and Entrepreneurship*, **9**(4), 2–13.

Fischer, E., A.R. Reuber and L.S. Dyke (1993), 'A theoretical overview and extension of research on sex, gender, and entrepreneurship', *Journal of Business Venturing*, **8**, 151–68.

Fletcher, J.K. (2004), 'The Paradox of Post Heroic Leadership: An Essay on Gender, Power and Transformational Change', *Leadership Quarterly*, **15**(5), 647–61.

Folker, C.A. and R.L. Sorenson (2000), 'Women's orientation to management: An empirical revisit to gender differences using family business owners', paper presented at the Western Academy of Management, Hawaii.

Fulop, L. and S. Linstead (1999), *Management: A Critical Text*, Sydney: Macmillan.

Gartner, W.B. (1988), '"Who is an entrepreneur?" is the wrong question', *American Journal of Small Business*, **12**(4), 11–32.

Gartner, W.B. (1990), 'What are we talking about when we talk about entrepreneurship?' *Journal of Business Venturing*, **5**(1), 15–28.

Gedajlovic, E., M. Lubatkin and W.S. Schulze (2004), 'Crossing the threshold from founder management to professional management: a governance perspective', *Journal of Management Studies*, **41**(5), 899–912.

Geeraerts, G. (1984), 'The effect of ownership on the organization structure in small firms', *Administrative Science Quarterly*, **29**, 232–7.

Gersick, K.E., J. Davis, M. Hampton and I. Lansberg (1997), *Generation to Generation: Life Cycles of the Family Business*, Boston, MA: Harvard Business School Press.

Gilligan, C. (1982), *In a Different Voice: Psychological Theory and Women's Development*, Boston, MA: Harvard University Press.

Global Entrepreneurship Monitor (GEM) (2004, 2007, 2008), available at: www.gemconsortium.org, retrieved 2 May 2008.

Gome, A. (2007), *Shouldering the drive and passion*, available at: www.smartcompany.com.au/Premium-Articles/Hot-Innovator/Shouldering-the-drive-and-passion.html, retrieved 30 May 2008.

Greer, M.J. and P.G. Greene (2003), 'Feminist theory and the study of entrepreneurship', in J.E. Butler (ed.), *New Perspectives on Women Entrepreneurs*, Greenwich, CT: Information Age Publishing, 1–24.

Habbershon, T.G. (2006), 'Commentary: A Framework for Managing the Familiness and Agency Advantages in Family Firms', *Entrepreneurship Theory and Practice*, **30**(6), 879–86.

Habbershon, T.G. and J. Pistrui (2002), 'Enterprising families' domain: Family-influenced ownership groups in pursuit of transgenerational wealth', *Family Business Review*, **15**(3), 223–38.

Habbershon, T.G. and M.L. Williams (1999), 'A resource-based framework for assessing the strategic advantages of family firms', *Family Business Review*, **12**(1), 1–25.

Habbershon, T.G., M.L. Williams and I.C. MacMillan (2003), 'A unified systems perspective of family firm performance', *Journal of Business Venturing*, **18**(4), 451–65.

Halamandaris, B. and W. Halamandaris (2004), *The Heart of America: Ten Core Values That Make our Country Great*, Deerfield Beach, FL: HCI Books.

Handler, W.C. (1989), 'Methodological issues and considerations in studying family businesses', *Family Business Review*, **2**(3), 257–76.

Harding, R. (2007), *The State of Women's Enterprise in the UK*, Norwich: Delta Economics and Prowess, available at: www.womenable.com/user files/downloads/PROWESS_State_of_Wmns_Enterprise_UK_2007.pdf, retrieved 21 November 2007.

Hills, G. (1995), 'Opportunity Recognition by Successful Entrepreneurs: A Pilot Study', in J.A. Hornaday, J.A. Timmons and K.H. Vesper (eds), *Frontiers of Entrepreneurial Research*, Boston, MA: Babson College, 205–17.

Hisrich, R.D. (1986), 'The Woman Entrepreneur—Characteristics, Skills, Problems, and Prescriptions for Success', in Sexton, D.L. and R.W. Smilor (eds), *The Art and Science of Entrepreneurship*, Cambridge, MA: Ballinger Publishing Company, 61–84.

Hisrich, R.D. and C.G. Brush (1983), 'The woman entrepreneur: Implications of family, educational and occupational experience', in J.A. Hornaday, J.A. Timmons and K.H. Vesper (eds), *Frontiers of Entrepreneurial Research*, Boston, MA: Babson College, 566–87.

Hollander, B.S. and W.R. Bukowitz (1990), 'Women, family cultures, and family business', *Family Business Review*, **3**(2), 139–51.

Hoy, F. and T.G. Vesper (1994), Emerging Business, Emerging Field: Entrepreneurship and the Family Firm, *Entrepreneurship Theory and Practice*, **19**(1), 9–23.

Hurley, A. (1999), 'Incorporating feminist theories into sociological theories of entrepreneurship', *Women in Management Review*, **14**(2), 54–62.

Iannarelli, C.L. (1993), 'The socialization of leaders: A study of gender in family business', *Dissertation Abstracts International*, **53**(9-A), 3283–84.

Indian Heroes (n.d.) Mallika Srinivasan, available at: iloveindia.com/indian-heroes/mallika-srinivisan.html, retrieved 30 May 2008.

Irava, W. Unpublished PhD, Bond University, in progress.

Jaffe, D.T. and S.H. Lane (2004), 'Sustaining a family dynasty: key issues facing complex multigenerational businesses and investment owning families', *Family Business Review*, **69**(1), 85–98.

James, H.S. (1999), 'Owner as manager, extended horizons and the family firm', *International Journal of the Economics of Business*, **6**, 41–56.

Jensen, M.C. and W.H. Meckling (1976), 'Theory of the firm: managerial behavior, agency costs and ownership structure', *Journal of Financial Economics*, **3**, 305–60.

Johnson, G.J. and R. McMahon (2005), 'Owner-manager Gender, Financial Performance and Business Growth amongst SMEs from Australia's Business Longitudinal Survey', *International Small Business Journal*, **23**(2), 115–42.

Kanter, R.M. (1977), *Men and Women of the Corporation*, New York: Basic Books.

Kanter, R.M. (1989), 'Swimming in newstreams: mastering innovation dilemmas', *California Management Review*, **31**(4), 45–69.

Kellermanns, F.W. and K. Eddleston (2006), 'Corporate venturing in family firms: Does the family matter?' *Entrepreneurship Theory and Practice*, **30**(6), 809–30.

Knight, F. (1964 [1921]), *Risk, Uncertainty and Profit*, New York: Sentry Press.

Kotey, B. (2005), Goals, management practices, and performance of family SMEs, *International Journal of Entrepreneurial Behaviour and Research*, **11**(1), 3–24.

Lansberg, I., E. Perrow and S. Rogolsky (1988), 'Family Business as an Emerging Field', *Family Business Review*, **1**(1), 1–8.

Lave, J. and E. Wenger (1991), *Situated learning: Legitimate peripheral participation*, Cambridge: University of Cambridge Press.

Leading Women Entrepreneurs of the World (2004), Program for Celebratory Gala Event, Sydney, p. 8, available at: www.leadingwomen.org/_File Library/File/MediaKit.pdf, retrieved 30 May 2008.

Litz, R.A. (1995), The family business: toward definitional clarity, *Family Business Review*, **8**(2), 71–81.

Litz, R.A. and R.F. Kleysen (2001), 'Your old men shall dream dreams, your young men shall see visions: Toward a theory of family firm innovation with help from the Brubeck family', *Family Business Review*, **14**(4), 335–51.

Lyman, A.R. (1988), 'Life in the family cycle', *Family Business Review*, **1**(4), 383–98.

Marceau, J. (1989), *A family business? The making of an international business elite* (1st edition), Cambridge, UK: Cambridge University Press.

Mass Mutual Financial Group (2007), Study: Family businesses growing steady and strong but face future risks: 2007 American Family Business Survey highlights opportunities and challenges for family firms across the US, press release dated 1 November 2007, available at: www.mass mutual.com/mmfg/about/pr_2007/11_1_2007.html, retrieved 8 June 2008.

Matterson, H. (2002), 'How to cash in and still keep a finger in the pie', *The Weekend Australian*, October 26–27, p. 36.

Meyer, M.W. and L.G. Zucker, (1989), *Permanently failing organizations*, Newbury Park, CA: Sage.

Miller, D. and I. Le Breton-Miller (2005), 'Management Insights from Great and Struggling Family Businesses', *Long Range Planning*, **38**, 517–30.

Minniti, M. and C. Nardone (2007), 'Being in Someone Else's Shoes: the Role of Gender in Nascent Entrepreneurship', *Small Business Economics*, **28** (2/3), 223–38.

Minniti, M., I.E. Allen and N. Langowitz (2006), The *GEM 2005 Report on Women and Entrepreneurship*, available at: www.gemconsortium.org/document.aspx?id=478, retrieved 30 May 2008.

Minniti, M., P. Arenius and N. Langowitz (2005), *The GEM 2004 Report on Women and Entrepreneurship*, available at: www.gemconsortium.org/document.aspx?id=419, retrieved 30 May 2008.

Moore, D.P. and E.H. Buttner (1997), *Women Entrepreneurs: Moving Beyond the Glass Ceiling*, Thousand Oaks, CA: Sage.

Moores, K. and J. Mula (2000), 'The salience of market, bureaucratic and clan controls in the management of family firm transactions: some tentative Australian evidence', *Family Business Review*, **13**(2), 91–106.

Moores, K. and M.A. Barrett (2002), *Learning Family Business: Paradoxes and Pathways*, Aldershot, UK: Ashgate Publishing.

Morck, R. and B. Yeung (2003), 'Agency Problems in Large Family Business Groups', *Entrepreneurship Theory and Practice*, **27**(4), 367–82.

Nelson, T. and L.L. Levesque (2007), 'The Status of Women in Corporate Governance in High-Growth, High-Potential Firms', *Entrepreneurship Theory and Practice*, **31**(2), 209–32.

Noe, R.A. (1988), 'Women and mentoring: A review and research agenda', *Academy of Management Review*, **13**(1), 65–78.

Numagami, T. (1998), 'The Infeasibility of Invariant Laws in Management Studies: a Reflective Dialogue in Defense of Case Studies', *Organizational Science*, **9**(1), 2–15.

Ogbor, J.O. (2000), 'Mythicizing and reification in entrepreneurial discourse: ideology critique of entrepreneurial studies', *Journal of Management Studies*, **37**(5), 605–35.

Olsson, S. (2006), 'We don't need another hero: Organizational Storytelling as a Vehicle for Communicating a Female Archetype of Workplace Leadership' in M.A. Barrett and M. Davidson (eds), *Gender and Communication at Work*, Aldershot: Ashgate Publishing, 195–210.

Randøy, T. and Goel, S. (2003), 'Ownership structure, founder leadership, and performance in Norwegian SMEs: Implications for financing entrepreneurial opportunities', *Journal of Business Venturing*, **18**, 619–37.

Reed, R. (1996), 'Entrepreneurial and paternalism in Australian management: a gender critique of the "self-made" man', in D. Collinson and J. Hearn (eds), *Men as Managers, Managers as Men*, London: Sage, 99–122.

Rosenblatt, P., L. de Mik, R. Anderson and P. Johnson (1985), *The family in business*, San Francisco: Jossey-Bass.

Rosener, J.B. (1990), 'Ways women lead', *Harvard Business Review*, **68**(6), 119–25.

Rugman, A.M. and A. Verbeke (2002), 'Edith Penrose's contribution to the resource-based view of strategic management', *Strategic Management Journal*, **23**, 769–80.

Salganicoff, M. (1990), 'Women in family business: Challenges and opportunities', *Family Business Review*, **3**(2), 125–37.

Salvato, C. (2002), *Antecedents of entrepreneurship in three types of family firms*, Jönköping: Jönköping International Business School.

Salvato, C. (2004), 'Predictors of entrepreneurship in family firms', *Journal of Private Equity*, **7**(3), 68–76.

Schulze, W.S., M.H. Lubatkin and R.N. Dino (2002), 'Altruism, Agency and the Competitiveness of Family Firms', *Managerial and Decision Economics*, **23**(4), 247–59.

Scott, J. and C. Griff (1984), 'Family, kinship and corporations', in J. Scott and C. Griff (eds), *Directors of industry: The British corporate network (1904–1976)* (1st edition), Cambridge, UK: Polity Press, 100–26.

Sexton, D.L. and N. Bowman-Upton (1990), 'Female and male entrepreneurs: Psychological characteristics and their role in gender-related discrimination', *Journal of Business Venturing*, **5**, 29–36.

Sharma, P. (2004), 'An Overview of the Field of Family Business Studies: Current Status and Directions for the Future', *Family Business Review*, **17**(1), 1–36.

Sharma, P. and P.G. Irving (2005), 'Four Bases of Family Business Successor Commitment: Antecedents and Consequences', *Entrepreneurship Theory and Practice*, **29**(1), 13–33.

Sharma, P., J.J. Chrisman and J.H. Chua (1997), 'Strategic Management of the Family Business: Past Research and Future Challenges', *Family Business Review*, **10**(1), 1–35.

Siggelkow, N. (2007), 'Persuasion with Case Studies', *Academy of Management Journal*, **50**(1), 20–4.

Silverman, D. (1985), Qualitative Methodology and Sociology, Hants, UK: Gower Publishing.

Sinclair, A. (2004), *Doing Leadership Differently: Gender, Power and Sexuality in Leading* (2nd edition), Melbourne: Melbourne University Press.

Sinclair, A. (2007), *Leadership for the disillusioned: moving beyond myths and heroes to leading that liberates*, Sydney: Allen and Unwin.

Smyrnios, K.X. and C. Romano (1994), *The PriceWaterhouse/Commonwealth Bank Family Business Survey 1994*, Melbourne: Syme Department of Accounting, Monash University.

Smyrnios, K.X. and R.H. Walker (2003), *Australian family and private business survey*, Melbourne: The Boyd Partners and Royal Melbourne Institute of Technology.

Sonnenfeld, J. (1988), *The Hero's Farewell: What Happens When CEOs Retire*, Oxford: Oxford University Press.

Stinchcombe, A.L. (1965), 'Social structure and organizations', in J.G. March (ed.), *Handbook of Organizations*, Chicago: Rand McNally, 142–93.

Stoy Hayward (1992), *Managing the Family Business in the UK: A Stoy Hayward Survey in Conjunction with the London Business School*, London: Stoy Hayward.

Thompson, P. and D. McHugh (1990), *Work organisations: a critical introduction*, Sydney: Macmillan.

US National Women's Business Council (2007), Key Contributions of Women-Led Businesses, available at: www.nwbc.gov/ResearchPublications/doc uments/NWBC_WLReport.Final.pdf, retrieved 21 November 2007.

Verheul, I., L. Uhlaner and R. Thurik (2005), 'Business accomplishments, gender and entrepreneurial self-image', *Journal of Business Venturing*, **20**(4), 483–518.

Villette, M. (1975), 'L'accès aux positions dominantes dans l'entreprise', *Actes de la Recherche en Sciences Sociales*, **1**(4), 98–101.

Ward, J.L. (1987), *Keeping the family business healthy: How to plan for continued growth, profitability, and family leadership*, San Francisco: Jossey-Bass.

Wenger, E. (1999), *Communities of practice: learning, meaning and identity*. Cambridge: Cambridge University Press.

Wenger, E. (2000), 'Communities of Practice and Social Learning Systems', *Organization*, **7**(2), 225–46.

Wenger, E. and W. Snyder (2000), 'Communities of practice: the organizational frontier', *Harvard Business Review*, **78**(1), 139–45.

Westhead, P. and M. Cowling (1997), 'Performance contrasts between family and non-family unquoted companies in the UK', *International Journal of Entrepreneurial Behaviour and Research*, **3**(1), 30–52.

Westhead, P. and M. Cowling (1998), 'Family firm research: the need for a methodological rethink', *Entrepreneurship Theory and Practice*, **23**, 31–56.

Whetten, D. (1989), 'What Constitutes a Theoretical Contribution?' *Academy of Management Review*, **14**, 490–95.

Yin, R.K. (1984), *Case study research: design and methods*, Beverly Hills, CA: Sage Publications.

Zahra, S.A. (2005), 'Entrepreneurial risk taking in family firms', *Family Business Review*, **18**(1), 3–40.

Zimmerman, M. and G. Zeitz (2002), 'Beyond survival: Achieving new venture growth by building legitimacy', *Academy of Management Review*, **27**(3), 414–31.

Index